# *Landmarks of*
# TOMORROW

A
Report
on the New
"Post-Modern"
World

# *Landmarks of* TOMORROW

*With a new Introduction by the Author*

# *Peter F. Drucker*

**TRANSACTION PUBLISHERS**
New Brunswick (U.S.A.) and London (U.K.)

Second Printing 1999.
New material this edition copyright © 1996 by Peter F. Drucker. Originally published in 1957 by Harper & Row, Publishers.

This book is printed on acid-free paper that meets the American National Standard for Permanence of Paper for Printed Library Materials.

Library of Congress Catalog Number: 92-7614
ISBN: 1-56000-622-6
Printed in the United States of America

Library of Congress Cataloging-in-Publication Data

Drucker, Peter Ferdinand, 1909–
    Landmarks of tomorrow / Peter F. Drucker ; with a new introduction
by the author.
        p.  cm.
    Originally published : New York : Harper, 1957.
    Includes bibliographical references.
    ISBN 1-56000-622-6
    1. Civilization, Modern—1950–  I. Title.
CB425.D77  1992
909.82—dc20                                           92-7614
                                                        CIP

# TO DORIS

to whose care, thought and judgment every page bears
witness, this book is dedicated in gratitude and love

# CONTENTS

# INTRODUCTION TO THE
# TRANSACTION EDITION

This book was called "futuristic" when it first appeared. But I do not believe in "forecasting" or in "predicting"; I consider them futile and self-defeating. This book should properly be considered an "early diagnosis." It looks at the society of the late 1950s, and especially at American society, and asks: Where have major changes already happened that will make the future very different from what most of us still assume to be "normal," from what most of us still take for granted? In fact, my first title was *The Future that has Already Happened*—and I dropped it only because it was too long to fit comfortably on a title page.

But the book did start out with the assumption that there had been a drastic change and that we had already moved out of one era, hence the book's subtitle, *A Report on the New Post-Modern World*. And the word "post-modern" was to the best of my knowledge first used in this book, was indeed coined by me. The book then went on to ask: In what areas have these changes occurred? Which ones are of major importance? What does each of them imply and mean? What do we have to learn, to unlearn, to do as a result of these developments?

In many ways this book represents a major departure from my earlier work. Eight years earlier I had published the last of three books analyzing and presenting the new industrial society that had emerged out of World War II, *The Future of Industrial Man* (1942); *Concept of the Corporation* (1946); and *The New Society* (1949)—all of which have since been reissued by Transaction. In the meantime I had begun work on the study of the constitutive institution of that society, management, and had, in 1954, published the first—and most fundamental—of my books on the subject, *The Practice of Management*, followed in later years by *Managing for Results* (1964), the first book on what we now call "strategy"; *The Effective Executive* (1966), the first book on what we now call "leadership"; *Management Tasks, Responsibility Practices* (1973), an attempt to pull together in one definitive volume all we know about management, both as a specific work and as a major social function; *Innovation and Entrepreneurship* (1986), the first presentation of entrepreneurship as a systematic discipline and of innovation as organized, systematic, purposeful work; and finally in 1991, *Managing the Non-Profit Organization*, the first attempt to project management, leadership, and entrepreneurship on the non-profit sector of society and its institutions. *Landmarks of Tomorrow* was thus different both from my earlier work in social analysis and from the books that over the next thirty years became the best known works of mine: the books on management, not "business" management but management as specific work, specific discipline, specific responsibility, specific social functions. *Landmarks of Tomorrow* did, however, set the format and approach followed since by all my later books on society: *The Age of Discontinuity* (1969), *The Unseen Revolution* (1976; both of which have also been reissued by Transaction), *The New Realities* (1989/90), and *Post Capitalist Society* (1993). They are all books dealing with basic changes in the foundations of society, all books that try to do what *Landmarks of Tomorrow* first tried to, that is, to present *the future that has already happened.*

Now, thirty-five years later, it is proper to ask whether events have since borne out this early diagnosis? On the whole, they have. The main findings of this book were the shift from nineteenth-century automatic progress to systematic, purposeful, organized innovation; the shift to knowledge as the new major resource; the emergence of a pluralistic society of organizations; the crisis in the effectiveness of modern government—rather amazing in that this finding was made just a few years before the Kennedy presidency seemed to enthrone government as the new "Enlightened, and All-Powerful Despot"; and finally the shift to a global economy and, indeed, a global society. Only one of the major findings has not been validated by events since—or rather only in part. And yet, it was the finding that evoked the most comment and interest when the book was first published: the finding that a new worldview, a new holistic philosophy was rapidly emerging. This finding that we were moving, and fast, from a Cartesian view of the world as a mechanical aggregate in which the whole is the sum of its parts to a worldview of configurations or *Gestalten* in which the whole is different from its parts has indeed happened in the disciplines that, in the last thirty-five years, have progressed the most: in biogenetics, biophysics and molecular biology; in psychology with its new focus on "personality"; in metereology and in the earth sciences; in the emergence of "ecology"; in mathematics with chaos theory and the mathematics of complexity. But it has not happened in philosophy itself. There we have been moving to even more extreme Cartesian atomism in which there is no whole at all but only parts: in philosophical linguistics and in deconstructivism. There is an old saying that philosophy follows the dominant scientific world

paradigm and transforms it into "worldview" and metaphysics—the best example is Immanuel Kant following Isaac
Newton. But Kant followed Newton a good fifty years later.
(Newton died in 1727 and Kant, born in 1724, did not pub-
lish a major work [*The Critique of Pure Reason*] until 1781).
If that is the pattern, we should expect the new philosophy to
be born around the year 2000—that is, more than forty years
after I had prematurely announced its arrival!

But worse than being premature in a diagnosis is to miss
and overlook a major development. And *Landmarks of Tomorrow* missed the information revolution. This is all the
stranger as the author, in those years, worked closely with
IBM, one of the leading computer manufacturers, lectured to
its managers, and altogether preached to all that the computer was not just a gadget but represented a veritable revolution in the way we were going to do work, be organized,
think, and that, indeed, the computer was but a symptom of a
basic change—the change from experience to information.
Indeed I gained a reputation as somewhat of a bore on this
subject and yet inexplicably there is not a word on information to be found in *Landmarks of Tomorrow*; that had to wait
until my next book of social analysis, the 1969 *Age of Discontinuity*. If the book were to be given a score as an "early
diagnosis" it would thus not get an "A+." But it probably
deserves an "A-"; in its main thesis—that here had been a
shift—and in identifying the main new developments, it was
on target.

There is one feature of the book, however, that will surprise today's reader—it surprised me when I reread the book
to write this introduction: the book's optimism. It deals with
weighty issues and major challenges, but it is a confident
book—whether in respect to economic development (where
it correctly saw the coming emergence of Japan as a devel-

oped and powerful economy), in respect to political structure and organization, or in respect to knowledge and education. It does not minimize the problems and challenges. But
it looks at them as work to be done—the title of the
penultimate chapter—rather than as burdens or crises. Six
years after the book was published, with President Kennedy's
assassination, we then entered the long period of agony, crises, despair, and horrors—and not only in American society.
Perhaps it is not too optimistic to look upon this long period
as a time of transition to the emergence of the "post-modern"
world on which this book first reported, and on all the horrors and crises of these thirty-five years as turbulences of
that transition. Perhaps it is not too optimistic to hope that
the period now ahead, after this reissue of *Landmarks of Tomorrow*, will justify the optimism with which the book was
written more than thirty-five years ago.

PETER F. DRUCKER

Claremont, California
November 1995

## INTRODUCTION

# This Post-Modern World

At some unmarked point during the last twenty
years we imperceptibly moved out of the Modern Age and
into a new, as yet nameless, era. Our view of the world changed;
we acquired a new perception and with it new capacities. There
are new frontiers of opportunity, risk and challenge. There is a
new spiritual center to human existence.

The old view of the world, the old tasks and the old center,
calling themselves "modern" and "up to date" only a few
years ago, just make no sense any more. They still provide our
rhetoric, whether of politics or of science, at home or in foreign
affairs. But the slogans and battle cries of all parties, be they
political, philosophical, aesthetic or scientific, no longer serve
to unite for action—though they still can divide in heat and
emotion. Our actions are already measured against the stern demands of the "today," the "post-modern world"; and yet we
have no theories, no concepts, no slogans—no real knowledge
—about the new reality.

Indeed anyone over forty lives in a different world from that
in which he came to manhood, lives as if he had emigrated,
fully grown, to a new and strange country. For three hundred
years, from the middle of the seventeenth century on, the
West lived in the Modern Age; and during the last century
this modern West became the norm of philosophy and politics,

society, science and economy all over the globe, became the first truly universal world order. Today it is no longer living reality—but the new world, though real, if not indeed obvious to us, is not yet established.

We thus live in an age of transition, an age of overlap, in which the old "modern" of yesterday no longer acts effectively but still provides means of expression, standards of expectations and tools of ordering, while the new, the "post-modern," still lacks definition, expression and tools but effectively controls our actions and their impact.

This book is a report on the new post-modern today we live in—nothing more. It does not deal with the future. It deals with the tangible present. Indeed I have tried to resist the temptation to speculate about what might be, let alone to predict what will be. I have not even tried to pull together into one order of values and perceptions what are still individual pieces. Till this is done, we shall not, of course, have a really new age with its own distinct character and world-view; we shall only be "post" something else.

As I saw the job, it was to understand rather than to innovate, to describe rather than to imagine. This is, of course, by far the smaller and less important of the tasks to be done; we still need the great imaginer, the great creative thinker, the great innovator, of a new synthesis, of a new philosophy and of new institutions.

This book encompasses a very wide horizon; yet it is incomplete. Essentially I have tried to cover *three big areas*, each representing a major dimension of human life and experience:

*The new view of the world, the new concepts, the new human capacities:*

The first part of the book (Chapters One, Two and Three) treats the philosophical shift from the Cartesian universe of mechanical cause to the new universe of pattern, purpose and process. I have also explored our new power purposefully to innovate, both technologically and socially, and the resulting emergence of new opportunity, new risk and new responsibility. There is a discussion of the new power to organize men of knowledge and high skill for joint effort and performance through the exercise of responsible judgment, which has given us both the new and central institution of the large organization and a new ideal of social order in which society and individual become mutually dependent poles of human freedom and achievement.

*The new frontiers, the new tasks and opportunities:*

The second part (Chapters Four through Nine) sketches four new realities, each of them a challenge, above all to the peoples of the Free World. The first is the emergence of Educated Society—a society in which only the educated man is truly productive, in which increasingly everybody will, at least in respect to years spent in school, have received a higher education, and in which the educational status of a country becomes a controlling factor in international competition and survival. What does this mean for society and the individual? What does it mean for education? The second is the emergence  of Economic Development—"Up to Poverty"—as the new, common vision and goal of humanity, and of international and interracial class war as the new threat. Third is the decline of  the government of the nation-state, the "modern government" of yesteryear, its increasing inability to govern internally and to act internationally. And fourth is the new reality of the collapse of the "East," that is of non-Western culture and civilization, to the point where no viable society anywhere can be built except upon Western formulations.

A short concluding section—only a few paragraphs—asks:

What does all this mean for the nations of the West and for the direction, goals and principles of their government and policies?

*The human situation:*

The third and last part (Chapter Ten) is concerned with the new spiritual—or, if one prefers the word, metaphysical—reality of human existence: the fact that both knowledge and power have become absolute, have gained the capacity for absolute destruction beyond which no refinement, no increase is meaningful any more. This, for the first time since the dawn of our civilization, forces us to think through the nature, function and control of both.

Though I have tried to be faithful to the facts I am certain that I have often misunderstood them—as any newcomer to a strange country is bound to misunderstand. Though I have tried to be objective I am conscious of my Western background, and of my bias—that of the great tradition of European and especially Anglo-American conservatism with its beliefs in liberty, law and justice, in responsibility and work, in the uniqueness of the person and the fallibility of the creature. I am equally conscious of the limitations of my knowledge and understanding—above all of my weaknesses in the creative arts. But, still, I hope that the aim of this book: to report and to give understanding, has been reached at least to the point where it conveys to the reader both the shock of recognition—how obvious the unfamiliar new already is; and the shock of estrangement—how irrelevant the familiar modern of yesterday has already become.

# Landmarks of Tomorrow

# CHAPTER ONE

# The New World-View

Some few years ago two brothers—intelligent, well-educated, graduate students in their twenties—went to see a play on the New York stage, *Inherit the Wind*. This was a dramatization of the notorious Scopes "Monkey" trial of 1925 in which a schoolteacher in rural Tennessee was convicted for teaching Darwin's Theory of Evolution, and in which the great nineteenth-century conflict between science and religion reached a climax of total absurdity. When the brothers came home they said they were much impressed by the acting but rather baffled by the plot. What, they wanted to know, was all the excitement about? Their father, when their age, had been so deeply stirred by the trial that he had given up the ministry and become a lawyer. But when he tried to explain its meaning and its excitement to his sons they both exclaimed, "You are making this up. Why, it makes no sense at all."

The point of this story is that one of the sons is a graduate geneticist, the other one a theological student in a Presbyterian and strictly Calvinist seminary. Yet the "conflict between science and religion" could not even be explained to either of them.

It is almost frightening how fast the obvious of yesteryear is turning incomprehensible. An intelligent and well-educated man of the first modern generation—that of Newton, Hobbes

1

and Locke—might still have been able to understand and to make himself understood up to World War II. But it is unlikely that he could still communicate with the world of today, only twenty years later. We ourselves, after all, have seen in recent elections how rapidly the issues, slogans, concerns and alignments of as recent a period as the thirties have become irrelevant, if not actually incomprehensible.

But what matters most for us—the first post-modern generation—is the change in *fundamental world-view.*

We still profess and we still teach the world-view of the past three hundred years. But we no longer see it. We have as yet no name for our new vision, no tools, no method and no vocabulary. But a world-view is, above all, an experience. It is the foundation of artistic perception, philosophical analysis and technical vocabulary. And we have acquired this new foundation, all of a sudden, within these last fifteen or twenty years.

### "The Whole Is the Sum of Its Parts"

The world-view of the modern West can be called a Cartesian world-view. Few professional philosophers during these last three hundred years have followed René Descartes, the early seventeenth-century Frenchman, in his answers to the major problems of systematic philosophy. Yet the modern age took its vision from him. More than Galileo or Calvin, Hobbes, Locke or Rousseau, far more even than Newton, he determined, for three hundred years, what problems would appear important or even relevant, the scope of modern man's vision, his basic assumptions about himself and his universe, and above all, his concept of what is rational and plausible.

His was a twofold contribution.

First, Descartes gave to the modern world its basic axiom

about the nature of the universe and its order. The best-known formulation is that in which the Académie Française, a generation after Descartes' death, defined science as "The certain and evident knowledge of things by their causes." Expressed less elegantly and less subtly, this says, "The whole is the result of its parts"—the oversimplification of the ordinary man who is neither scientist nor philosopher.

Second, Descartes provided the method to make his axiom ②effective in organizing knowledge, and the search for it. Whatever the significance of his Analytical Geometry for mathematics, it established a universal, quantitative logic concerned with relationship between concepts, and capable of serving as universal symbol and universal language. Two hundred years later Lord Kelvin could redefine the world-view of Cartesianism by saying, "I know what I can measure."

That the whole is equal to the sum of its parts had been an axiom of arithmetic for almost two thousand years before Descartes (though it no longer is an axiom of all arithmetic today). But Descartes' formulation also implied that the whole is determined by the parts, and that, therefore, we can know the whole only by identifying and knowing the parts. It implied that the behavior of the whole is caused by the motion of the parts. It implied above all that there is no "whole" altogether as apart from the different sums, structures and relationships of parts.

These statements are likely to sound obvious today; they have been taken for granted for three hundred years—even though they were the most radical innovations when first propounded.

But though most of us still have the conditioned reflex of familiarity toward these assertions, there are few scientists today who would still accept the definition of the Académie

Française—at least not for what they call "science" in their own field. Every one of our disciplines, sciences and arts today bases itself on concepts which are incompatible with the Cartesian axiom and with the world-view of the modern West developed therefrom.

## From Cause to Configuration

Every one of our disciplines has moved from cause to configuration.

Every discipline has as its center today a concept of a whole that is not the result of its parts, not equal to the sum of its parts, and not identifiable, knowable, measurable, predictable, effective or meaningful through identifying, knowing, measuring, predicting, moving or understanding the parts. The central concepts in every one of our modern disciplines, sciences and arts are patterns and configurations.

Biology shows this more dramatically perhaps than any other science. The tremendous development of biology in the last fifty years is the result of the application of strict Cartesian method—the methods of classical mechanics, of analytical chemistry or of mathematical statistics—to the study of the living organism. But the more "scientific" the biologist has become, the more has he tended to talk in terms such as "immunity" and "metabolism," "ecology" and "syndrome," "homeostasis" and "pattern"—every one of them describing not so much a property of matter or quantity itself as harmonious order, every one therefore essentially an aesthetic term.

The psychologist today talks about "Gestalt," "ego," "personality" or "behavior"—terms that could not be found in serious works before 1910. The social sciences talk about "culture," about "integration" or about the "informal group." And all talk about "forms." These are all concepts of a whole, of a pattern or of a configuration which can be understood only as a whole.

These configurations can never be reached by starting with the parts—just as the ear will never hear a melody by hearing individual sounds. Indeed, the parts in any pattern or configuration exist only, and can only be identified, in contemplation of the whole and from the understanding of the whole. Just as we hear the same sound in a tune rather than C♯ or A♭, depending on the key we play in, so the parts in any configuration—whether the "drives" in a personality, the complex of chemical, electrical and mechanical actions within a metabolism, the specific rites and customs in a culture, or the particular colors and shapes in a nonobjective painting—can only be understood, explained or even identified from their place in the whole, that is, in the configuration.

Similarly, we have a *"Gestalt"* pattern as the center of our economic life, the business enterprise. "Automation" is merely a particularly ugly word to describe a new view of the process of physical production as a configuration and true entity. "Management," similarly, is a configuration term. In government we talk today about "administration" or "political process"; the economist talks about "national income," "productivity" or "economic growth," much as the theologian talks about "existence." Even the physical sciences and engineering, the most Cartesian of all our disciplines in their origins and basic concepts, talk about "systems" or—the least Cartesian term of them all—about "quantum" in which, in one measurement, are expressed mass and energy, time and distance, speed and direction, all absorbed into a single indivisible process.

The most striking change perhaps is to be found in our approach to the study of speech and language—the most basic and most familiar symbol and tool of man. Despite the anguished pleas of teachers and parents, we talk less and less about "grammar"—the study of the *parts* of speech—and more and more about "communications." It is the *whole* of speech, including not only the words left unsaid but the atmosphere in which words are said and heard, that alone communicates. It is only this whole that has any existence at all in communications. One must not only know the whole of the message, one must also be able to relate it to the pattern of behavior, personality, situation and even culture in which communication takes place.

These terms and concepts are brand-new. Not a single one of them had any scientific meaning fifty years ago, let alone any standing and respectability in the vocabulary of scholar and scientist. All of them are *qualitative*; quantity in no way characterizes them. A culture is not defined by the number of people who belong to it, or by any other quantity; nor is a business enterprise defined by size. Quantitative change matters only in these configurations when it becomes qualitative transformation—when, in the words of the Greek riddle, the grains of sand have become a sand pile. This is not a continuous but a discontinuous event, a sudden jump over a qualitative threshold at which sounds turn into recognizable melody, words and motions into behavior, procedures into a management philosophy, or the atom of one element into that of another. Finally, none of these configurations is as such measurable quantitatively or capable of being represented and expressed—except in the most distorted manner—through the traditional symbols of quantitative relationships.

None of these new concepts, let me emphasize, conforms to the axiom that the whole is the result of its parts. On the contrary, they all conform to a new and by no means yet axiomatic assertion, namely that the *parts exist in contemplation of the whole.*

*The Purposeful Universe*

Moreover, none of these new concepts has any *causality* to it. Causation, that unifying axis of the Cartesian world-view, has disappeared. Yet it has not, as is so often said, been replaced by the random and happenstance. Einstein was quite right when he said that he could not accept the view that the Lord plays dice with the universe. What Einstein was criticizing was only the inability of the physicists—including himself —to visualize any concept of order except causality, that is, their inability to free themselves of their own Cartesian blinders. Underlying the new concepts, including the new concepts of modern physics, is a unifying idea of order. It is not causality, though, but purpose.

Every one of these new concepts expresses purposeful unity. One might even state as a general principle of all these postmodern concepts that the elements (for we can no longer really talk of "parts") will be found so to arrange themselves as to serve the purpose of the whole. This, for instance, is the assumption that underlies the biologist's attempts to study and to understand organs and their functions. As a distinguished biologist, Edmund W. Sinnott, puts it (in his *The Biology of the Spirit*): "Life is the imposition of organization on matter." It is this arrangement in contemplation of the purpose of the whole that we mean today when we talk of "order." This universe of ours is thus once again a universe ruled by purpose —as was the one which the Cartesian world-view overthrew and replaced three hundred years ago.

But our idea of purpose is a very different one from that of Middle Ages and Renaissance. Their purpose lay outside of the material, social, psychological or philosophical universe, if not entirely outside of anything man himself could be, could do or could see. Our purpose, by sharp contrast, is in the configurations themselves; it is not metaphysical but physical, it is not purpose *of* the universe, but purpose *in* the universe.

I read a while ago a piece by a leading physicist in which he talked about the "characteristics of subatomic particles." A slip of the pen, to be sure; but a revealing one. Only a half-century ago it would not have been possible for any physicist, no matter how slipshod, to write of anything but the "properties" of matter. For atomic particles to have "characteristics," the atom —if not matter and energy altogether—must have a "character"; and that presupposes that matter must have a purposeful order within itself.

The new world-view, in addition, assumes *process*. Every single one of these new concepts embodies in it the idea of growth, development, rhythm or becoming. These are all *irreversible* processes—whereas all events in the Cartesian universe were as reversible as the symbols on either side of an equation. Never, except in fairy tales, does the grown man become a boy again, never does lead change back to uranium, never does business enterprise return to family partnership. All these changes are irreversible because the process changes its own character; it is in other words self-generated change.

Only seventy-five years ago the last remnant of pre-Cartesian thinking, the idea of spontaneous generation of living beings, was finally laid to rest by the researches of Louis Pasteur. Now it comes back to us in the research of respectable biologists who look for clues to the origin of life in the action of sunlight and cosmic particles on amino acids. Now respectable mathematical physicists seriously talk about something even more shocking to the Cartesian world-view; a theory of constant and spontaneous generation of matter in the form of new universes and new galaxies. And a leading biochemist, Sir Macfarlane Burnet, the Australian pioneer of virus research, recently (in the *Scientific American* of February, 1957) defined a virus as "not an individual organism in the ordinary sense of the term but something that could almost be called a stream of biological pattern."

In this new emphasis on process may well lie the greatest departure from the world-view of the modern West that has been ruling us for the last three hundred years. For the Cartesian world was not only a mechanical one, in which all events are finitely determined; it was a static one. Inertia, in the strict meaning of classical mechanics, was the assumed norm. In this one point the Cartesians, otherwise such daring innovators, were the strictest of traditionalists.

It had been an accepted doctrine ever since Aristotle that the Unchangeable and Unchanging alone was real and alone was perfect. The proudest achievement of the Cartesian world-view was to make this traditional axiom usable. Motion so obviously exists; yet on the basis of the axiom of the primacy of immobility it can simply not be explained, understood and measured—as was first pointed out two thousand years ago in the famous paradoxes of Zeno, such as the paradox of Achilles and the tortoise. Only calculus (together with Descartes' own Analytical Geometry the foundation of modern mathematics, and the first result of the new, Cartesian world-view of the seventeenth century) could find a way out of the impasse between the axioms of immobility and inertia and the experience of motion. This it did by the most ingenious trick: by explaining and measuring motion as an infinite number of infinitely small and perfectly static "stills."

It is far from true that this solved Zeno's paradox as the textbooks assert. Indeed we are becoming only too painfully aware today that the solution is inapplicable to genuine movement, that is to development—whether it be biological or economic growth—which cannot be explained away as a kind of optical illusion. But for three hundred years the modern world-view could do what no one before had been able to do— assert the axiom of inertia and yet handle motion with growing assurance. It could point to its success in analyzing, predicting and controlling motion as evidence of the validity of its axiom of the immovable and the unchangeable as alone perfect and real.

In *our* idea of process, however, we assume—and are increasingly conscious of the assumption—that it is growth, change and development that are normal and real, and that it is the absence of change, development or growth that is imperfection, decay, corruption and death. We are breaking, therefore, not only with the "obvious" common sense of the world-view of the modern West, but with much older and much more fundamental Western traditions.

## Toward a New Philosophy

These new concepts have, within the last twenty or thirty years, become the reality of our work and world, if not the small talk of the popular newspaper. They are obvious to us. Anyone rash enough to suggest that they are anything but obvious, and are indeed almost incomprehensible—methodologically, philosophically and metaphysically—would at best be stared at as an egghead and more likely be curtly dismissed as a hairsplitter.

There are beginnings toward the new synthesis we need—in biology and physics, in operations research and modern mathematics, in general systems theory, in semantics, linguistics and mathematical information theory. We are beginning to move from the old mechanical concept of discipline as determined by static properties of the subject matter, to new disciplines dealing with such universal configurations and processes as "growth," "information" or "ecology."

Anticipation of the new vision can be found in many great thinkers—Aristotle, Leonardo, Goethe, Bergson, Whitehead. The first to comprehend it, however, was probably that astounding South African, Jan Christiaan Smuts—the closest to the "whole man" this century has produced—with his philosophy of Holism twenty-five or thirty years ago. Physicists increasingly grope for it, as do Lancelot Law Whyte in his *The Next Development of Man* and Erwin Schroedinger, the Nobel Prize winner, in his *What Is Life?* The latest and most persuasive expression of the new view is *The Image*, by the distinguished economist Kenneth Boulding. The contemporary philosopher whose books sell best in paper-back editions in the United States is the late Ernst Cassirer, though his works are anything but popularly written—indeed a veritable thicket of Teutonic abstractions. His writings deal with patterns, configurations and symbols of order as the essential human experiences.

Yet though we take the new world-view increasingly for granted, we do not yet understand it. Though we talk glibly of "configuration," "purpose" and "process," we do not yet know what these terms express. We have abandoned the Cartesian world-view; indeed it is rapidly becoming almost incomprehensible to us. But we have not, so far, developed a new synthesis, a new toolbox of methods, or new axioms of meaning, order and inquiry. We have certainly not yet produced a new Descartes. As a result we are in intellectual and aesthetic crisis in every area.

The people working in a given discipline see the new process and configuration concepts; indeed, they often see little else. But for rigorous work they have only methods based upon the old world-view and the old concepts, methods which are quite inappropriate to the new vision.

In the social sciences this lag shows itself in the glaring discrepancy between the talk of "culture," "personality" or "behavior" and the inability to produce much more than vast collections of empirical data about particular—and by definition meaningless—manifestations.

In a discipline that is much closer to my own daily interest, the study of management, the situation is equally frustrating. The discipline only exists because we have configuration concepts such as "business enterprise" and "the process of managing." All of us stress that the really important things are process-characteristics, such as the climate of an organization, the development of people in it, or the planning of the nature and purposes of a business enterprise. But whenever we try to be scientific we are thrown back either on purely mechanistic and static methods, such as work measurement of individual operations, or at best on organization rules and definitions.

Or take the physicists: the more they discover about the various subatomic particles of matter, the more confused, complicated and inconsistent become their general theories of the nature of matter, energy and time.

Another result is that the very disciplines that are advancing the fastest, in which therefore there is the most to learn, are rapidly becoming unteachable.

There is no doubt that medicine has made giant strides during this last generation. But every experienced teacher of medicine I know wonders whether the young medical school graduate of today—the same one who gets "the best medical education the world has to offer"—is as well taught and as well prepared as his more ignorant predecessor thirty years ago. The reason is simple. Medical schools are still organized around the idea of disciplines as static bundles of knowledge. A hundred years ago, when the modern medical school came into existence in Paris, Vienna and Berlin, there were at most six or seven such "bundles." But there are fifty or more today. Each has become in its own right a full-blown science, which it takes a lifetime to master; even to acquire a smattering of ignorance in any of them takes more than the five years of medical training.

This crisis, it should be firmly said, is not the natural result of advancing knowledge as some academicians assert. The natural result of advancing knowledge should be, as it has always been, greater simplicity—and greater ease of understanding, learning and teaching. This is the first, if not the foremost, aim in advancing knowledge. That our knowledge becomes constantly more specialized, more complicated, rather than more general, proves that something essential is lacking —namely a philosophical synthesis appropriate to the world we inhabit and see.

What may well be the most serious affliction of this time of philosophical transition is the maddening confusion of tongues among the various disciplines, and the resulting cheapening and erosion of language and style. Each discipline has its own language, its own terms, its own increasingly esoteric symbols. The unity of the universe is gone for twentieth-century man—for the first time, perhaps, since Thomas Aquinas, seven hundred years ago, wove together into one pattern the religious and the secular heritage of Western Christianity. Whenever we try to re-establish such a unity all we can do is to go back to Cartesian, that is to ultrapositivist or mechanistic concepts of the world, which deny the very insights and knowledge that make the unification desirable and indeed necessary.

No wonder that the layman is confused, bewildered and sullen. We hear a great deal today about the anti-intellectual public. But what else can the public be if it cannot understand? Yet to understand, it would need the unifying general concepts which the experts themselves do not have.

Fortunately we already can foresee—as only a decade or two ago we could not—what form the new integration will take.

We can see first what it will not be. It will go beyond and encompass the Cartesian world-view rather than repudiate it. The great shift to the Cartesian world-view became necessary because its predecessor, scholasticism, had become sterile and had ultimately failed. The new world-view, however, has become necessary largely because of the great success of its predecessor, the mechanistic, positivist Cartesian "Science." We are abandoning the whole-parts concept of the Cartesian world-view, its mechanical causality, its inertia axiom. But while modern physics leads us, for instance, to rediscover Aristotle on an entirely new level of understanding, it does not make us any more appreciative of astrology. Modern biology and modern Operations Research make us conscious of the need to accept and to measure quality, value and judgment. They have not made us repudiate strict methods of demonstration and proof or abandon the quest for impersonal measurement.

Another negative conclusion: the Cartesian dualism between the universe of matter and the universe of the mind will not be maintained in the new integration. It was never fully accepted in this country. But it was certainly the most potent, as it was the most central, part of Descartes' own system. For three hundred years it has paralyzed philosophy—if not thinking altogether—by creating meaningless but increasingly bitter splits between idealist and positivist, with each building ever-higher spite fences around his own little plot of reality.

If there ever was a useful distinction here, it ceased to be meaningful the day the first experimenter discovered that by the very act of observing phenomena he affected them. Today our task is to understand patterns of physical, biological, psychological and social order in which mind and matter become meaningful precisely because they are reflections of a greater unity.

We can also say affirmatively what the new integration needs to be.

It must give us a concept of the "whole" as a universal and yet specific reality—whether it be "system," "organism" or "situation." We need a discipline rather than a vision, a strict discipline of qualitative and irrevocable changes such as development, growth or decay. We need rigorous methods for anticipation of such changes. We need a discipline that explains events and phenomena in terms of their direction and future state rather than in terms of cause—a calculus of potential, you might say, rather than one of probability. We need a philosophy of purpose, a logic of quality and ways to measure qualitative change. We need a methodology of potential and opportunity, of turning points and critical factors, of risk and uncertainty, constant and timing, "jump" and continuity. We need a dialectic of polarity in which unity and diversity are defined as simultaneous and necessary poles of the same essence.

This may sound like a big order—and one we are as yet far from being able to fill. Yet we may well have the new synthesis more nearly within our grasp than we think. On it are based powers we already exercise: the power to innovate, and the power to harmonize individual and society in a new dynamic order.

If there is one thing we have learned, it is the truth of the old injunction of the seventh-grade mathematics teacher: Don't worry about getting the right answer; what matters is setting up the right problem. In philosophy, science and methodology—and even more perhaps in art—a problem begins to be solved the moment it can be defined, the moment the right questions are being asked, the moment the specifications are known which the answers must satisfy. For then we know what we are looking for, what fits and what is relevant.

And that, in one after another of the areas of human endeavor, we already know.

# CHAPTER TWO

# From Progress to Innovation

## 1 · THE NEW PERCEPTION OF ORDER

Where is "inevitable progress" now? Only a generation ago, despite the shock of the First World War, the belief
in history's built-in progression was still ingrained. The French-
men of the generation of Briand and Herriot believed in it,
as did the well-meaning Social Democrats of the Weimar
Republic, the English middle class that flocked to the "Left-
Wing Book Club" in the thirties and the Liberals who then
dominated the American university faculties.

Today the very expression sounds odd—half macabre mockery, half plain foolishness. Occasionally a faint rumble of the
old belief echoes in the set phrases of political rhetoric; but
these are the phrases the city editor cuts out first when he prepares the speech for newspaper publication. Only the truly
convinced Communist doctrinaires still profess belief in the
historic inevitability of progress. But what they mean is the
inevitability of universal cataclysm. And that, one suspects, is
truly hoped for only by the old men now on top, men whose
beliefs were formed thirty or more years ago. Even in their
mouths it has a hollow, archaic ring—somewhat of a piece
with their stubborn clinging to Edwardian ornament or

17

"*Jugendstil*" in architecture, late-Wagnerian self-intoxication in music, and pre-Impressionist monumental painting.

As for the rest of us, including, all evidence indicates, most of the younger leaders in the Communist countries, we no longer accept the blithe optimism of "inevitable progress," nor its blind denial of the tragic in human life and the evil in human nature. We no longer believe that anything happens automatically except perhaps trouble. We are no longer sure of the direction we are going, let alone of the destination we are bound for.

But do we believe in anything?

No answer can be found in what we say and write. There everything is confusion, doubt, contradiction. But a clear, though unexpected answer is found in our deeds. We do not, indeed, believe any more in the inevitability, let alone the automaticity, of progress. But we practice innovation—purposeful, directed, organized change.

Innovation, as we now use the term, is based on the systematic, organized "leap into the unknown." Its aim is to give us new power for action through a new capacity to see, a new vision. Its tools are scientific; but its process is of the imagination, its method the organization of ignorance rather than that of known facts.

The impact of this new power on our lives is already great. It changes our technology and gives us new opportunities to make technological advance to order. It is giving us an altogether new ability for nontechnological innovation in society and economy.

Old basic institutions of human society—the government, the armed forces, the school—have been converted from organs of preservation into organs of innovation. And new institutions expressly designed for innovation, such as business enterprise and research organization, have become of central importance.

But innovation is more than a new method. It is a new view of the universe, as one of risk rather than of chance or of certainty. It is a new view of man's role in the universe; he creates order by taking risks. And this means that innovation, rather than being an assertion of human power, is an acceptance of human responsibility.

## The Research Explosion

The visible expression of this new belief in innovation is the activity aimed at producing new knowledge that we call "research." With the belief in progress in collapse, research, one should have expected, would slow down, perhaps even disappear. Instead there has been a research explosion.

Within the last forty years expenditures on technological research in American industry have risen almost a hundredfold, from less than $100 million a year in 1928 to $10 billion or more today. This represents only nonmilitary research on new technologies, new products and new processes for the civilian economy. From being a marginal factor, industrial research has become a powerhouse of economic energy. From being confined to a few large companies in a few highly technological industries such as electrical engineering or chemicals, it has become general—pursued alike by small and large business, by old or new industries. Proportionately industrial research expenditures have grown faster than any other item in the nation's budget, excepting only military research. Industrial research took 0.1 per cent of national income thirty years ago; today it takes almost 2 per cent of an income four times as large. There is little doubt that the trend is toward continued further growth, both absolutely and in terms of national income.

This is by no means a uniquely American development. It is closely paralleled in Great Britain—the only other country for which figures are published. In Switzerland and West Germany the trend has been the same. One large Dutch business concern, Philips, has increased its research efforts fiftyfold during this period despite depression, war and enemy occupation. Even in Soviet Russia industrial nonmilitary research has been expanding fast in the last few years—though the Russian economy, except for military purposes, is still largely imitative.

Nor has the explosive expansion of research effort and expenditures been confined to economy and business. Medical research expenditures have probably increased even faster. We all know the story of research in military technology; it has changed warfare more in the last fifteen years than it had been changed in the century before. Nontechnological research and inquiry, aimed at social innovation, which were almost unknown thirty years ago, are also growing to major proportions: organized research into accounting concepts or educational methods, into hospital administration, theories of organization or marketing practices.

Only a few years ago *Punch*, the English comic weekly, commented on the new "fad" by listing the numerous advantages and the one single disadvantage of industrial research. Among its main advantages were these:

It does no harm.
It reduces unemployment.
Visitors and shareholders alike are impressed by the sight of so much science and the smell of hydrogen sulfide.
One of these days someone may find something that will make all the difference in your business. At least according to statistics this is not altogether impossible.
Scientists are nice quiet lads without vice.
The only real disadvantage is *cash*.

*Punch* went on to say that it could not visualize any business-man comparing these advantages with the one slight imped-iment and remaining long in doubt what to do. After all, money is not everything.

When this comment appeared there were already many readers who did not think it funny—who, on the contrary, thought that the attitude behind it was the real reason why Great Britain had lost her economic leadership. Today there would be few who did not feel that the joke, if any, was on *Punch*. Indeed the Labour party won the election in the fall of 1964 largely by accusing the Conservative government of taking *Punch's* view on research.

## Man and Change

In the shift from yesterday's "progress" to today's "inno-vation" the new post-Cartesian, post-modern world-view finds its clearest expression. And in the new capacity to aim at and to bring about innovation—however crude and primitive it still may be—the new concepts of pattern and purposeful process have first become effective and operational.

Innovation views change as controlled, directed and pur-poseful human activity.

This is a new view, different alike from the traditional as well as from the "progress" view of change. However sharply opposed in other respects, both considered change as uncon-trollable; if purposeful at all, its direction and purpose were outside and beyond man.

Man has of course always lived in change. Consciousness of impermanence, of becoming and passing, and the faculty to adapt to both, are among his most distinct traits. Yet throughout most of history change was considered catastrophe, and immutability the goal of organized human efforts. All social institutions of man for thousands of years had as their first purpose to prevent, or at least to slow down, the onrush of change. Family and church, army and state, were built to be ramparts of security against the threat of change. All through history, "from time immemorial" has been the seal of approval and the hallmark of perfection, the "return to the good old days" the flag in which the very demand for the new had to wrap itself to be respectable.

Thus the Renaissance, for all its creative energy, for all the great changes it produced, saw itself as a return to the changeless perfection of classical antiquity. The contemporary Reformation saw itself as a return to the perfection of early Christianity. Any departure from the ways of the primitive Church was automatically a corruption. Much later still, the American Revolution justified itself as a restoration of the traditional "rights of Englishmen." And even after World War I, Europe instinctively aimed at the return to the "golden age" of 1913 rather than toward something new and in the future— which was surely one of the reasons for the resultant catastrophe.

The belief in inevitable progress reversed this attitude toward change; but it left unaltered the character of change as something outside man—in history, in social forces or in evolution. All it did, so to speak, was to change the minus sign into a plus sign without changing the equation. As has often been said, it secularized the Christian view of history as the progression of God's plan; but while the fullness of time was now to be measured by historical periods rather than by the clock of eternity, the process itself was still self-initiated and self-controlled rather than humanly initiated and humanly controlled.

By contrast we today no longer even understand the question whether change is by itself bad or good. We start out with the axiom that it is the norm. We do not see change as altering the order—for better or for worse. We see change as being order in itself—indeed the only order we can comprehend today is a dynamic, a moving, a changing one. And because change itself defines any order we can see, change can be anticipated, can be foretold to a considerable extent, and can therefore even be controlled.

Innovation itself is not new; it has gone on as long as man has existed. All of man's institutions except the family, all his thoughts, all his art, all his tools, once were innovations, developed consciously and introduced purposefully. What is new is the view of man as the order-maker, working consistently through the anticipation, control and direction of change.

Even the idea of organizing innovation is not so very new. In respect to social innovation it goes back almost two hundred years. The Northwest Ordnance of 1787, which innovated the pattern of settlement and government for the empty North American Continent, was an early example. The American Constitution was an essay in purposeful innovation with its concepts—at once so conservative and so radical—of a republic built on all three principles of legitimate rule: of law and courts as the true sovereign; of the simultaneous allegiance of the citizen to Union and to individual state; and of the self-regulation of the system through a prearranged process of constitutional amendment and revision.

Technological innovation based on science goes back as much as a century. It was in 1857 that a young Englishman, William Perkin, discovering by accident the first synthetic dyestuff, first set about consciously to apply scientific knowledge to industrial production and thereby became the father not only of science-based industry but of modern technology and of industrial research.

Among economists Karl Marx was the first perhaps to see the role of the businessman as innovator; to this insight he owes in large measure his power as an economic historian. But to admit this as meaningful would have destroyed the myth of progress. Hence Marx explained away his own insight by making the "objective logic of the class situation" the determining factor and dismissing the innovating act as mere self-delusion or conscious deception.

Today this seems to us incomprehensible. For we now take innovation for granted, and see change as the norm, instead of the occasional, the extraordinary and often the fearful. We hardly understand any more the "logic of history" or any other of the conceptual trappings of the age of progress.

But do we really *understand* innovation?

### Innovation and Knowledge

There is obviously a close link between science and innovation. Indeed the most common current definition of innovation would be that it is purposeful change by means of the systematic inquiry we call scientific method and of the new knowledge gained thereby. Innovation is clearly a result of the scientific breakthrough, that is of the emergence of scientific method as fundamental method, and of scientific knowledge as a main tool of human and social action.

But things are not quite so simple. One sign of this is the new relationship between pure and applied research in innovation.

Innovation aims at application; its goal is not knowledge in itself but effective change. This would argue for applied research which extends and makes usable pure knowledge as the appropriate tool of innovation. But increasingly we find—in the military, in industry, in society—that pure research has the greatest innovating impact. Today, especially in the United States, we talk a good deal of the mistake of slighting pure research. But contrary to public belief, we are not spending proportionately less effort or less money on pure research than has been spent traditionally. Proportionately we spend a good deal more, since historically pure research was always limited to a mere handful of people in a few universities. Still it is true that we have been slighting pure research as measured against today's innovation needs and opportunities; pure research has simply become the most effective form of applied research.

At the same time applied research too has changed its meaning and character. Just as pure research is increasingly concerned with application, applied research is increasingly concerned with fundamental knowledge, is indeed increasingly productive of new fundamental knowledge. Work on the dosage of antibiotics, for instance, would be considered applied research by any definition. Yet this work raised such fundamental questions as the genetic character of microorganisms, that it produced new fundamental insights into the nature of infection and the body's defenses against it. The conventional picture of pure and applied research is somewhat analogous to the relationship between radio transmitter and receiving set. The transmitter sends out its signals whether any set is tuned in or not. It is a one-way relationship in which knowledge radiates out to be converted and applied, but where nothing feeds back from application to knowledge. By contrast innovation assumes a circular process. Application, in trying to make existing fundamental knowledge effective in action, uncovers both needs for new knowledge of a fundamental kind and the necessary insights.

One example: the application of well-known theoretical statistics to the marketing problems of business uncovered the need both for a fundamental and nonstatistical theory of consumer behavior and motivation and for new fundamental insights needed to go to work on it. The pure research thus stimulated produces not only the necessary fundamental knowledge but new opportunities for new applications and the tools for them—which in turn uncovers new needs for fundamental knowledge, and so on.*

This shift in the relationship—or in our understanding thereof—will change the organization of systematic research and inquiry. We will have to provide for systematic feed-back from applied to pure knowledge. It will have profound impact on the relationship between disciplines and on the education of the people engaged in research and inquiry.

Yet this is only a symptom of something much bigger, though far less tangible: a change in the meaning of "knowledge." In the traditional concept the aim of the systematic search for knowledge was new facts (whatever this slippery metaphysical term might mean). The knowledge derived from innovation and the goal of its systematic, organized, purposeful search is, however, a new vision, a new pattern, a new attitude.

I shall—intentionally—take my examples from the economic rather than from the technological field.

Among the most potent and most visible changes in an industrial economy are the new tools and practices developed for the very old job of selling a product or a service: consumer credit, packaging, advertising, market research, brand promotion, chain stores, supermarkets and discount houses. Within thirty years they have changed the behavior of business, the behavior of consumers, the very face of our towns and cities—and in significant measure the structure of the economy, its strength and vulnerability, and the division of national income.

Yet these are not the real innovations, they are consequences and results of two big changes in basic view. We shifted first from a traditional view of selling as the specialized effort that persuades

---

* This circular relationship would of course always have been a more correct picture than the conventional one-way street—even in that purest of disciplines, theoretical mathematics. What matters here is, however, less which picture is correct, but which is seen, held and understood.

an individual customer to buy whatever it is the business produces, to one of marketing, which is a business-wide function aiming both at creating customer and market for the company's product and at adapting the product to customer and market. And now we are shifting again from this product-focused to a customer-focused concept which sees marketing as the "demand half" of the economy, that is as the sum of all efforts and activities necessary for the fullest and yet most economical satisfaction of customer wants.

Obviously each of these views sees the same elements—the market, the product, the customer, the producer, the distributive chain between the two, and so on. But each sees these elements in a different pattern. And it is this view of the pattern that is knowledge and the foundation of innovation, this view of the pattern that creates both the need for new knowledge and new approaches, and the opportunities to develop new tools, new methods and new distributive systems.

Another big change in our economic system during this last generation is the new view of the business enterprise as a human and social organization, the shift that underlies the emergence of human relations, of the new concepts of management and organization, and the rise of such new disciplines as industrial psychology and industrial sociology. Again there were no new facts; indeed all the elements had been known and understood for many years. What was new was a view of the relationship between men at work—the vision of the new human organization we shall discuss later on in this book.

Few innovations, whether technological or social, are as sweeping as these. But even the more modest innovation— the new "major medical expense" insurance policy, for instance, or a new plastic—results from such a new view: of the function of insurance or of the nature of illness as an economic problem for the family; of the structure of large molecules or of textile demand. If there is no such new view there is no innovation; there is only adaptation.

But there is also no innovation if the new view is accidental, is entirely hunch or guess rather than the result of a deliberate, systematic organized effort to reach it.

We believe today that such vision can, in all areas of human knowledge, be aimed at purposefully and brought about systematically. This is why we believe in innovation. But are we capable of planning, organizing and working for informed and systematic intuition?

### The Power of Organized Ignorance

Sixty years ago the great French physicist Henri Poincaré first pointed out the role of intuitive insight in scientific discovery. But to Poincaré this was essentially a "flash of genius," unpredictable and indeed subconscious. All one could do, Poincaré thought, was to train oneself to watch out for it. Today we increasingly believe that there is a conscious discipline—already learnable though perhaps not yet teachable—for the imaginative leap into the unknown. We are developing rigorous method for creative perception. Unlike the science of yesterday, it is not based on organizing our knowledge. It is based on organizing our ignorance.

The best example is an old one which antedates today's innovation by many decades: Mendeleev's formulation, between 1869 and 1872, of the Periodic Table of Chemical Elements—the great creative act of order on which rest both modern physics and modern chemistry. Mendeleev did not discover a single new element, nor a single new property of any of the then known sixty-three elements. He did not propound a new theory of elements, their structure or their relations. He did not, in other words, organize the then existing knowledge and build on it. All earlier efforts to bring order out of the chaos of nineteenth-century chemistry had tried to do just that; and though great men, such as Lothar Meyer, had spent years on it, they only added confusion. Mendeleev asked instead: What unknown and as yet undiscovered elements *must* we assume to make order out of those we know? Science textbooks quite rightly stress that Mendeleev's theory was proven through its power to predict the "blank spaces," the twenty-nine then undiscovered and unknown elements, their weights and their properties. But they rarely stress that it was the blank spaces that ordered the known sixty-three elements rather than the known sixty-three that provided the blanks. It was this organization of ignorance on which the whole tremendous accomplishment rested.

Few achievements can compare with Mendeleev's. Yet on a smaller scale we do today systematically what ninety years ago was an isolated and uncomprehended feat of individual genius. One example is the development of the atomic bomb in the Manhattan Project during World War II. Most nuclear scientists apparently understood right away that Hahn and Meitner by accomplishing nuclear fission had made possible an atomic bomb. But the development of the bomb itself required the systematic organization of our ignorance, the determination of the things that would have to become known, the inference of what they would be and would mean, and the organization of work on each piece of ignorance. Similarly the development of a vaccine against infantile paralysis was conscious and directed innovation based on the organization of ignorance over a twenty-year period. Again the question was: What, that is today unknown, do we have to assume to make order out of the chaos of our fragments of knowledge? What, in other words, are the specifications for future knowledge?

To discuss the various approaches and tools we are developing would go far beyond my purpose here. There is Operations Research for instance. It can be defined as the application of systematic method, especially of logic and mathematics, to risk-taking decisions. It is no accident that its original development in wartime Great Britain started with the idea of putting to work on strategic or weapons problems people who, while possessing rigorously trained minds, had no knowledge of the subject matter. Biologists, psychologists and mathematicians were for instance set to work on the allocation of aircraft or on antisubmarine defense.

There are methods such as "critical-factor analysis" which enable us to say both what new knowledge we need, and what new developments in other, apparently unrelated fields would have meaning for our problem.

We cannot yet build efficient solar-energy plants. But Dr. Kenneth Kingdon of the General Electric Company's Research Laboratory has shown, first, that there is enough solar energy to provide power for every house in the United States; second, how much such energy could cost and yet be competitive; third, that the only feasible system would need devices that do the jobs of photovoltaic cells and storage batteries; and finally, that the cost of these devices would have to be one per cent of present cells and 16 per cent of present batteries. This does not of course give us solar energy. But starting out with what we do not know, we arrive at a specification of what we need to know. As a result we can decide whether the project is feasible, what it requires in terms of knowledge, effort, and manpower, and how to allocate our time and money. It is even possible to predict how long it will take to get the new knowledge, what specific breakthroughs we need and where they might come from.

But the essential things are not the new tools but the new concept. It assumes that there is order—order in the universe, order to our imagination and order in the development of knowledge. It further assumes that this order is one of pattern, so that it can be perceived before it is known. It assumes that this perception of order is the basis of innovation. It finally assumes that we can "leap-frog" to this perception through the systematic organization of our ignorance from which we then can develop the necessary new specific knowledge and tools.

✍ ✍ ✍

## 2 · The Power of Innovation

Innovation adds; it does not replace. It cannot and will not take the place of the creative act, of the *"Eureka"* of sudden insight by the genius. Neither does it render superfluous organized work on the refinement and the adaptation of knowledge.

On the contrary: Innovation is used properly to multiply the power both of the flash of genius and of the steady slugging away on improvement, adaptation and application. It catches, so to speak, the flash of lightning of individual insight that streaks across the horizon, and converts it into permanent light. At the same time it can give direction to the work of improvement and can sense when the small, unimaginative steps in expanding existing knowledge reach the threshold of new imagination. Indeed it can organize for this leap.

The story of antibiotics is one illustration of the power to convert the flash of genius into systematic innovation. The flash of genius was Fleming's discovery of the bacteria-killing properties of the penicillium mold. The innovation was Waksman's insight, gained by the process of organizing ignorance, that here was a whole new view of biological action in the organism, and a whole new approach, the "antibiotic" one, to the treatment of disease. This took ten years. But once gained, it made possible, almost overnight, the organized search for new antibiotic microorganisms,

the development of specifications for them, the theoretical understanding of their action and of their risks.

An illustration of the impact of innovation on adaptations of
present knowledge is the development of a theory of the change
from an underdeveloped preindustrial and static economy to a
growing advancing, industrializing one. Ten years ago there was
no such theory. Today we have a theory, admittedly crude and
primitive, but adequate enough to win general acceptance among
economists, regardless of their other views, regardless even of the
side of the Iron Curtain they work on. Yet, unlike all other major
economic theories, there is no one great economist to whom the
theory of Economic Development can be credited. Rather it represents the achievement of a method: defining the aim, specifying
what we have to know, and analyzing a great many small improve-
ment-efforts to spot the threshold where adaptation turns into
doing something new.

Innovation does not change the permanent limitations of
human existence. But within them it adds a new dimension:
that of setting an objective beyond our power and knowledge
today, defining what needs to be done to make it attainable,
and organizing work to get it done. Again—this cannot be said
too often—there has always been innovation. What is new is
only that we are becoming capable of doing systematically
what before has usually been a streak of lightning, and that
we can organize ordinary mortals to do what before could
usually be done only by the rare genius.

There are two major areas of innovation: the created universe of nature and man's own society. There is technological
innovation, the finding of new understanding of nature and
its channeling into new human capacity to control, to prevent
and to produce. And there is social innovation, the diagnosis
of social needs and opportunities and the development of concepts and institutions to satisfy them. In both areas innovation
gives us new capacities. It makes technology open-ended. And

it makes it possible to go beyond reform and revolution in society.

## The Open-Ended Technology

Innovation makes technology open-ended and capable of being designed. We now can organize for technological innovation, both to obtain new basic resources of material civilization and to develop new material end products to our specifications. This in turn gives us, to an increasing degree, freedom to arrange the elements of the physical environment to fit predetermined human, economic and social ends rather than letting the available elements determine what is possible.

If we look at the history of modern technology, that is at the last two hundred years or so, we can see readily that the important breakthroughs were changes in the foundations. Some of these actually opened up fresh physical resources, such as the development of new sources of mechanical energy beginning with the steam engine, or the use of electromagnetic and electronic phenomena for communication and control. Some created new attitudes, that is new mental resources. Such were the application of system and knowledge to agriculture that began in England in the early eighteenth century, the application of thought to work—from Eli Whitney's interchangeable parts around 1810 to today's automation—and the application of science to create new products for the market, which began with Perkin in 1857.

Our industrial civilization rests on ten or fifteen such basic technological breakthroughs of the last two hundred years. The chronometer which made possible controlled navigation, the machine tools developed in the late eighteenth century, and the industrial production of steel invented around 1860 were the only ones among them that were improvements within the then existing technology; these three made it possible to do better, faster and more cheaply something that was already being done. All the others were innovations; they made it possible for us to do what we had never done before. They contributed a new power rather than better performance.

The same is true of medicine. There have been a dozen or so medical breakthroughs since Harvey discovered the circulation of the blood, and Jenner the smallpox vaccination. Every one of them was a true jump, every one created a new vision and a new power—quite apart from flying in the face of all that passed for medical knowledge and practice in its time.

Yet despite its fundamental importance, work on new foundations was peripheral rather than central to our effort to understand and to control nature. The bulk of our manpower, time and money has always been spent on improvement of existing knowledge. The breakthroughs, with rare exceptions, came from outside the going technological effort, came from the flash of genius. The popular picture of the lonely inventor starving in his garret is a caricature. Most of the men who contributed the breakthroughs did very nicely; and quite a few— Watt, Liebig, Perkins, Siemens, Bell and Edison, for instance —built flourishing industrial empires. Even in medicine, where up till 1880 or so, resistance to change was much more pronounced, few of the great innovators were denied their due recognition. But the popular impression senses rightly that the great technological breakthroughs were not themselves the product of organized technological effort but came from the outsider.

Innovation makes it possible to organize for such breakthroughs to new foundations within the organization of economy and technology.

We know that the food supply of the world can be greatly increased within the existing technology: by applying, world-wide, already available and tested methods of the technology and of the social organization of farming; by applying the research concepts and tools developed for the temperate zone to the largely unimproved crops and animals of the tropics which support half of mankind; and by cutting waste, loss and spoilage which now destroy half of everything produced in most of the world, through the application of well-known and tested methods and tools of farm finance, crop handling, farm marketing and transportation. Indeed we know that world supply can at least be doubled, and probably tripled this way.

We also know that all such applications may within fifty years have become inadequate to feed a rapidly growing world population on an increasing nutrition level.

We can, however, define clearly—*and this is innovation*—what other, new major source of food is already available to us. We know (though we do not fully understand) the basic process by which the mechanical energy of light is converted into the biological energy of food; we know above all that it is light rather than soil that produces biological energy. Hence we can determine that there is a major, largely unused source of food—the oceans—and that we can develop aquaculture, the systematic farming of the surface of the sea, to complement agriculture, the systematic farming of the surface of the land. Indeed we can say that aquaculture is capable of producing more biological energy than agriculture. Since light is the source of biological energy, the sea must be as productive, acre for acre, as is the land; it may well be more productive. There is of course more than twice as much sea surface as there is land surface; and, excepting only the arctic wastes, the entire sea surface is productive, whereas most of the land surface is not.

All this is theoretical argument: a new view of old and well-known facts. And it is not based on any sizable knowledge of marine biology. But now we can specify what knowledge we need and where to search for it. In agriculture we have two major sources of food: plants and vertebrate animals. In aquaculture we have three: plants such as algae, vertebrate animals (though they are mainly fish rather than birds or mammals) and, specific to the sea, invertebrate animals such as the small shellfish known as "krill," which exists in abundance in most oceans and furnishes the staple food of the large whales. Incidentally, these marine invertebrates have, of all known animals, the highest efficiency in converting fodder into meat, carbohydrates into protein.

We therefore can specify that we must explore all three potentially feasible areas of aquaculture; we know what specifications as to cost, production methods and yield each must satisfy to become practical; we can predict what knowledge we need, and so on. We can, in other words, organize for systematic work. We can even estimate how much time, effort and money it might take to produce large-scale practical results.

This is but one example. We can—and do—similarly organize innovation with respect to new sources of mechanical energy. Increasingly we should become capable of organizing innovations in other material foundations of human life: soil and water supply, weather and space. In respect to human life itself we are becoming capable of organizing innovation to maintain health in addition to curing or preventing disease. We are at work on developing means for cheap and effective self-control of human fertility.

In every one of these areas the process of organizing innovation, if spelled out step by step, might sound as simple as that of organizing for aquaculture (though, needless to say, the actual work is complex and difficult, will take many decades and may indeed never succeed). Yet though it sounds simple, it is a rigorous process which we did not possess fifty or even thirty years ago.

At the same time innovation opens up technology at the other end: that of materials and products. It enables us to make new products to specifications, indeed to arrange nature according to man-made stipulations:

Polymer chemistry, the branch of chemistry that deals with large organic molecules, has produced synthetic rubbers and plastic fibers, and underlies our fastest-growing industry. Here we increasingly start out with specifications: We need a material that has certain properties not found in any existing material or in nature. We can define what structure of the molecule this is likely to require. Then we can organize to build it. This, for instance is the process by which a German chemist, Ziegler, recently developed the new low-pressure polyethylene in which the atoms of an old substance, polyethylene, are rearranged to produce a new substance with new, planned properties.

The same approach is taken increasingly in pharmaceutical research—for instance, in the attempts to build, according to specifications, chemical substances that will "fool" a diseased organ or a cancer, that will be sufficiently close to its normal food to be snatched up hungrily, but will be sufficiently different not to nourish disease or cancer but to starve it. We are increasingly building to specifications materials and products in electronics and metallurgy, and in many other fields. And much that is of great impact is not in fundamental and big areas but in ordinary, everyday products and materials which too are increasingly being designed and redesigned according to theoretical specifications—of performance, of the market, of style, of price and cost.

Open-endedness with respect to the foundations, combined with open-endedness with respect to end products enables us to plan and design a business, a technology or even a national economy rather than adapt to existing resources or existing products.

It was axiomatic to traditional economists (including Marx), and is still taken for granted by most, that available resources determine what can be produced, and conversely that existing products require specific resources. This is the characteristic economic expression of the Cartesian world-view. If you have steel there are certain things you can produce; and to produce them you have to have steel. The only choice is between the alternative uses of steel. At any one time there is an optimum allocation of steel between these alternative uses, a fixed, determined, "best" utilization of equally fixed and determined resources.

This determinist view is changing rapidly under the impact of innovation. We can increasingly decide what end products we want and then find the raw materials for them. We can increasingly decide what raw materials we have available and then develop the uses for them. There are, obviously, real limitations. But these are being rolled back steadily; the space between them is already so large that it is sounder today for a country, a technologist or a business to start out with the assumption that there are no limitations than to start out with the determinist strait jacket of tradition and existing knowledge.

Thus paper, which as material for writing, printing and packaging is as basic to industrial civilization as is steel, has been a product of temperate-zone trees. Countries without such trees had to import paper or do without. Today we ask: What is it that the substance called "paper" does, and how can locally available materials be made to produce this? As a result we are today making paper from sugar-cane wastes. We can make paper from any source of cellulose, even from noncellulose raw materials if we have to. We can produce plastics that do the job of metals, or use glass to make textile fibers, and so on. These are not only technical possibilities but economic possibilities; indeed we can define what the costs should be, what conditions of raw-material supply, market and process would be needed, and how probable is their attainment.

We already feel the impact of this new reality in which the traditional mutual determination of resource and end product is being replaced by the ability of planned, purposeful substitution of both resources and end products. The traditional idea of the one "best" allocation of resources is being replaced, for every national economy, every industry and every business, by a choice between a number of optima which themselves are the result of human decision and action rather than of God-given resources. We do not yet have any economic theory based on this new capacity to choose. But a powerful new tool of economic analysis, input-output analysis, clearly assumes that we can choose between optima, can indeed create new ones. This is also what businessmen assume when they talk of "long-range planning."

### From Reform to Social Innovation

The invention of "lend-lease" rivaled all the new weapons as a contribution to Allied victory in World War II. It made possible a unified war effort for maximum production under central direction; and yet it strengthened national pride and initiative, indeed built on it. Similarly the Marshall Plan rather than the atom bomb restored the Free World. These are social innovations, and they have had an impact on the life of our generation as great as any technological innovation.

The emergence of Soviet Russia as a superpower rests neither on Marxist ideology nor on technology but on social innovations such as the farm-machine station which made possible the political suppression and economic exploitation of the farmer without complete collapse of food production; the Five-Year Plan; and the concept of mass education as a tool of both economic development and military prowess (none of these, needless to say, "Marxist" or even easily compatible with Marx). Economic Development, which marches over the world today, is another new social vision, a social innovation.

The great changes in the economy of the developed countries during the last twenty-five or fifty years have resulted primarily from similar social innovations. Cartels as well as antitrust laws are social innovation. In the United States the development of mass production, mass distribution, mass research and mass ownership of industry through pension funds and investment trusts has brought the great changes. All are social rather than technological innovations, as is the new concept of the role of government in the economy. "Productivity" is a social innovation even though its tools are, in part at least, technological.

All through the Free World—but in Soviet Russia as well —there is the new institution, the business enterprise, and the new process of making human resources fully effective, the process of management.

On a lower plane: Most businesses that have been outstanding successes during the last generation or two, and have grown from corner-store to giant size, have been based on social innovation. Marks and Spencer in England or Sears, Roebuck in the United States are based on a vision of the mass market; the Volkswagen on a vision of a European transportation revolution; IBM on a vision of the organization of information and office work; Philips of Holland on a new concept of the international economy and its new subsistence needs.

Social innovation is the mark also of the spectacular individual success stories—the "great millionaires" who so captivate the common imagination. From the English Press Lords or Henry Ford in the early years of our century to the Greek tanker kings today who built their fortunes on the realization that the world's energy economy had become an essay in transportation, they all started out with a new configuration of social elements, a new vision of social opportunities and social needs. Then they created the needed technology, invented new financial instruments or new methods of selling and servicing, and so on.

It could be said that social innovation is nothing new, that all along it has been at least as important as technological innovation, and has had at least as much impact. We could not even dream of an industrial economy but for the social innovation of insurance sometime late in the seventeenth century. For we could not take the economic risks of economic change if we also had to take, unprotected, the economic risks of natural catastrophe, of fire and flood, shipwreck and hailstorm. But social innovation has in the past decades become much more frequent, much more rapid, much more "normal."

We are today organizing for it—in every large business, in every large labor union, in every government. Few businesses have yet recognized this clearly (I know only of one, the General Electric Company, that has set up its headquarters staffs deliberately as social innovators). But every large company—and many a small one—works on social innovation in one or the other area: organization structure or marketing, managing technological research, distribution costs or financial policy, human relations or data processing, management education or international economic development. The same is true of governments and of universities, of hospitals and of military forces.

All this would mean little but for the fact that we are gaining the ability to make social innovations systematically, purposefully and effectively. We may not yet really understand what our new capacity is. But we do know that it is method rather than flash of genius, disciplined imagination rather than artistic temperament, and organized effort rather than lucky break. Above all it is a method that enables us to set objectives and to organize work for their attainment.

One sign of this advance is the conscious and deliberate integration of social with technological innovation in the new independent research organizations that have grown so spectacularly in this country since the end of World War II. Stanford Research Institute, Arthur D. Little and the Rand Corporation (a subsidiary of the U.S. Air Force) all combine technological and social innovation. Their staff includes social scientists and political scientists, management and marketing experts, economists and historians, working together with physicists, geologists, chemists, biologists and mathematicians.

Only twenty years ago this would have been unthinkable. When the research activities of the U.S. Department of Agriculture—the oldest, largest and most versatile research organization in this country—were reorganized and expanded during the thirties, for instance, natural-science research and social research were sharply separated. The very successful regional research institutes in the South or Southwest included in their program only physical research in raw materials, products or processes. Yet the postwar institutes owe their phenomenal growth and success precisely to the inclusion of social innovation.

The impact of social innovation is similar to that of technological innovation. It makes social organization open-ended. It makes possible the organized leap to new social ends, and the organized development of new social tools and institutions to specifications. It gives us a choice between ways of accomplishing social ends and a choice of ends to be accomplished by given approaches or institutions.

Twenty-five years ago we knew only one way to provide for the cost of modern medical and hospital care in industrial society: through a government-run compulsory national health service. The only question seemed to be whether there was a problem; and the evidence was clear that the rise of modern medicine—by making universal access to medical and hospital care desirable and possible—had indeed created a medical expense problem for all but the wealthy. Every European country followed the logic of this argument into a government-run national health service.

We in the United States would have done the same had we been "logical." Instead we defined the problem: to make the direct expenses of illness bearable for all. We defined the requirements: medical care had to be prepaid, and the risk had to be spread. We established easily that both were feasible; sickness has a predictable probability distribution. Indeed all national health plans then in existence were based on an insurance principle. We defined our specifications: to maintain the free choice of doctors by patients, the professional relationship between the two, the doctor's freedom to set his fees within the limits of professional ethics, and the principle of local and private control. Then we designed, one after another, new concepts and tools: voluntary hospital insurance, first for employee groups, later for whole communities; voluntary medical-care insurance for the "normal" illnesses; major-medical expense insurance for the infrequent but financially catastrophic prolonged illness; and so on. We created institutions: the voluntary community co-operatives such as "Blue Cross" and "Blue Shield" in free competition with medical-care plans and insurance companies. Every one of these steps served a specific partial purpose; yet each was taken with the end objective of universal total coverage firmly in mind.

By now we know the problem: The specifications cannot be satisfied completely; there are some marginal areas where government aid is needed to achieve the aim of financial protection for everyone: in reinsuring such marginal major-medical risks as the very aged, or in the care, treatment and expense of prolonged mental illness. One group—the very poor who are only casually employed—cannot be covered by insurance but must be cared for free, as charity patients, or helped out by governmental relief funds. We do not yet know how to insure the widow with small children unless she has a job. There are weaknesses in our system, just as there are weaknesses in every governmental system.

But we know that we are capable of solving the problem—have indeed solved most of it—at no more expense than the most efficient governmental system. And we have done so in a way that strengthened social values: professional independence, local initiative, self-government and pluralist competition, which we rightly or wrongly consider valuable and important.

The social problem to be solved was the same here and in Europe. The aim was the same. But the resources which we used to design the "product" were our own natural resources: the values and habits of American society.

There are also examples where the same resources are being used to design very different social end products. The Marshall Plan, for instance, used nothing new: loans, expert advice, intergovernmental committees. But the "product" was new indeed—and was the result of conscious design to satisfy a truly innovating vision. Another example is some of the international businesses being built today—by European as well as by American firms—who use very old means such as loans, patent licenses and investments, to build manufacturing businesses designed both to act as generators of economic development in underdeveloped countries and to prosper as "a stake in economic growth" rather than through a specific technology or product-line.

There is the prospect of European unification—not through conquest, not through the dazzling diplomacy of a Bismarck or through revolutionary uprising, but through the planned design and development of common bonds; of common institutions for specific purposes such as the Iron and Steel Community, the Common Market, or Euratom; of common interests and common experiences. The resources used for this creation of a Europe commonwealth are precisely the same national interests, national loyalties and national traditions that have always kept Europe apart.

On a smaller scale, but perhaps as important, are the efforts today to create the habit of voluntary co-operation for mutual improvement in the poor peasant communities of the world. These communities do have strong habits of co-operation, but only to maintain custom. New things are traditionally begun only by government from above. So many of the things that should be done are so easy: to dig a well, to grade an approach road, to use better seed. The impact of these simple things is greatly out of proportion to the effort. To do them, however, requires that the habit of community co-operation, which always operated to prevent change and to forbid initiative, now be directed toward promoting change and spurring initiative. The innovation lies in making the old traditions of the peasant the very means by which he acquires the vision and the power to do new things.

This last example brings out, I think, wherein social innovation differs from our old ways of producing social change: reform and revolution. Unlike reform it does not aim at curing a defect; it aims at creating something new. Unlike revolution it does not aim at subverting values, beliefs and institutions; it aims at using traditional values, beliefs and habits for new achievements, or to attain old goals in new, better ways that will change habits and beliefs. But it also tries to do something neither reform nor revolution could do: to give us a method for defining both the new that is possible or needed and the things that can be done to achieve it.

We need social innovation more than we need technological innovation. The new frontiers of this post-modern world are all frontiers of innovation. Neither reform nor revolution can solve these great problems; only genuine social innovation can do the job.

ᴘ ᴘ ᴘ

## 3 · INNOVATION—THE NEW CONSERVATISM?

Innovation is risk. Present resources are committed to future, highly uncertain results. Present action and behavior are subordinated to the potential of an as yet unknown and uncomprehended future reality.

Innovation can best be defined as man's attempt to create order, in his own mind and in the universe around him, by taking risk and creating risk. It can be defined as the organized, indeed deliberate, seeking of risk to replace both the blind chance of premodern times (as symbolized in the Renaissance belief in *Fortuna* as the presiding genius of human destiny) and the certainty of the more recent but still outdated belief in inevitable progress, both chanceless and riskless.

This is bold, very bold. It entails not just one heavy risk, but three: the risk of being overtaken by innovation, which one might call the risk of exposure; the risk of failure of the innovating attempt; and, heaviest of all, the risk of innovation's success.

### The Risks of Innovation

Innovation can change, almost overnight, the established order, render obsolete what only yesterday seemed impregnable, make dominant what only yesterday was negligible.

Economists tell us that the large business enterprise of today has a built-in momentum that may give it an advantage way beyond anything deserved by efficiency or managerial excellence, and may keep it strong, powerful and big long after it has ceased to be aggressive and competitive. There is something in this. Yet, of the hundred largest manufacturing companies in the United States only thirty years ago, more than half have disappeared from the list today. Some have vanished altogether, others have fallen way behind. Their places have largely been taken by companies which, thirty years ago, either did not exist at all or were insignificant. The newcomers owe their present position not to financial manipulation but to new technology, new processes or new products—that is, to innovation.

The risk of exposure in innovation changes the nature of international politics and international economics. There is always present the possibility of a sudden landslide that can completely alter the international landscape and the position and balance of forces. This might be a change in the international economy, in international resource-geography or transportation-geography. It might be a change in political constellation, in military or industrial balance of power, or national policy—all capable of changing, almost overnight, the international position of a whole country, even of the biggest and mightiest.

Such dramatic changes have of course occurred throughout history—but they came fairly infrequently. The cause may have been that mysterious historical event, one nation's decline in vigor or another nation's sudden outburst of creative energy. It may have been foreign invasion or a sudden shift in trade routes. Once in a long while it was the result of new technology, especially military technology. But what was rare "turning point" in the past has now become ever-present danger. What happened as by-product is now capable of being purposeful goal. What was *Fortuna*, in other words, is now risk.

This not only applies to a country internationally. It applies fully as much to institutions, groups and forces within a country, within an economy. Each technology, each industry, each business lives under the risk of being made obsolete without warning, of being destroyed or damaged by innovation, technological or social.

This risk cannot be avoided. On the contrary, any attempt to prevent innovation, even any attempt to ignore it, can only make the risk greater. Nor can the risk be shrugged off as "all in the day's work." It must be accepted and provided for.

Little needs to be said about the second risk in innovation, that of failure.

Innovation must anticipate the future and must commit

resources, efforts and destinies to this anticipation. But no human being can possibly predict the future, let alone control it. Innovation must therefore have a high failure rate. It may fail because the innovation was faulty in vision, insufficient in design or premature in timing. It may fail because of inability to produce the planned results or to produce them in the available time. Or—perhaps the cruelest but also the most common risk—the innovating attempt may succeed brilliantly, only to be obsolete by the time it is completed, overtaken by events, by the growth of knowledge, or simply no longer appropriate. Thus very few of the main lines of medical research that would have appeared to a well-informed man as most important and most promising thirty years ago have contributed much to the great medical advances since.

These two risks lead to a paradoxical conclusion. More and speeded-up innovation alone can protect against the risk of being overtaken by the innovation of others. But this necessity only commits even more resources to a gamble in which failure is more probable than success.

Yet, both the risk of exposure and the risk of failure are minor compared to the third risk: that of the success of innovation.

Innovation does not create new laws of nature. It is not even primarily concerned with finding such laws. It aims, however, at directing and channeling the forces of nature according to human needs and human vision. It aims furthermore at directing and channeling the values, beliefs, institutions and human resources of society according to those needs and that vision.

What impact beyond the desired one will a successful innovation have? What new and unexpected changes will it produce? What will it do to the fabric of society, its beliefs, its bonds of community?

A minor example: The development of effective insecticides such as DDT was rightly considered a great achievement. It made possible the truly innovating vision of control of disease-bearing and destructive pests. But unexpectedly, the new insecticides killed beneficial insects as effectively as destructive ones, bees as well as malaria-bearing mosquitoes. This unforeseen result not only threatens bird life deprived of its food; it threatens all the trees and flowers—among them our major fruit trees—dependent on insects for pollination.

Innovation is thus not only opportunity. It is not only risk. It is first and foremost responsibility. No one is responsible for chance; no one can do anything about it. One can only welcome inevitable progress or bemoan it; at most one can attempt to delay it. But innovation is deliberate choice; and we are responsible for its consequences.

The essential choices are between values, in respect both to aim and to means. Precisely because it makes technology and social structure open-ended, innovation poses the continuous question what its values are. Should we aim at strengthening our traditions or at weakening them? Should we aim high or be expedient?

There may be areas where the values are given and outside the innovating decisions. Industrialists in a free economy might claim that they must and do operate under an objective rule of profitability. Industrialists in a socialist economy might similarly claim that production determines their decisions. Neither is a clear and unambiguous measure. Profitability over the long run is, for instance, something quite different from profits this year or next; the difference is one of basic values. Similarly production may be measured by units, value, quality or cost—and all Soviet sources indicate that there is as much disagreement over the concrete meaning of production in that country as there is in a free economy over profitability.

But inevitable to all social innovation is a value decision in respect to the objective, the specifications selected, the institution built and the methods chosen. Every social innovation— whether by government or school district, business or labor union—expresses a view of what man and society are and what they ought to be.

Innovation is therefore always ethics—as much as it is intellectual process and aesthetic perception. It needs ethics (as a perceptive book* recently pointed out) as much to decide what value considerations are relevant as to decide which are right. Traditional ethics, regardless of school, looked for the right response to a given situation. We need ethics today that concern themselves with the problems of creating the right situation. Ethics, most philosophers would agree, have been rather arid since Spinoza, though hardly for want of books written on the subject. The climate of "inevitable progress" could not have been congenial to a discipline that assumes choice to be both relevant and rational. Now, perhaps, we can expect new fundamental and fruitful work in ethics—we certainly need it.

## Plan or No Plan?

The risks and responsibilities of innovation require themselves major innovations. The first risk, that of exposure to innovation, makes planning necessary. The second risk, that of failure in innovation, prohibits, however, any *central* planning and demands a competing multiplicity of local plans. The third risk, that of the impact of successful innovation,

---

* *Ethics for Policy Decisions* by W. A. R. Leys, New York, 1952.

demands a new attitude to change, a new politics of change in society. It demands essentially a new conservatism.

Twenty-five years ago an English Socialist economist, Barbara Wootton, wrote a pamphlet, *Plan or No Plan*, which had a profound impact on public and policy-makers, at least in the English-speaking countries. Her thesis was simple: Planning is a necessity; therefore centralized Socialist dictatorship, controlling alike society and economy, is a necessity. For the only alternative to centralized planning by fiat from above is the mad, self-destructive chaos of "no plan."

There were quite a few things wrong with the argument even then—it was naïve to the point of being disingenuous. But the syllogism appeared almost a truism only a few short years ago—and by no means only to Communists and Socialists. In those days American business also shared the view. The National Recovery Administration (NRA) through which, with enthusiastic business support, Franklin D. Roosevelt first attempted to overcome the Depression, was in essence centralized planning from above for the entire economy.

Today even the Communists, to judge by Russia's recent actions, have considerable doubt. The rest of us have none. Wherever the people in a country that had experienced centralized planning were given a free choice—in most of Western Europe for instance—they repudiated it. They had seen how little resemblance the reality of planning from above bears to the theoretical picture of an orderly and harmonious efficiency. But the alternative to planning by centralized fiat is not "no plan." It is *planning by self-control.*

Wherever we look today, we see planning. Long-range planning is the central theme of today's businessman. Every day my mail contains yet another speech or article on the long-range planning of a well-known company—in English, in German, in French, in Italian, in Dutch, in Spanish or Por-

tuguese or in Japanese. Company after company is setting up
a long-range planning department. And so is city after city.

Most universities work on a long-range plan. So do hospitals
and school districts, research laboratories, professional societies, newspapers and magazines, international bodies, the
military, political parties, government departments and law
firms. Indeed long-range planning threatens to become something of a fad. There is more than a grain of truth in the
Washington gibe: "We don't want to do the job so let's set
up another long-range planning study."

In many cases planning is still weak in its understanding
of the job and of the methods used. There is the tendency to
confuse planning with the futile attempt to outguess the fluc-
tuations of the business cycle. There is the tendency to try to
do planning by projecting the trends of the past into the
future whereas the starting point of planning must always
be the recognition that the future will be different. There is
the all-too-common belief that planning eliminates risk—
the most dangerous delusion of all, since planning is actually
risk-creating and risk-taking.

But there is also a growing understanding of the nature and
function of planning, and growing knowledge of the proper
tools and methods. We are learning the difference between
planning and prediction or forecast, and between what we
would like to see happen and what we can try to make happen.
We are learning the difference between blind gambling and
rational choice among risks based on informed judgment.
We are learning that the aim of planning is not to perpetuate
the present but to anticipate and force the new. The purpose
is innovation.

Above all we are learning that the only protection against
the risk of exposure in innovation is to innovate. We can
defend ourselves against the constant threat of being overtaken

by innovation only by taking the offensive. The best statement of this new attitude comes perhaps from the world of business: The time to change the theory of the business on which a company operates, and to innovate in respect to its character, function, objectives, product, market and organization, is when the company is most successful and most profitable. For every theory of the business eventually becomes obsolete. If a company waits until it starts to go downhill, it has usually waited too long.

This process requires an attitude that has been far from common. It requires that rarest of human insights: the willingness to question one's own success. But it is the only attitude that can make productive—can indeed make bearable—the risk of innovation. It is easy, for instance, to think through a country's foreign policy when it has failed—any editorial writer can do that. It is much more difficult to innovate a new concept of the country's foreign policy when the present one is highly successful. Yet this is the only way to prevent failure. And the aim of long-range planning is to make effective this attitude in an organized, systematic, continuous effort of innovation.

## Local Plan or No Plan

Because of the risk of innovation our choice is not between centralized plan and no plan but between centralized plan and localized plan. But the risk of failure in innovation converts this into a choice between local plan (which alone can work) and no plan, into which central planning degenerates. The risk of failure in innovation makes centralized planning impossible, indeed converts it into chaos and tyranny, and makes its certain outcome collapse. The odds are simply too heavy against the success of any one plan. We have to commit present resources to highly uncertain future results, stake ourselves on our ability to perceive the as yet unknown and to do the as yet impossible. Therefore we have to plan. But to expect any one such plan to come out right is folly, and so is the expectation that any one group of planners will come out right no matter how many alternative plans they develop. Elementary mathematics shows that the outcome of such a gamble must be worse than to have no plan at all and to play random chance.

At the same time the very stake in his planning forces the centralized planner to try to control everything; anything uncontrolled becomes a danger. Centralized planners would probably tend to become tyrants anyhow; absolute power always hungers for more power. But even if the planners did not want to tyrannize, centralized planning for the entire economy or for the entire society propels them inevitably toward it. The more the central plan embraces, the riskier the venture, the greater the odds against its success.

The inability to foresee, thirty years ago, the recent breakthrough areas in medicine may, at first glance, sound like an argument against organized systematic innovation. But the major breakthroughs that did occur were all the result of genuine innovation rather than of chance. The breakthroughs would not have been made if one man, or one group of men, no matter how knowledgeable, responsible or wise, had been the central planners of medical research. They were achieved only because the planning was multiple, pluralistic, autonomous, local. The example is thus both a cogent argument *against* centralized planning and a cogent argument *for* local planning.

We are concerned here with control, not with ownership, with centralized planning rather than with nationalization (though the two may tend to go together). Centralized planning by nation-wide industrial cartel—such as Roosevelt's NRA attempted—would be just as bad as centralized planning by the dictatorship of the proletariat. Altogether this is not just a matter of the economy where it has traditionally been fought out, but of all innovation, technological and social, by economic, by political, or by cultural institutions.

There are, it should be said, qualifications. As long as an economy is purely imitative of other, more highly developed economies—as Soviet Russia was and largely still is—centralized planning is possible. It is wasteful. It is beset with serious risks—Russia's economy has broken down unnecessarily into famine, uncontrolled inflation or paralyzing purges every five years or so. It is inevitably tyrannical. But it is not impossible. The moment, however, that innovation becomes as necessary as it is highly desirable, centralized planning becomes impossible. It is no accident that the Russians are now busily engaged in decentralizing their planning.

Centralized planning is also possible where the objective is sharply defined, the planning period very short and the costs not very important. The best example is war. It is no accident that the very idea of planning came out of the experience of World War I, especially out of the work of the American and German War Industries Boards. Even for war, however, experience argues against centralized planning for innovation; what can be planned centrally is the use of resources available, in existence and known. One of Churchill's strengths as a wartime leader was to understand this. He centralized decisions, even on details, in his own hand. He set up complete controls over existing resources. But he encouraged, initiated, pushed and fought for decentralized, autonomous, competing planning for all innovations, technological, strategic and social.

The argument against central planning is not an argument against planning by the central organ—whether the government of a country, the general staff of an army or the top management of a business. On the contrary, without effective planning by the central organ, planning altogether is impossible. The central organ must plan in respect to its own jobs: foreign policy and defense in the case of a government for instance, or basic objectives, financial policy and organization structure in the case of a large business—for it too faces both the risk of exposure and the risk of failure in innovation. In addition the central organ must represent the common interest in respect to local, autonomous planning. It must co-ordinate, balance and guide. It must make the final risk-taking decisions. It must set standards of conduct and of performance. Above all it must stimulate the local organs to plan rather than to drift. But it must not be *the* planner, must not even insist on conformity in the local planning efforts, but rather encourage diversity, competition and independence.

There is plenty of room to disagree where the line should be drawn between the sphere and authority of the center in planning, and the sphere and authority of local planning. We find this disagreement in international and national affairs. It is a live issue in a university between the central administration and the faculties, departments and individual scholars, and in a large business between top management and divisions, functional staffs and individual managers or professionals. There is also plenty of room for argument over the best pattern of co-operation, competition and autonomy between the pluralist innovating efforts of a society, a government, an army, a university or a business. But the principle is simple and clear: The risk in innovation is too great to allow uniformity and centralization; it requires different, autonomous, alternative, competing, local efforts.

Despite all the ink spilled over it, central planning is no longer the real issue. More real and much more difficult is the question: how "local" should local planning be? If too small or too narrow, a local organ will have neither the vision nor the resources to plan for innovation. If too large or too diverse, it will in itself become a central planner.

The Soviet Union has recently announced a policy of decentralizing planning by large geographic regions. It is almost certain that this is wrong and will work badly. On the one hand, the unit is both too large and too diverse. On the other, it is also too small and too narrow—both for industries that are national in their economic character and for real technological innovation. Peter Kapitsa, the Soviet Union's most distinguished physicist—and by no means a friend of planning—warned publicly against the decentralization of technological research which, he predicted, would become subordinate to regional expediency and immediate need and thus slight real innovation. Many managers of important businesses in the Soviet Union have at the same time—though much more discreetly—protested that the decentralization did not go far enough; the region is still a central planner whereas genuine local planning autonomy for each major business is needed. To anyone familiar with government, armed services, universities or business in the Free World these arguments will sound familiar.*

What makes the question of the best unit of local planning so difficult—but also so important—is that different purposes require different definitions of what "local" means and different organs for the job. There is no formula; and there should be no uniformity.

This concept of local planning may seem disorderly, wasteful, illogical. But the greatest planner of all knows otherwise. Nature provides against the risks of life by multiplicity and competition. It would be so much more orderly if there were only one plant and one animal. But when the mighty dinosaurs succumbed to a change in environment, there were available some obscure, wretched creatures, ancestors of the present mammals, to take their place—for they had produced an ap-

* This was written in 1957; only seven years later, in the fall of 1964, the failure of the geographic regions became one of the causes of Khrushchev's

parently useless innovation: self-control of their body temperature. It would be much less wasteful if the female frog laid only two or three eggs, or if there were just one sperm cell in the human semen to fertilize the female ovum. But rather than eliminate the overwhelming odds against the embryo frog's surviving to maturity or against the sperm's reaching the ovum, nature provides millions of both. And it is this multiplicity, this purposeful duplication, this result-focused logic, this co-operative competition, that is the true order.

Centralized planning was a first reaction to the new power of innovation and its new risks. But it attempted to organize a manifestation of the post-Cartesian world-view by Cartesian means: Centralized planning sees the world as a machine. Planning we need; but the risk in innovation alone forbids centralized planning and demands autonomous, competing, local innovation. Centralized planning attempts to order our search for new vision and a new capacity of achievement on the model of mechanical order, the measure of which is efficiency. But productive planning has to be modeled after a higher order—that of life, the measure of which is creativity. The aim of innovation is not a static conversion of input into output but a dynamic transmutation of ignorance into knowledge and of impotence into power. Its operational problem is not efficiency but risk.

### Innovation as Responsibility

Perhaps the most important—though the least tangible—consequence of innovation is the new responsibility it requires. It is above all a political responsibility.

If value choice is both inevitable and meaningful, a genuine, constructive conservatism becomes both possible and necessary. For then it becomes essential to take responsibility for the strengthening of basic values and the observance of fundamen-

---

fall—and the "genuine local autonomy for each major business" the central plank of the economic policy of the new leaders who succeeded him.

tal principles; to demand respect for the historical roots of a society but to despise its self-glorification; to respect one's fellow man but to know one's own weaknesses, limitations and fallibility; to demand a high goal and to take the long view. These are traditionally the qualities of the conservative temperament.

Conservatism found its profoundest spokesmen in the age of "inevitable progress": Burke and Acton, John Adams, Marshall and Calhoun, Stahl and De Tocqueville. It was the creed of great statesmen: Washington, Hamilton and Lincoln; Castlereagh and Disraeli; Metternich. But it could not be fully effective as a political force—not even in the countries of the Anglo-American tradition—because it either became pure reaction or it resigned itself to the role of retarder and brake, rather than creative force. Individual conservatives—George Washington is the great example in this country, Disraeli in England—could rise above this by becoming great and yet truly conservative innovators. But conservatism as such could only be an antibody (though a badly needed one). The age belonged to the liberal, the radical, the progressive, if not to the revolutionary.

Today both liberalism and conservatism in their traditional meaning are moribund. Indeed ideological parties are probably obsolete and certainly meaningless. And any revival of traditional conservatism is most unlikely.

We need something new: the conservative innovator, who accepts innovation and with it accepts, indeed asserts, responsibility for its risks and results. Precisely because an age of innovation can no longer ask whether there should be change or even how fast, but only argue over what it should be, aim for and do, this may well be the age of those who believe that responsibility rather than success is the measure of man: the age of the conservatives.

# CHAPTER THREE

# Beyond Collectivism and Individualism

## 1 · The New Organization

The medieval morality play is staging a comeback. During the last ten years our popular literature has become increasingly concerned with the ethics of human relations and the morals of power. But the actors are no longer the great of the earth, the bishops and kings, merchant princes and feudal lords. They are the great of organization: corporation vice presidents and battalion commanders in the army, engineers and sales managers. They wear neither coronet nor miter, but carry brief case and slide rule; they are clearly middle class in income and wealth, mores and behavior.

Yet their struggles for power and position, and the ethics of their relationship, have become almost overnight an absorbing and popular topic. They were the subject of Herman Wouk's *The Caine Mutiny*. Beginning with *Executive Suite* by Cameron Hawley, one popular novel after the other has focused on organization ethics in big business. The popular and much-discussed American television play *Patterns* had the same topic. Twenty or thirty years ago the most widely read books in the social sciences dealt with economics, psychoanalysis or cultural anthropology. Now we have James Burnham's *The Managerial Revolution*, Kenneth Boulding's *Organizational Revolution*, William H. Whyte's *Organization Man* and David Riesman's *The Lonely Crowd*—all four dealing with the ethics of man in large-scale organization.

The two best-selling novels published in Soviet Russia during the short relaxation of thought control after Stalin's death, Ehrenburg's *The Thaw* and Dudintsev's *Not by Bread Alone*, also dealt with the ethics and morality of men in the new organization. In England this has been the main concern of at least one outstanding writer: C. P. Snow. Himself a leading figure in the "new organization" (as Civil Service Commissioner in charge of scientific personnel), he has, in such novels as *The Masters* and *The New Men*, written searching studies of the problems of power, of responsibility, and of the behavior of men working together in organization.*

The new organization is hardly yet seen in its full meaning and impact. We take it for granted. But we rarely realize that it represents a new capacity we have gained within the last generation. Fifty short years ago, with few exceptions, only simple, repetitive, regimented work could be brought together in large-scale organization; any work requiring skill and knowledge, let alone judgment, could be performed only by the individual working alone. Today we have the capacity to organize men of high skill and knowledge for voluntary, joint performance through the exercise of responsible judgment.

* How recent all this concern is I myself can testify. For the first attempt to study one of these new organizations was a book of mine: *Concept of the Corporation*. When it appeared less than twenty years ago (in 1946), the very idea that anyone could seriously study the big-business enterprise as a social institution, and management as a central social function in society and economy, was considered strange if not revolting.

This is the new organization, the inevitable setting for the new, systematic innovation of our times.

This new organizing ability has already created a new social reality. It has given us a new leadership group and a new leadership function: the employed professional specialist and the employed professional manager.

It creates a new central issue of power, demands a new organization ethics and a new organization law.

It creates a new social problem—the integration of the professional men, both specialists and managers, into the organization—which bids fair to become *the* social question of the twentieth century.

It creates the need and opportunity for a major new field of human knowledge, and for a major new discipline, that of managing. This discipline should be, indeed must be, both systematic and humanist, both a special study and in itself a general, liberal education.

The new organizing capacity creates a middle-class society of men who are professionals in their work but rank as employees, managerial in their responsibility but middle class in their outlook, expectations, rewards, opportunities and values. This professional middle class is becoming the characteristic, if not the dominant, group in every developed society. Its emergence creates a new economics. Organization knowledge and professional knowledge are becoming the real "factors of production"; "land, labor and capital," the three factors of production of traditional economics, are increasingly becoming merely limitations on the effectiveness of knowledge.

Finally the new organizing capacity has by-passed the age-old fixed positions of individualism and collectivism alike, and is giving us a new vision of the nature of individual and of society, and of the bond between them.

This chapter will discuss this new organizing capacity and the new social reality that results from it.

## The Capacity to Organize

There may not be much substance to today's common plaint that the ablest and best-educated college graduates increasingly look for their life's work and career to a job in a large organization, especially the large business enterprise. But two things are certain: First, the large organization—whether business, civil service or armed force—has developed an apparently insatiable appetite for men of skill, knowledge and responsible judgment. Second, the young people of high skill and knowledge are increasingly convinced that what they have learned and know can be used effectively in the large organization, can be made productive in and through the large organization. Obvious today, almost taken for granted, these are brand-new and radical facts. They bespeak the new powers and capacities of large-scale organizations.

A good example of the new capacity to organize is today's air base. The traditional titles of rank of a military organization are of course still maintained. The Table of Organization still portrays a neat downward flow of decisions, knowledge and orders from the commandant at the top who "gives the orders" to the soldiers and noncoms at the bottom who "obey the orders." But what orders can the commandant actually give to a crew chief who is in charge of maintaining the jet planes of a squadron? Though only a sergeant, the crew chief applies his own skill and his own knowledge, both of a very high nature. He uses his own judgment. He, rather than the commandant or even the squadron commander, decides whether a plane can be flown and what has to be done to make it air-worthy. The commandant can discipline the crew chief, can demote him, can replace him. But he cannot "command" him; he can, at most, overrule him. Indeed it is one of the major jobs of the commandant to make possible the fullest contribution of the crew chief's skill and knowledge, the fullest exercise of his judgment. Conversely the more the crew chief knows and the more responsibility he accepts, the greater is his usefulness and contribution.

There are literally thousands of such people of decision-making skill and self-governing judgment on a modern air base: fliers and meteorologists, radio men and doctors, armorers and photographers, metallurgists, statisticians, operations researchers and psychologists. Each of them plies his own trade or profession. At the same time he is a member of the organization, working closely with men of different skill and knowledge, informed in his work by the direction, quality and purpose of the organization and of the other men in it, and in turn having immediate impact on the direction, quality and purpose of the work of the entire organization and on its performance.

Such military organization is today increasingly typical. Old-style military organizations may still be the major employers of men in all armed forces. But the new branches, on which the fighting and striking power of a modern armed service increasingly depends, are all of the new type: the aircraft carrier, the armored division, the parachute battalion, and now the guided-missile unit.

How radical a break this is, is shown by the picture of Napoleon's army in the movie made recently from Tolstoy's *War and Peace*. Here the French infantry attacks the Russian cannon on the heights of Borodino. Unprotected, out in the open, the infantry marches up the hill: eight men to a line, eight lines to a square, eyes forward, two steps to the drumbeat. Heads, arms, legs fly through the air; line after line is literally mowed down. But those left standing keep on like automata, eyes forward, two steps to the drumbeat. Napoleon's generals well knew that it would have been both more effective and much less costly for the men to take cover and then race uphill between salvos in loose formation. They even admired the

occasional "irregulars"—such as the American Revolution-
ists—who could do this. But they could not imitate them—
no army could. To organize large numbers of men for joint
effort required "drill," that is total subordination to iron
routine, and indoctrination in one regimented behavior until
it became a conditioned and compelling reflex.

This had been the principle of effective military organization
all along. Armies are the oldest large-scale organizations for
joint effort; the conduct of war has, for thousands of years,
been one task that could not be left to individuals or small,
local communities operating on their own. And for most of
recorded history armies were the only large-scale organizations.
They were—from their first beginning at the dawn of recorded
Egyptian, Chinese or Greek history until well into World War
I—based on the repetitive, almost automatic discipline of drill,
command and obedience. Now this traditional and simple organization of command is rapidly being infiltrated by a new
organization by responsible judgment.

The army is the most dramatic example of this new capacity
to organize, because, having been based so long on the old
ideas, it shows the contrast between the two so clearly. But
for the origin of the new concepts we must turn to a different
and much younger institution: the business enterprise. It is
there that the new concepts were first—though dimly—perceived. The earliest attempt can be found in the works of the
students of business organization fifty years ago—such as
Rathenau in Germany or Fayol in France. A generation earlier,
a few of the industrial masterbuilders of the late nineteenth
century—Carnegie and Rockefeller in this country, Renold
and Mond in England, Siemens and Abbe in Germany—had
already been applying some of the principles in crude form.
But only in the last thirty years has the business enterprise,
especially in its managerial structure, become the chief car-

rier and the chief developer of the new concepts.

Because it stands for the new capacity to organize, the business enterprise has emerged as a central institution everywhere, under free enterprise and under Communism, in developed countries and in underdeveloped ones. This key position of business enterprise in the organizational revolution explains why the older institutions, the armed forces, the government service, even the Catholic Church, today increasingly look to the business enterprise as their model of organization, and try (sometimes rather unwisely) to apply the new principles of management to their own structure and operations. This key role in developing the new capacity to organize has made business employment the preferred career for many able young people; even in the United States this represents a sharp change from the situation only a generation ago.

And yet even business enterprise, when it first emerged, depended on the old "regiment and drill" concept. Certainly, the first effective large-scale organization for economic performance, that is for the production and distribution of goods and services, was based on this concept. The pioneers of Scientific Management—such as Taylor and Gantt—groped for the new concept fifty years ago, and talked of tapping the human knowledge, individual responsibility and voluntary dedication of the worker. But they could not do it. Instead they gave us the assembly line. Their achievement rested on their breaking down productive work into simple, repetitive, routine tasks. It was the great and enduring contribution of Scientific Management to have seen that productive work, like fighting work, could be studied rationally, analyzed systematically and organized purposefully. But then they organized through the same old regimentation and drill, and broke down jobs into repetitive, simple, mechanical motions. The "assembly line robot," that favorite manikin of the twenties and the thirties, was nothing but Napoleon's soldier moved into Henry Ford's plant.

Organization created energy and performance vastly superior to what any individual, no matter how skillful or how experienced, could have produced—just as the ancient Greek army of part-time, nonprofessional citizens, outperformed the professional "artists" of warfare who had met in single combat under the walls of Troy. But fifty years ago we could not have organized had we not been able first to reduce work to drill, skill to obedience, knowledge to training, and co-operation to the assembly line. Today the assembly line is obsolescent. Today we know that even mechanical work is best organized as joint effort of men of high skill and knowledge exercising responsible, decision-making, individual judgment in a common effort and for a joint end.

This is the essence of automation as a concept of human organization for work. Automation may well eliminate the unskilled worker from the production floor. But it replaces him by an equal number of men of high skill and judgment: machinists, instrumentation specialists, programers, engineers, mathematicians, business analysts and so on. Each of them works in his own field of knowledge with a broad discretionary area of judgment. Each of them, however, must of necessity work closely with all the others—in constant communication with them, constantly adjusting to their decisions and in turn making decisions that affect their work.

The principles and concepts which automation applies to mechanical production work had earlier been developed for nonmechanical work in the business enterprise. They are fast becoming the rule for all those who are not "workers" in the traditional usage of the word, but who labor productively as technicians, professionals and managers.

*Individual Work and Teamwork*

The new organization is transforming work that was previously confined to individual effort. It does not replace the individual by organization; it makes the individual effective in teamwork.

It has always been axiomatic that work of skill and knowledge, and above all work requiring judgment, has to be done by the individual on his own. This "self-evident truth" was the basis of all individualist philosophy. Insofar as organization was seen to apply at all, its purpose was to make it easier for the individual to work by himself and to produce his own individual results.

The finest example is the traditional university in which the individual scholar is given the greatest freedom of work and thought, and in which the institution provides the common student body, the physical plant, the housekeeping and the financial means to make fully effective an essentially self-contained effort of individuals who share only the commitment to intellectual integrity. Similarly the modern research laboratory, as it emerged around 1850, made the individual master scientist more effective by supplying him with housekeeping and with trained assistants.

The Civil Service—also an invention of the nineteenth century—was at first designed to make effective the individual acting alone and by himself rather than in and through an organization. The British Civil Service in India succeeded in running a whole subcontinent with a mere handful of men—never more than a thousand. Each of them was on his own, usually after the briefest period of apprenticeship; he rarely even saw another official from one month to another.

Even the one big step beyond purely individual work of skill, knowledge and judgment did not change the accepted theorem. This advance was functional specialization—the idea that one could organize a number of people of like skills and knowledge for group effort.

This concept came originally out of the military. Since the eighteenth century different kinds of fighting work—infantry, cavalry or artillery—had been increasingly organized as separate branches. This made possible great advances in the effectiveness of each branch and of the entire military organization. But it required that the working together of different branches be held to a minimum. Each developed its own skills, its own weapons, its own tactics, its own traditions, its own officer corps with its own education and careers; but they came together only in the plans and orders of a commander outside and above them. And since even with functional specialization we could organize only very small numbers of people of skill and knowledge to work together, to advance meant of necessity constant fission of fields of knowledge into separate and separately organized specialties.

The same principle was followed when functional specialization came to be applied to the economic tasks of production and distribution—at about the same time that Scientific Management was applying the much older organizing principle to unskilled work. In business too we could only organize work of skill and knowledge by setting it up in self-contained and isolated functions. We still could not organize more than very small groups for joint effort, and were then forced to set up more and more separate and autonomous subfunctions. Any of our business functions—whether engineering or accounting, manufacturing or marketing—shows the same limitations and underwent the same development.

In functional specialization, in other words, we tried to organize skill and knowledge work as if it were performed by one man—with each branch or department acting like one man in its relations to the entire organization and to all other branches and departments. We never attempted to organize people of different skills and different knowledge, making different contributions, in one joint effort.

Contrast this with today's organization. Contrast this for instance with the organization of the work that went into the production of the atom bomb, where thousands of high-grade professionals of all kinds of knowledge—physicists, mathematicians, chemists, design engineers, soldiers, procurement specialists, financial people, personnel people, production experts, and so on—worked together, organized not by functional specialization but by the stage of the project. Increasingly this is becoming the preferred organization of our research laboratories. Indeed it is the only effective organization for purposeful and systematic innovation.

In the army functional specialization, while still providing the background of education and career, is gradually giving way to interfunctional integration, for instance in the Regimental Combat Team.

Even in the university—the most specialized of all our organizations, and the one where, as a rule, department and specialty lines are most rigidly drawn—interdisciplinary courses and research are becoming increasingly common. Here a number of scholars from different disciplines work together on a common subject matter to which each contributes his own knowledge. In one of our large Eastern universities, for instance, there were in 1957 more than four hundred such interdisciplinary courses, studies, seminars or projects. Among them was a course in Western civilization bringing together historians, philosophers, natural scientists, painters, musicians, political scientists and economists; a graduate seminar on labor problems run jointly by a lawyer, a cultural anthropologist, an economist and an engineer interested in automation; and a research project on electronic-computer design headed by a linguist and embracing psychologists, engineers, mathematicians and physiologists.

In business we have similar approaches. For specific assignments we increasingly use the "task force" or the team composed of men from different functions and specialties working together. For permanent operations we use decentralization which organizes within the business large numbers of men of different specializations for joint work, common performance and maximum contribution around an objective, common, nonfunctional concern, such as a line of products or a market.

The clearest example of the new team concept is the gradual transformation of the hospital. When it first emerged from being a place for the poor to die in—Florence Nightingale and the Crimean War of 1854 were the turning point—it was organized as a facility for the individual master doctor. The nurses existed to carry out his commands, the medical staff to assist him. As late as 1880 even the "first assistant" in a major hospital had to wait for the "chief" rather than perform an operation himself or make a diagnosis.

This soon turned into functional specialization: Until quite recently, advances in hospital care resulted primarily from increasing specialization, and from the increasing isolation of specialty from speciality.

Today we have the diagnostic clinic in which specialists work together as a team—with the patient the unity rather than the specialized field of knowledge. Increasingly nonmedical professionals are becoming partners in the team: dieticians, psychologists, social workers, biologists, physical therapists. The nurse is changing from "servant" of the doctor into executive officer of the team—the one who co-ordinates the efforts, watches the patient, measures the effectiveness of the treatment, and so on.

In one large hospital, the nurse is given the diagnosis and the plan of treatment decided upon by the doctor in charge. It is her job both to organize the efforts—to provide the medication, arrange for the clinical tests, mobilize dietician, therapist or psychologist—and to inform the doctor should the course of the illness deviate from the stated expectations.

Indeed this shift of the nurse's role has gone so far that one order of Catholic nuns, founded expressly to nurse the sick, thinks of withdrawing from nursing. "The change in the nurse's role is wonderful for the patient," says the Mother Superior, herself an experienced hospital administrator, "but we were not founded to serve the body but to serve God through being humble and through doing work that the world despises and spurns. And now we all have advanced degrees. Now we are becoming professionals and managers if not 'bosses.'"

Equally indicative of the change is the emergence of the hospital administrator—less and less often a medical man himself—as the "manager" of the large organization that today's hospital has become, and of hospital administration as an area of study in which we apply the new concepts of organization.

Perhaps most significant of all is the fact that today's doctor can hardly practice medicine any more unless he have access to, and membership in, the big, organized, managed joint effort that is today's hospital. He has not ceased to be an individual professional; indeed the hospital multiplies his effectiveness as an individual professional. But only in and through the organization can he any longer be effective as an individual; he has become as dependent on the organization as the organization used to be dependent on him.

Nowhere, it should be said, is the new organization yet to be found in perfect or pure form. The new capacity to organize is everywhere still mixed in with old forms and concepts of organization. Many doctors for instance still try to practice pretty much the way their grandfathers did; many hospitals are still organized as they were in 1910. Most men in uniform in all countries are in organizations much closer to the basic concepts of Napoleon's infantry than to the needs of the modern air base. Even at the air base the formal structure of organization is closer to tradition than to its own new needs or to its own informal but effective way of life. The same is true of most small business.

Yet numbers are not very relevant; statistics tell us where we have been rather than where we are, let alone where we will be. The institutions that are dynamic in, and characteristic of, our society are organizing on the new concept. The social problems, the social ethics, the social knowledge of our age all are the problems, ethics and knowledge of the new organization.

⚑ ⚑ ⚑

## 2 · FROM MAGNATE TO MANAGER

The best-known and most spectacular American financier of our age, Robert R. Young, committed suicide early in 1958. It was not ill-health that drove him to take his own life. He had not lost his money; on the contrary, he was a very rich man at the time of his death. There was no threat to his control of a number of large and important businesses. But it had apparently dawned on an ambitious man that all he had was money rather than power, prestige or even public respect. He had always craved power and prestige, had indeed become a financial manipulator as the best way to power. Ten years before his death, it was rumored, he had even expected to be the presidential candidate of one of the major parties. At the very least he expected high public office.

Fifty, even thirty, years ago this would not have been an unreasonable ambition. The businessmen who then attained power and public office in American life were often financial operators—Bernard Baruch under Wilson, for instance, or Andrew Mellon and Eugene Meyer a decade later under Herbert Hoover. Businessmen have indeed been more prominent in American public life these last fifteen years than at any earlier period. But they are no longer financial magnates but professional managers—men whose ability is not financial manipulation but the capacity to organize, men whose distinction is not their wealth but proven performance in leading men of professional skill and knowledge in joint effort.

Ironically, Robert Young started out on the right road to power and public position; as a young man, he had been a major executive of General Motors, the world's largest manufacturing company, and was slated to go to the very top. For all his brilliance he misjudged his world, however. Wanting power, he switched from manager to magnate just when the tide of history began to flow the other way. Thirty years later he had become the era's outstanding financial operator and the one tycoon in the railroad industry. But when a committee of Congress started hearings on the financial plight of the American railroads in 1957, the man whose battles for control of the railroads and crusades for railroad reform had made headline news for twenty years was not even called to give his opinion. Railroad managers, economists, engineers, labor leaders, tax experts, all were invited to testify; but it did not, apparently, occur to anyone to ask the man who looked upon himself as the savior of the American railroads. This, it seems, decided Young to give up; his failure, which his suicide admitted, was echoed by the keynote of the obituaries in the newspapers: "What a waste of talent and ability this life has been."

*Specialist and Manager*

This too is a morality tale, straight out of *Pilgrim's Progress.* But it is above all an example of the shift brought about by the new capacity to organize. The employed professional is fast emerging as a center of authority and responsibility, and as a symbol of achievement in our society.

The two kinds of employed professional—the professional specialist and the professional manager—are mutually dependent on one another. They must exist and work together to be effective at all. The same man may do both kinds of work in his job; but the two functions are different and distinct.

The professional specialist is an expert in one area of knowledge. There are few of the traditional areas of human knowledge and endeavor which are not tapped by today's organizations: all the natural sciences and all the humanities, engineering and mathematics, logic and the law, writing, teaching, architecture and economics, the military arts and the new disciplines of business such as accounting, marketing and manufacturing. Each of these is a discipline in itself, a large and growing field of organized knowledge and systematic accomplishment. In each of these specialties and in many others today's organization needs men of expert knowledge and professional standing.

The specialist must apply his knowledge as a professional. This means not only that he has to be good at his trade and to try constantly to be even better. He has above all to take responsibility for his own performance and his own contribution; for only the man who contributes knowledge can truly measure his own effort and contribution.

There is an old story which illustrates this. In the wilds of Afghanistan, the big car of an American tourist broke down and refused to start. No one could figure out what was the matter;

even the factory representative who was flown in gave up. The tourist was ready to abandon the car and go home when someone remembered that an old blacksmith who lived beyond the mountains some fifty miles away had, in his youth, tinkered with engines. In his despair the tourist sent for him. Three days later the old man appeared on a mule. He took one look at the car and asked for a hammer. He gently tapped one spot on the engine twice, and said, "Start her up"; and the engine purred as smoothly as if it had just left the test stand.

"What do I owe you?" the grateful tourist asked.

"A hundred dollars."

"What, a hundred dollars for two taps with the hammer?"

"Well, I can itemize it for you," the old man said:

*For two taps with hammer—ten cents;*

*For having known where—99 dollars and 90 cents.*

In the work of the professional specialist the ten cents' worth of hammering can always be measured easily, but not the "having known where" of knowledge, dedication, initiative and responsibility.

For this reason the professional specialist needs the manager. The specialist works in a field of knowledge and accomplishment that, like every field, sets its goal in its own terms: engineering or biological knowledge, sales or functional buildings. It is the job of the manager to bring all of these together, to make them effective and weld them into one performance. His professional knowledge is the capacity to organize. He is certainly dependent on the specialist. But the specialist is equally dependent on him.

This is the reason why the professional manager has emerged as a new focus of social order, of social mores and of individual aspirations. The manager's position is grounded in the objective needs of the job and his authority is grounded in results and knowledge. It cannot be explained away as "delegated" either by property owners or by elected representatives; it can barely be controlled by them. The manager's position is, in other words, a professional rather than a property or a political position. Yet, unlike the traditional professional, such as doctor or lawyer, he must exercise power over people. His decisions have not only individual but broad social impact.

The manager is the agent of both economic and social development. The absence or shortage of managers is the critical deficiency of underdeveloped countries and the supply of managers a foremost asset of the developed ones. For the manager is the carrier of our new capacity to organize.

It makes little difference if the manager is not an employee but an owner. He must act as a professional, must subordinate his ownership interests and his ownership rights to the objective need of the organization for managerial performance. Otherwise the organization will fail.

The classic example is Henry Ford. His refusal to be a professional manager, or to allow others to manage, his insistence on acting in the role of owner, all but destroyed his company. Its resurgence after his death in 1945 resulted primarily from the deliberate and thorough introduction of systematic, professional managing and from the employment of professional managers in large numbers, who were given full authority and responsibility despite being employees.

The rise of the professional specialist and the professional manager creates new opportunities. It creates a new social mobility. It creates a new ladder of advancement. It creates new concepts of accomplishment, and new authority. It creates new educational opportunities and needs. But it also creates new problems of responsibility and justification of power.

## Power and Responsibility in Organization

We have here a new situation. The new organization needs both professional manager and professional specialist; but it must also exercise power over them. Both manager and professional must be true to their values and their vision. Yet the organization is not a tool for their own individual ends; it has ends of its own—objective and impersonal—toward which the individual has to direct his own vision and efforts. Moreover, manager and specialist each has his own distinct, necessary work; but they depend on each other to do it. And both need the organization.

Each of the three—organization, manager and specialist—is a power center.

The organization has to have power over people. Yet in a free society it must never be allowed to become an end in itself for which the individual is just a means. It must never be allowed any power over individuals other than what is absolutely necessary for its function in, and contribution to, society. It must never be permitted the dangerous delusion that it has a claim to the loyalty or allegiance of the individual—other than what it can earn by enabling him to be productive and responsible.

Every organization serves but a partial function in society and satisfies but one of many human needs—defense or economic production for example. As such it can exercise only partial power even in a despotic society, let alone in a free one. It must never substitute its partial interest for the common weal. It must never, for instance, demand or expect of a man that he do his job at the expense of his responsibility as a husband and father, a citizen, a church member or a member of a profession.

Altogether organization must never be allowed to consider its relationship to the individual member as an indissoluble union; it must treat it as existing only for a specific purpose and therefore revocable. Rousseau's deep insight that the right to emigration is the ultimate safeguard against tyranny applies perhaps more to the new organizations than to any other community, precisely because they are partial, limited-purpose communities. Whenever an organization restricts this right, it abuses power.

We are in this country today greatly (and understandingly) exercised over corruption, racketeering and profiteering in some labor unions. But crooks are nothing new—and the law usually catches up with them. Much more dangerous is the claim of the "decent" labor union to the total allegiance of its members and to control of access to a trade or industry. Increasingly, for instance, labor unions in this country and in Great Britain, abusing the closed shop, expel members for opposition to the incumbent union leadership, and thereby deny them access to their living. A good many of the powers which the law grants to the labor union today can no longer be tolerated.

But a business which through bonuses, pensions or stock option plans puts such a penalty on quitting as to make it virtually impossible for an executive to "emigrate," also usurps power and practices antisocial restraint of mobility. It is understandable that an executive bonus be paid in ten annual installments rather than dissipated entirely in income tax. But if, as a result, the executive cannot quit for ten years without losing a bonus already earned, concern for his tax problems becomes an antisocial stranglehold on him. These fetters are no less binding for being golden, no less intolerable for having been forged in the interest of the individual and at his request.

The professional manager too has power—has to have power. But this power too must never go beyond what he needs to perform. It must never be allowed to become personal power over people, let alone power to manipulate, to "adjust" or to make over personality.

It makes no difference whether abuse of the manager's inherent power is hidden or in the open, whether it is brute oppression or affable manipulation of consent. Nor does it matter whether the motives are selfish or genuine altruism, desire for self-aggrandizement or mistaken kindness. It is abuse, if not despotism, for a manager to aim at power rather than at responsible performance.

The manager has a responsibility to the people working with him. He has the responsibility to build the structure in which men can achieve the most, and to find the right spot in the structure for each of the professional specialists. He must make most effective whatever skill and knowledge the specialists have, and give full scope to their judgment. He has to keep them informed of the common goal toward which their efforts are to be directed; and he has to keep himself informed of the new potentials of contribution and performance opened up by advances in areas of specialized knowledge. He has the responsibility to create, in other words, the conditions in which the professional specialists can both achieve the most and develop themselves the most. And he has the responsibility— both to the individual and to the organization—to demand superior performance and to condone nothing less.

The issues of power and responsibility of organization and manager are widely seen and discussed. But the even more crucial issue of the power and responsibility of the individual professional specialist in organization is just coming into the open.

So far, we have worried most about the responsibility *to* him.

"How should we manage research scientists?" is the question I am always asked.

Everyone seems surprised when I say: "I can't answer that till you tell me what you expect *from* them."

When the United States Department of Defense recently brought in a senior executive from a big company to head up the work on missiles, it stressed his ability to get along with scientists whereas his ability to get performance from scientists is really what will count.

The professional specialist has been regarded as something old and familiar: the independent professional such as small-town lawyer or family doctor. As he moved onto organization staffs all that appeared to change was legal form: He worked under an employment contract rather than in a client relationship. Actually the professional moved from a position of social isolation and purely personal responsibility into one of social power and community responsibility when he became a professional employee in the organization.

The professional specialist must contribute voluntarily. But he cannot contribute arbitrarily. He too has power: his effort, his knowledge, his willingness and ability to convey knowledge in usable form, and his exercise of judgment determine the capacity and achievement of others. He has a responsibility toward his area of knowledge—he has to be a professional and not just a technician. He has a responsibility toward the organization, for without the organization there would be no opportunity for him to work as a man of skill and knowledge (and get paid accordingly). He has the responsibility to make his contribution most effective and most productive for the joint effort and the joint result, and to direct his own vision and work toward the objective of the whole.

The new organization thus requires an organization ethics—for the organization itself, for the professional manager and for the professional specialist. Such an ethics must demand self-respect, self-discipline and humility appropriate to the new great power and the new high responsibility. It must be operational rather than "preachy"; it must enable people to act, to decide and to judge their own behavior against commonly accepted standards. The new organizing capacity creates both the need and the opportunity for the development of new ethical concepts, new ethical principles, and above all of new living examples of responsible conduct.

Law is also needed wherever authority and responsibility have to be defined.

A large labor union—the United Automobile Workers—has set up an independent board of outsiders to hear appeals from members against decisions of union officers. A large company—Continental Can—gives each employee the right of direct appeal to the president against managerial decisions on promotion, job-assignment, demotion or firing. An automobile company—Ford—establishes a mixed tribunal of company officials and dealers to hear appeals against decisions on a dealer franchise.

All these are judicial processes set up to develop a "common law." So is the grievance procedure under a union contract; indeed arbitrators appointed under such contracts in major American industries consciously try to develop a coherent body of common law through their decisions. But the organization manual of large organizations—whether businesses, government agencies or armed forces—also is a "legal" document, a primitive constitution; increasingly such documents not only define the limits of authority but provide for organized procedure to settle conflicts.

This, as any historian of the law knows, is the way legal concepts and legal institutions have usually come into being. That this is not clearly understood is the result of a modern misconception which—contrary to historical experience—defined "law" as "enactment of the sovereign government." Such a public enactment our new organization law is not and must not be. It must be private not only in its origin but in its sphere and scope.

Governmental legislation can provide orderly process—but not the substance of organization law. Government-enacted organization law could establish the demand for internal safeguards against abuse of power, and provide for judicial review of internal decisions. To go beyond, and to try to legislate substantially for the internal power relations of the new organizations, would lead to laws to enforce morality, that is to sumptuary legislation, which has always been ineffectual. To try to regulate internal power relations administratively must lead to arbitrary bureaucracy which is not only ineffectual but subverts law in the end.

The law we need must deal with the function and limits of power which is public rather than private law. But it is the public law largely of autonomous, self-governing bodies such as we have not known, by and large, since the Middle Ages. We have little legal theory, few precedents and, except for Canon Law and the codes of military justice, few examples. Yet this organization law may well be the most rapidly growing area of common law today. It is genuine law—i.e., impersonal, objective and general—but "layman's law" rather than "lawyer's law."

## The Organization Man

Not much is heard these days of that favorite bogeyman of the twenties and thirties: the assembly-line robot, the helpless human being destroyed or at least bored to death by the repetitive monotony of the assembly line. Only twenty years ago, Charlie Chaplin in his last great movie, *Modern Times*, gave artistic expression to the protest of human creativity and human dignity against the regimentation of traditional organization. Today the assembly-line robot is gone.

His place in the folklore of industrial society is now increasingly taken by a very different figure: the organization man—the bright-eyed, gray-flanneled junior executive of high education and good income, who succeeds in imposing conformity and the riskless monotony of "perfect adjustment" on a challenging and responsible, if not creative job.

This new manikin is of course just as much a caricature as

was the assembly-line robot. But however distorted it reflects a real problem: that of the professional in the new organization.

Organization ethics and organization law will not by themselves come to grips with the problem which organization man presents if only in caricature. Organization ethics and organization law deal with power structure and constitutional processes. But the question of the professional in organization is a social issue.

One good example of the nature of the social question we face is to be found in the large modern corporation-law firms which have become centers of legal practice in the United States. A common problem here is the middle-aged lawyer who is not a partner and will never be one. By the standards of the nineteenth century this man would be judged a success. Financially he is at least twice as well off as most independent lawyers. He has job security. He is usually expert in one branch of the law. This is not, in other words, the problem of a Willy Loman—the tired, unsuccessful "hero" of *Death of a Salesman.*

Yet the middle-aged lawyer in the big law firm, despite his income, despite his security, despite his knowledge, is only too often a frustrated, bitter and bored man. He may be all but irreplaceable; but at the same time he tends to become increasingly resentful of the organized practice of law, increasingly unwilling to contribute his knowledge to the partner who, in charge of the law work for a client, has to pull together all legal knowledge available within the firm into one legal strategy.

When he was younger this man may have enjoyed the intense competition within the large law firm which subjects all juniors to the constant scrutiny of the partners, makes them jockey for recognition and for promotion, makes them hope for the "one break." In middle age the days of promotion are over, and the competitive struggle is nothing but the increasingly unbearable tension of the "rat race."

An intelligent law firm will avoid this problem by getting rid of those associates who are not "partner material" by the time they are forty. It will place such men in good jobs with a client's legal department. It will help them to set up in practice for themselves or to join a smaller firm as a partner. This is laudable acceptance of responsibility—but still an admission of defeat. If the only thing you can do in conscience with your highly expert people is to get rid of them just when they should reach their peak, there is something badly wrong with the structure or the spirit of your organization.

One issue is status.

Here is a man who decides much bigger issues than many independent lawyers ever hear about. He has, for instance, a real impact on the behavior and fortune of large businesses. Yet he is an employee, is subject to somebody else's decisions, is a dependent.

Another issue is opportunity—for fulfillment rather than for advancement. The large organization actually creates many more opportunities for advancement than any previous social structure. Yet more and more, professional people have to be satisfied and effective as subordinates, have to gain pride, status, fulfillment in a job that ranks way down.

There is a subtle quality problem here. As long as there have been organized armies the great majority of officers who have become majors have retired as majors. It has always been true that not everybody can become a general. But there is a difference between a major who remains a battalion commander while another battalion commander moves on to become general, and a meteorologist-major who remains a major because this is the furthest any meteorologist can go under the existing system. The first may feel personally aggrieved, may feel that he is a better man than the general, and that he owes his bad luck to favoritism and intrigues, if not to the proverbial stupidity of the higher-ups. But his job, whatever his personal feelings, is a subordinate job; it is, within a much smaller sphere, the same kind of job as the general's. The meteorologist's job, however, is not subordinate. It is a specialist's job requiring highly advanced scientific knowledge. In his own field he is asked to function as a general while enjoying the status only of a major.

We have the same situation in industry in respect to the professional specialists: engineers, chemists, accountants, production planners, sales forecasters, purchasing agents and hundreds of others.

Opportunities for advancement, recognition and status—and of course largely also for rewards—have been primarily managerial opportunities. We have a major job ahead to create opportunities for status, recognition and reward for people who become leaders in their field of professional knowledge, without at the same time becoming decision-making, risk-taking managers. We have to create these opportunities without destroying the necessary authority and responsibility of the decision-maker, the unity of action and the discipline of joint effort and performance.

To a considerable extent this is a problem of welding different value systems into the common goal of one organization. The meteorologist who perforce remains forever a major, the contract expert who will never become a law partner, the metallurgist who will never be more than a senior engineer, all of them are likely to accept the need for the general, the partner, the department head or vice president. But as professionals they resent the inferior position which, so it appears to them, their own inferior status assigns to knowledge. They see a conflict between organization logic and the professional integrity of their discipline and of their own work. Yet a man of skill and knowledge, exercising responsible judgment, must be dedicated, must strive to make a contribution, must believe in what he is doing. Mercenaries can be satisfied with pay, promotion or plunder. Professional people if they want to respect themselves must see their work as serving no mean end, and as part of a grand design.

Perhaps an even more important social question is the competitive pressure and tension within the modern organization.

There is a widespread popular myth that the large organization offers security—contrasted with an equally mythical individualist society fifty or a hundred years ago, in which men supposedly fought it out on their own in a competitive system. But to the young people in our universities this is not how the world looks at all. They see life today, life in the organization, as intensely competitive.

"Our grandfathers had it easy. They started as lawyers, as doctors or as shopkeepers on their own, and had no one to satisfy but themselves. If they did not do so well, then they were content to live modestly—and were still lawyers, doctors and shopkeepers in the eyes of the neighbors." But now— so the argument runs—you are in competition even before you are hired, in competition against school grades and college grades, in competition with all the others for the trainee job. As soon as you are hired you come under constant scrutiny, are perpetually appraised, set one against the other. You are under constant pressure and tension: Will you get the raise, will you get the promotion, will you get the transfer, will you get the "break"? You are being pitted against the very people who should work with you most closely. They lose out if you go ahead; and conversely they benefit by your being passed over.

The young people are right. I am convinced that it is this competitive tension of the large organization which is largely behind the desire of the young to impose conformity on the universe, to play it safe, to do what is expected of them. It may be the only defense of the individual against pressures which are wrong socially and individually, because they put emphasis on getting ahead and promotion rather than on the work itself.

It is of course easy to exaggerate both the extent and the tension of this competitive pressure. Moreover we can do a great deal to alleviate the competitive pressure within the large organization, for example by making the individual professional job bigger, especially in the earlier years. But the large modern organization will remain a competitive world.

A country doctor does not compete against a Park Avenue or Harley Street diagnostician; nor does a small-town lawyer compete against the leader of the tax bar in the capital. They have different rewards which are commensurate to the very different risks they take. They have different satisfactions. But they have the same status in society. Both say of themselves, "I am a doctor" or "I am a lawyer"; neither is the other man's boss. In the new organization however the individual doctor reports to the medical director, the individual lawyer competes for both status and income with all the other men in the legal department.

The old social question of the nineteenth century was one of classes, the new one is one of individuals in society. The old one focused on economic justice, the new one on social justice. The old one was concerned with economic opportunities, the new one is primarily concerned with the value decisions and the value priorities of the social order.

The old social question expressed a blind conviction in the reality of worldly success, indeed a conviction that success solved all social problems. The new social question is a problem of success—and the issue is precisely what success means.

For this reason incidentally the new social question is, individually, a concern of the middle-aged, whereas the old one was primarily a concern of the young. The manifestation of the new social question is not rebelliously militant youth—that unique nineteenth-century phenomenon—but people twenty years older, who quietly retire on the job.

The slogans, theories and pat answers of the nineteenth-century social question may still dominate our political rhetoric. Indeed that stubborn relic of 1850 society, the dedicated Communist, may refuse to admit that there can be any other issue. In socially and economically developed countries, however, the new capacity for the organization of men of skill, knowledge and judgment for joint work and common performance has largely made irrelevant the social problems and social concerns of the nineteenth century. But the very success of the new organizing capacity has created a new problem, a new social question, that of the individual professional in large-scale organization. It is increasingly the social question of our world.

## The Discipline of Managing

We have been organizing for thousands of years. Yet little, if any, attention has been given to the systematic study of organization. Even in the military field the emphasis has usually been on leadership—that is, on personal individual impact—rather than on managing—that is, on systematic, purposeful, organized, sustained effort. Within the last fifty years, however, with the emergence of the new organization, managing has become a major field. The works on the subject run into the thousands. Schools that promise to teach business administration or public administration are the most rapidly growing of all our educational institutions, and attract more students than any of the schools in the older professional fields.

Perhaps even more important, we are going in for advanced manager education in which mature and successful managers go back to school, in some places for a whole year. The demand for advanced management education greatly exceeds the available supply.

Twenty or even ten years ago this might have been shrugged off as an American fad more expensive but not much more significant than flagpole sitting. Today education for management, whether for young people or for mature managers, is growing as fast in Western Europe as in the United States, in Latin America, in Australia or in India. Advanced management schools are to be found in England, in Switzerland, in Germany, in Holland, in Italy, in Chile, in Australia, and so on. In India the education of managers is recognized as one of the central problems of economic development—especially of managers for government-owned enterprises.

Most amazing perhaps is the spread of this development to Communist countries. The whole idea of management is still officially nonsense and heresy to any good Marxist; yet one of the first things the Poles did when they loosened the Russian fetters a little in 1957 was to ask for advice and assistance on management education. The Yugoslavs too—though carefully and quietly —are bringing in management experts from the West to advise them. A major theme of Khrushchev's demand for decentralization of Russian industry was the need for systematic education and development of managers, and for a systematic discipline of managing.

Yet while institutions for management training multiply, the discipline they are set up to teach remains rudimentary. We still need a discipline of managing, that is, a systematic body of knowledge that can be taught, learned, increased and improved by systematic work and study. This is a discipline of the new, post-Cartesian world-view. Its subject matter is a process. It starts out with a purpose of accomplishment. No matter how much we can quantify, the basic phenomena are qualitative ones: change and innovation, risk and judgment, growth and decay, dedication, vision, rewards and motivation. And the end product of the knowledge we are trying to gain is value decisions affecting individual and society.

Take "Operations Research." In its application of quantitative, that is mathematical and statistical, tools to entrepreneurial situations, its goal is to identify clearly the risk-taking value decisions among which the manager can choose. The goal is to inform his judgment and to educate his imagination, rather than, as in a Cartesian discipline, to replace both by rigorous, quantified "facts."

The discipline we need cannot be a technical discipline—though it will have many technical areas. It cannot even be a specific discipline such as physics, for instance. It must be truly humanist: of human beings united in common vision and common values and working for a common goal, yet acting individually. It must focus information, knowledge, judgment, values, understanding and expectations onto decision, action, performance and results. It must deal with men as thinking, doing, feeling and appraising beings, and must therefore pull together intellectual, emotional, esthetic and ethical knowledge. Thus—in important respects not unlike the discipline of medicine—the discipline of managing must both be fed from all fields of knowledge dealing with man's experience and, in turn, feed new knowledge back to all of them.

One of the central areas that the discipline of managing needs to explore is how an organization functions. Here are hundreds, if not thousands of people, each doing his own work according to his own knowledge. Yet their end product is common performance. What must they know to be able to direct their efforts toward the common end? What must others know about their work and their knowledge? What decisions have to be taken, when and where? And how are they to be conveyed to all the people who have to take action to make the decision effective?

The new organization, whether an army or a business, is above all an information and decision system. Information, ideas, questions, flow from the outside environment as well as from the people within. They not only have to be perceived and transmitted; the relevant has to be separated from the merely interesting. Then somebody has to make a decision which in turn has to flow back to the places where it can become effective action. Information and decision systems are around us everywhere; every living being is one, and so is every machine. But the organization is probably the most complex. In the first place, it is composed of human beings rather than biological organs or machine parts. In the second place, unlike any other system, its responses and goals are largely determined from within and can be changed by conscious decision. The study of information and decision systems is rapidly becoming a central discipline—one of the unifying disciplines of the new world-view. Its toughest problems, but also its greatest application, will be found in the new organization.

The new organization, almost by definition, commits present resources to future and highly uncertain results. The time span of decisions thus presents a perennial problem. Virtually every decision in these organizations—on a new weapon or a new arrangement of units in the regiment, on a new product or a new training program, on a new subsidy or a new tax schedule—is a long-range decision. Usually years must pass before the decision is fully effective, years during which it produces only costs and pains and no results. And then further years are required before the decision has paid for itself, years during which it therefore must still be the "right decision." How does one make such decisions? What has to be known?

When is the right time? And what kind of people are needed to make them and to see them through? How should they be educated? What should they know and what should they do? How are they to be motivated, measured or rewarded?

The new organization is subject to a pathology of its own: its own diseases and limitations, its own periods of aging and decay. It is, for example, congenitally prone to degenerate into bureaucracy.* In this disease emphasis shifts from accomplishing something in society and economy to keeping things from being done.

Some of the familiar symptoms of bureaucracy are: mistaking efficiency for effectiveness, as in measuring the performance of the post office by the pieces of mail it handles rather than by the speed and cost of their delivery; confusing "getting along with people" and endless meetings with teamwork and co-operation; mistaking size for importance, as in the standard Washington saying: "This can't be important; it doesn't cost enough"; mistaking "our way" for the right way—the "we have always done it this way" school of managing; mistaking administration, that is the internal workings of the organization, for its business; and "busyness"—the filled brief case, the long hours, the four telephones on the desk, the swirling chaos of assistants—for enterprise, performance and work.

An organization belongs on the sick list when promotion becomes more important to its people than accomplishment in the job they are in. It is sick when it is concerned more with avoiding mistakes than with taking the right risks, with counteracting the weaknesses of its members rather than with

---

* C. Northcote Parkinson, an English economist and sometime bureaucrat, has recently catalogued the major forms of the bureaucratic disease in his *Parkinson's Law and Other Studies in Administration*, a book that is at the same time extremely funny and deadly serious.

building on their strength. But it is sick also when "good human relations" become more important than performance and achievement.

To see that an organization is sick is not very difficult; one has only to listen to the language and style within it. The moment people talk of "implementing" instead of "doing" and of "finalizing" instead of "finishing," the organization is running a fever. But prevention and cure are still almost unknown.

Another organization pathology is that of growth and decay. In biology, psychology, in crystallography, in economics, scientists talk of a "normal growth curve"—a process of growth, maturing, aging and decay. Historians from Thucydides to Toynbee have applied the concept to civilizations. Does it apply to the new social organization too? It applies to individual technologies, to individual markets, to individual products; but it does not apply universally. Fields of knowledge (law, for instance, or astronomy) and all the arts have kept on growing; and so have animal species. Where then does organization belong? How far can innovation change the growth curve of a business enterprise, for instance rejuvenate it, or at least delay its aging? Here too we need knowledge.

The new discipline of managing needs to define the limits of organization. Organization is not appropriate to all work. It has rather created new institutions for new tasks. But what are the tasks for which organization is superior? What work is best done by teamwork, and what by the individual? And of great and immediate importance—what are the limits on size and complexity of organization?

The mammoth universities of 50,000 students that we are going to build in this country will be way too large. But what should be done with them? Break them up? Would a university of, say,

25,000 students be manageable? Or would 5,000 be better and more effective? Should we run each "school" within the university —e.g., medicine, law, science, education, business, engineering, dentistry, divinity—as a separate autonomous institution, while retaining the "university" for bookkeeping and housekeeping purposes only? Or should we organize autonomous units across the "schools" around fields of study and research such as history or genetics?

The Department of Defense of the United States has so far been incapable of organizing for any effective joint performance other than to destroy a succession of Secretaries of Defense. But is this because it is too large? Or because it is not large enough, that is, because we still retain three armed services instead of merging them into one? Could we manage both the size and the pluralism of services if only we replaced the traditional functional specialization of Army, Navy and Air Force by performance-oriented, result-oriented, new service units? I incline to the latter view; but I cannot prove it.

Maybe the problem of giant university and armed forces is not size at all but diversity. Any organization, to perform and to survive, must excel in something. In how many areas can one even try to excel without setting up strains, conflicts and internal contradictions that tear the organization asunder? Somewhere there is a limit. Clearly, some of the diversified businesses in the United States that were so popular in the boom after World War II have exceeded that limit. But where is it? And what determines it?

## The Principle of Organization

The biggest challenge for the discipline of managing is the question: What is the nature of this new organization, what is its governing principle?

A recent newspaper story highlights one aspect: On one of the military research installations there is a young Ph.D. in physics who was drafted into the army as a private. To the scientist in charge he is "doctor"; to the commanding general he is "soldier." He sits on technical meetings alongside the general. But he does not eat in the same mess.

The earlier instance of the meteorologist and the general illustrated one side of the problem, that is, the question of individual status. But there is an organization problem here too. Authority is necessary; it must be recognizable; that is, it must carry rank. The organization needs clear foci of decisions for the whole; someone must take the risks so that others can act. Every professional who applies skill, knowledge and judgment to his job makes decisions that affect others. But there are top jobs; there are—and must be—final decisions. There is a final responsibility for the whole to which over-all authority must be given.

We still express the structure of authority, responsibility, function and rank in organization in the typical organization chart, which shows the chief executive at the top and the lesser executives as exercising authority delegated by him. It is still customary to explain the existence of organization by the fact that there is more work to be done than any man can do, so that he has to delegate to others what is really part of his job.

But this is nonsense in modern organization. The individual people of skill, knowledge and judgment cannot exercise somebody else's authority or somebody else's knowledge. They exercise their own knowledge and should have the authority that befits their contribution. It is the job that determines the authority and responsibility of the holder—and this is original authority grounded in the needs and objective requirements for performance rather than in the power of the man above. The only power the top man must have is that of deciding whether a certain contribution is needed—

and even that, increasingly, must be an objective decision according to objective needs of the organization rather than a power decision.

It is also untrue, however, that the superior is only a "servant" of those under him, that his main job is to make it possible for them to do their job, that is to supply them with the knowledge, the information and the tools they need. It is the first job of a manager to make sure that those under him can do their best and can do it most effectively; but he also has a genuine responsibility of his own which requires authority.

Any man of professional standing in the modern organization, whether he be manager or individual professional, has three equally important responsibilities. Each of them then needs its own authority. He has a responsibility to make it possible for subordinates to do their own work most effectively. He has a responsibility to the entire organization. And he has a responsibility to people who do not stand in any authority relationship to him, who work in other areas and in other jobs, and who yet depend on him for knowledge, information, advice, ideas or teaching.

Here is a subtle structure. Rank, authority, function and rewards are all distinct rather than inseparable as they have always been. This structure answers no known organization design. It has a pattern of its own. Its emergence is both a result of the new world-view of pattern and process and in itself a major part of it.

In asking for the principle of the new organization we ask for the principle of human order in society. The elements of this new configuration, which we have here called the "new organization," are human beings. Its process is human dedication, human knowledge and human effort. Its purpose is the creation and satisfaction of human values. And its principle of organization must therefore be a vision of man in society.

ϟ ϟ ϟ

### 3 · BEYOND COLLECTIVISM AND INDIVIDUALISM

The new organization exists in society, is indeed an organ of society for the performance of social purposes. What does its emergence mean for today's society?

There are two answers.

The new organization creates a new social structure, a middle-class society of employed professionals. This is the sociological and political answer.

The new capacity to organize heralds, though still with uncertain and confused voice, an order of society that goes beyond collectivism and individualism. This is the philosophical answer.

### The Middle-Class Society

Few social prophecies in history have had greater impact than the apocalyptic vision of Karl Marx; that capitalist society would inevitably impoverish and expropriate until nothing would be left but vast masses of the "exploited proletariat" and a mere handful of "exploiters." And few have so rapidly and so completely been disproven by history.

The important fact is not even, as the Revisionists in Socialism pointed out fifty years ago, that the lot of the worker improves steadily the more capitalism progresses. The important fact is the emergence of a new class which is neither capitalist nor worker but which is rapidly becoming dominant in all industrially developing countries: the employed middle class of professional managers and professional specialists.

This class rather than the capitalists has power and control (as the Robert R. Young story illustrated). The capitalist, that is the man who has property title to productive resources, must, to be effective, behave as a manager. And progressively the ownership titles are being held by this new middle class rather than by the capitalists. In the United States today the important capitalists are the institutional trustees for the savings, pension-claims and investments of the little people: insurance companies, pension funds and investment trusts.

At the same time this new class is absorbing the worker—socially, economically and culturally. Instead of becoming a proletarian, today's worker joins the middle class of employed professionals—in his tastes, his way of life, his aspirations.

Above all, this is the class that does the work. Marx's society of capitalists and workers is inconceivable in an industrial country. It is a preindustrial society compatible only with conditions of extreme underdevelopment such as exist still in India, for instance, or in China. In a developed country we can quite easily conceive of a society without either capitalist or proletarian, a society composed entirely of the middle class of employed professionals. This is fact rather than fancy; a fully automated large company with its securities held by institutional trustees would be such a society. In the United States today there are quite a few companies, employing well over a hundred thousand people each, which virtually answer this description. No one doubts that they work effectively.

It is no longer even true that this new class is a "middle class" in the sense that it sits between an upper and a lower class. It is today's society—or, at the least, it will be the society of tomorrow.

Census classifications are a crude and sluggish gauge of social processes, but they show the development quite clearly.

Sixty years ago the United States was still a rural country; half the population lived on the land and by farming. Then, for twenty-five years, the industrial worker—Marx's proletarian —multiplied; from one census period to the next this classification grew rapidly, both in numbers and as a percentage of the total population. Since 1925, however, this group has not grown as a percentage of total population; and since 1945 it has been slowly shrinking even in total numbers. The next group to rise sharply were white-collar employees, mainly clerical and sales personnel. This group is still growing in numbers, though quite slowly; but as a percentage of the population it reached its peak by 1940.

Since 1935, however, the classification known as "managerial, professional and technical" employees has grown fastest and at an increasing pace, both in total numbers and as a proportion of population. Managerial, professional and technical employees already compose the largest single group in the American working population, having passed the industrial workers around 1955. Twenty years hence they may well be as numerous as all other nonfarm groups taken together. Already our largest employee group is teachers—primary, high school and college—who are themselves professional employees par excellence, and employed to train others to be professional employees. To satisfy the demand for their services, this group will have to rise three or four times as fast as any other group in our working population over the next twenty years.

The American development may be the most dramatic, because it has been compressed into such a short time. But it is paralleled in all other developed countries—in Great Britain, in Germany, in Italy, in Switzerland and Holland, in Japan. It goes on in the rapidly developing countries such as Australia or Mexico. In such countries, the managerial, professional and technical group, the employed, professional middle class, grows by two or more percentage points for every percentage point of economic growth.

Marx, only a hundred years ago, predicted the continuous growth of the proletarian class, and did not foresee the managerial, professional, technical group at all. And he was no blinder than his contemporaries. This development could not have been imagined within the knowledge and experience of the nineteenth century, could not have happened within the limitations of nineteenth-century capacities. It is a development of the post-modern world; it results from our new capacity to make skill, knowledge and responsible judgment effective in organization.

In matters of social structure, however, values are more important than numbers. That this new professional middle class has become the leader is therefore the real measure of the change. No one is as sensitive to such value changes as a minority group struggling for recognition and acceptance. Thus the shifting values of the American Negro provide a useful barometer here.

When first released from slavery, the Negro in America reflected the traditional values of the preindustrial, agrarian Old South; his leader was a politician, a lawyer or a preacher. Later, around 1900, came a powerful effort to produce Negro capitalists, especially bankers. Today the focus of Negro efforts to obtain acceptance is the fight for admission of members of their race to professional and managerial positions within the large organizations: the higher ranks of government service and armed forces (where the greatest success has been attained), research laboratories and hospitals, universities and business enterprises.

Thirty years ago the Negro community in the suburban area where I live was led by lawyers and preachers. Today the most prominent Negro leader is a physicist employed by one of the large industrial research laboratories. In another suburban area the prominent Negro leaders today are the bursar of a large white college and his wife, a social worker employed by the town. When Jackie Robinson of the Dodgers retired—the first Negro player in major-league baseball and a hero to his people—he did not, as earlier Negro sports heroes had done, open his restaurant; he joined a white-owned restaurant chain as personnel vice president.

The best comment, perhaps, on the shift and its meaning was made by a leader of one of America's most militant industrial labor unions, the only one of our large unions that could truly be called "working-class conscious." "Where will our leaders of tomorrow come from?" he asked at a recent union convention. "Today's leaders are in their fifties. When they started, twenty-five or thirty years ago, union office was the most accessible and the most promising opportunity for a young worker. Today a man of similar drive and ability goes to college at night, gets himself a little education and in no time has a job as a management trainee or as an industrial engineer. Five years later he has forgotten that he ever was a union member; he thinks like a manager, lives like a manager, behaves like a manager." The remedy? "Union leadership must become a professional, managerial career."

The capitalists, the men "who are in business for themselves," have not disappeared, of course. We have not only the Texas oil millionaires and the Greek tanker barons. In this country more people have gone into business for themselves during the last ten years than during any comparable period in our history, just as more have become lawyers, preachers, doctors in private practice, and so on. The new organizations themselves create constantly new independent entrepreneurs or professionals; the vast number of consultants in all fields, for instance, or the small, independent tool-and-die makers that surround the automotive and aircraft plants. But the tanker barons get their financing from the anonymous employed managers of large investment institutions such as insurance companies; the financial power rests in their hands, rather than in those of the millionaires. Moreover, the entrepreneurs are successful only if they act as managers; the largest single reason for the failure of new businesses, study after study has shown, is managerial incompetence.

The "poor" also have not disappeared. But in a developed country they no longer represent the "masses"; rather they constitute isolated special-problem groups. In this country the hard core of poverty is in such groups—the Negroes, the Puerto Ricans and the Indians in the Southwest—racial minorities of poor educational background, suffering from discrimination; a widely scattered group of small farmers on worn-out submarginal lands, who do not have enough knowledge to farm well or enough schooling to get jobs in the cities; single, old people with no one to support them; and widows with small children. Essentially these are "nonemployable" people, if only for reason of prejudice, rather than "poor" people. The cure is overcoming prejudice or individual rehabilitation rather than social or economic reform.

There are of course tremendous differences of status and income within the middle class. But there is also increasing equality of opportunity and increasingly a common way and style of life. The president of a large company may have a very high income. But unless he reached the top well before World War II—that is, unless he be today at least middle-aged—he is unlikely to be a very rich man, income taxes what they are (in all countries except Soviet Russia). He will measure his financial status more by his life insurance and his pension than by his wealth. And while he may be surrounded at work by imperial splendor, he is apt, like the president of our largest business enterprise, to live in a nine-room house in a residential suburb, to help his wife with the dishes on the maid's day out, and to baby-sit with his grandchildren so that his daughter and her husband, a young chemist, can go to the movies. It is not private wealth any more that supports the luxury trades; it is the expense account of the great or not-so-great organization which goes with the job and which "the office" pays for.

The president of the large business enterprise does not look upon himself as a capitalist—even if he owns a sizable share of the stock. He looks upon himself as a manager, and is so regarded by society. The least successful of employed professionals, who never gets beyond the position in which he started, does not look upon himself as a worker; he looks upon himself as a professional or as a member of management.

This is an open-ended society in sharp contrast to the rigid, inescapable classes Marx saw—a vision which, we know now, mirrored the past rather than predicted the future. The new society makes possible great and genuine equality of opportunity, for all who can gain access to enough education to qualify for an entrance job are in the running for the prizes. Indeed it is a society that demands equality of opportunity—simply because the more professional men of knowledge we use, the more we need. We have told ourselves for a hundred years—with little effect on our practice—that racial discrimination against the Negro is a denial of elementary justice and a betrayal of all the values of American life. But the recent realization that we just cannot afford to waste the potential of professional ability and skilled performance the Negro has to offer has, within a short period of fifteen years, transformed both popular attitudes and the actual opportunities for the Negro. Indeed it is likely today that the Negro will attain substantial equality of opportunity as an employed professional long before he attains equality of opportunity for nonprofessional work, as an industrial worker, for instance. This may be an ironic commentary on humanity; but it is also a measure of the shift in social structure. For in the society of the professional employee equality of opportunity ceases to be a demand of the individual against society, an ideal of social justice. It becomes a demand of society on itself, and a measurement of its operational effectiveness.

The middle class society is not free from problems and weaknesses. But they are new problems. Earlier in this chapter I talked about the social problem of the post-modern world: the status of the professional employee in organization. To this corresponds a very real problem of his status and function in the larger society.

Any previous society would have denied the status of professional to an employee—would at least have restricted it to a few gentleman's employments such as the church, the civil service, the university and the army. Snobbery, of course; but even snobbery has its reasons. Can an employee be a professional? Or will he become a mere technician—a barbarian in thrall to his tools? Will he, though employed, be a citizen thinking of the common good and working for it? Or will he see only his dependence, follow narrowly his self-interest, and live by the creed that "what is good for quality-control engineers is good for society"?

I recall the president of a large American university who, in the spring of 1933, witnessed the taking over of an old and famous German university by a newly appointed Nazi commissar. "The fellow," my friend reported, "made the most outrageous, most illiterate speech, insulting systematically every senior member of the faculty and sneering openly at learning, intellectual honesty and all the things the university stood for. Yet when he asked for questions, one full professor after the other got up and asked: 'Will there be more money for plant biology?' 'Will we get a bigger law library?' 'Will we get more assistants?' When they were assured that there would be plenty of money for anyone willing to 'co-operate,' they all sat down, smugly content.

"What haunts me," the college president went on, "is the question: would my own faculty back home, so very liberal, so very brave in passing resolutions, act differently in a similar situation? Or would they too only be concerned with their own pet projects, see only their own shop, take responsibility only for their own footnotes?"

This question goes back all the way to Aristotle. Aristotle first extolled the virtues of the "middle estate," first claimed special qualification as a citizen for the man of the middle class. But his definition of "middle class" was someone neither so rich as to be dominated by his wealth nor so poor as to have to work for a living, let alone to be employed. Whoever had to work for a living could not be a citizen. Our new middle class by definition works for a living and as an employee.

Aristotle, most of us today would think, was too pessimistic. But the problem is a real one—and it cannot be dismissed by resounding platitudes about social responsibility. It is the specific problem of "virtue" in this post-modern society.

To state the problem shows how much the new sociological dimension that results from our capacity to organize has already changed the nature of society. For this problem is not one of "social forces" as were those of the older "modern" society. It is a problem of individual values and conduct. Its solutions are not to be found in economic or social reform but in the ideals of the educational system, the ethos of the community and the living examples of its leaders. The problem is not one of social justice or economic opportunity but of the meaning and responsibility of power and knowledge. Above all the problem is no longer to gain victory for a democratic society but to make effective the aristocratic value of unique responsibility in a democratic reality of general opportunity.

## Freedom in Dynamic Order

The philosophical dimension of a society, its principle of order, is much less tangible than sociological structure, status, opportunities or economic facts. But it is far more powerful. Sociological structure may determine how people act. But the philosophical ideal of order determines why people act, what they expect and what they accept—their ideals and their values.

The new organization changes our vision of the good society. It implies a new ideal of man in society and gives to social order a new goal and meaning. It makes untenable the fixed positions of social thought which we have occupied for centuries, the positions respectively of collectivism and individualism.

The new organization is incompatible with either concept. It must go beyond both, and develop a new expression for the relationship of individual to society. The relationship will have to be one of mutuality rather than of opposition. Individual and society will have to be seen as extensions, respectively, of each other, benefiting and strengthening, rather than limiting, each other. Collectivism and individualism express static and mechanistic concepts of the social order (even the so-called "organic theory of state" is not organic at all but rather sees the biological body as a mechanical assembly). The new organization expresses a dynamic order; it expresses a configuration of wills, decisions, responsibilities whose whole is much greater than the individual parts—but only if each "part," each professional, takes true professional responsibility for the whole.

Neither individualism nor collectivism was ever a very satisfactory concept of social order. The basic limitation of individualism was the reality of organized society. It is simply an obvious fact that collectives are not just aggregates of individual contracts for specific purposes but genuine entities that outlive the individual, have their own behavior, their own logic, indeed their own being. There is something called "Germany," and individuals are willing to die for it, no matter how contrary to their belief the collective acts or how little that entity serves their interest.

The basic limitation of collectivism was always the reality of the individual. A Hans Mueller could be destroyed by the collective called "Germany," but he could not be entirely controlled by it and could not be contained within it.

The either/or between collectivism and individualism has always been more rhetorical than real. The two have always been slogans rather than genuine principles. If treated as absolutes, they always became untenable in theory and unworkable in practice. Every time they were carried through by the doctrinaires they collapsed into tyranny or dissolved into catastrophe. But both were close enough to actual experience to serve as preferences; each was operational within the traditional power to organize. Either was valid enough to serve as a fixed position from which to explore the central problem of freedom and order in human society.

This is no longer possible. It is no accident that the insight of "human relations" thirty years ago has had such an impact on our managerial thinking. There is nothing remarkable in the perception that people in a work situation behave like people. And yet this came as a shock both to the individualist, who had seen only the worker but not the community of work, and to the collectivists, who had seen only the common task but not the power and control of the individuals in it and over it.

Today's organization bases a collective—that is, a genuine social whole—on the individual acting as an individual and committing himself as an individual. His act must be voluntary; the more of a "man" and the less of a "cog" the individual member, the stronger the organization. The individual also needs internal, personal resources—of knowledge, of initiative, of responsibility, of values and of goals—way beyond anything an individualist society requires.

But conversely the individual, in order to be effective as such, not only has to find access to the organization; he has to accept its reality, has to affirm its objectives and values, has to focus his values, knowledge and efforts on its needs and opportunities.

The traditional view of social order, whether that of collectivism or of individualism, sees society and the individual as restraints or limits on each other. At the best it seeks a compromise between them, through "concession" to society or to the individual. In the new organization the two are functions of each other, mutually strengthening and complementing each other. The traditional view, so to speak, subtracts society from individual or vice versa; the new organization multiplies the two.

The more the individual in organization grows as a person, the more can the organization accomplish—the insight underlying all our attention to manager development and advanced manager education today. But, conversely, the more the organization grows in seriousness and integrity, objectives and competence, the more scope is there for the individual to grow and to develop as a person. This is a dynamic rather than a static relationship. It is determined by a future state and future purpose and focused on the growth and development of both.

No organization comes close to living this vision today. We are confused, preach one thing and do another, guess, blunder, stultify. But even the most mismanaged of our new organizations seeks for this concept and gropes for this vision, even the most disorganized already measures its actions against this ideal of freedom in dynamic order, however dimly it perceives it, however rudely it understands it.

The new organization deals with the relationship between individual and society, between freedom and order. This makes it hazardous both if it fails and if it succeeds. In this it shares the risk of all innovation.

But it is also a challenge and an opportunity to overcome the old, sterile conflict between individual and society, between freedom and order, in a new synthesis. This task demands social thought and political theory of high imagination and originality. But at the same time it permits us to build the new social order on the best of our traditional values, and to live up to the best in our ideals.

# CHAPTER FOUR

# The New Frontiers

No one born after the turn of our century has ever known anything but a world uprooting its foundations, overturning its values and toppling its idols. No one younger than this century has known anything but an age of revolution.

In the political, the social, the economic, even the cultural sphere, the revolutions of our time have been revolutions "against" rather than revolutions "for." *The Revolution of Nihilism* was the title of a best-selling book thirty years ago. The specific application was to Nazism (the author, Herman Rauschning, had been a prominent Nazi politician), but the title would apply generally. The revolutions of the twentieth century have been driven by enmity; they have been aimed at destroying rather than building; their slogans have been "death to" or at best "independence from" rather than "life for" or "freedom to." There were some exceptions: The New Deal owed its world impact in the gloomy thirties to its hope and positive faith, to its standing for rather than against. But on the whole throughout this period the man—or party—that stood for doing the positive has usually cut a sorry and rather pathetic figure; well-meaning but ineffectual, civilized but unrealistic, he was suspect alike to the ultras of destruction and the ultras of preservation and restoration.

Now, for the first time, in this age, there are new things

to achieve; for the first time there is constructive work to do.

The Marshall Plan, to give an illustration, was designed to restore. Its targets were Europe's production figures of 1938, the last "peacetime" year. Its aim was to undo the ravages of war and to go back to where Europe had been. The official measurements of achievements used the prewar figures right to the end. But virtually from the start, vision and goal shifted. Almost everyone engaged in the effort, American and European alike, soon focused on building a new future rather than on restoring the past. Everyone began to work on Europe's potential, began to think about the institutions, habits, methods needed to create a new industrial economy and a new industrial society, and in the end, something even newer: a European community. Soon this appeared to be the only practical approach; restoration and revolutionary overturning alike became impractical dreaming.

Only a few years later we had forgotten that restoration had been the original aim; when President Truman in his Point Four program called for systematic action on a new task, the economic development of underdeveloped areas, he assumed that he was simply extending the Marshall Plan.

We could not do anything like this in the twenties. We could not do it in the thirties. We could not even do it in the postwar planning that occupied so many good people in London and Washington during World War II. We did not lack good will, knowledge, intelligence or even leadership. We lacked tasks. And now we have some.

There are new frontiers outside and beyond both the established order and the revolutionary's power-greedy vacuum. There is need to build and room to build in—even if it is only in the open spaces left by the leveling of old structures. Increasingly these new frontiers are the realities of today. It is there that the conflict between the Free World and Communist tyranny will largely be decided; increasingly the world conflict becomes a conflict over the leadership in the new tasks.

There are four areas in which we face new demands: an intellectual area where a new "educated society" is emerging; an economic area in which economic development "up to poverty" presents both an opportunity of advance and unity and the danger of international and interracial class war, setting the underdeveloped against the developed peoples; a political area in which we face the need for new institutions of social order; and a cultural area in which the disappearance of the "East" as a viable culture and civilization has created a vacuum.

Failure in any of these areas would be catastrophic—above all for the free West. Only in the economic sphere do we yet know how the demands of the task can be met. But in all four areas the work to be done can be defined.

These areas of challenge, threat and opportunity to our post-modern world will be described in the next chapters. The preceding chapters focused on perceptions, ideas and new capacities. Now we are going to discuss policies. So far we have asked: "What *is* the new reality?" Now we shall ask: "And what does it *demand* of us?"

# CHAPTER FIVE

# The Educated Society

## 1 · THE EDUCATIONAL REVOLUTION

An abundant and increasing supply of highly educated people has become the absolute prerequisite of social
and economic development in our world. It is rapidly becoming a condition of national survival. What matters is not that
there are so many more individuals around who have been
exposed to long years of formal schooling—though this is
quite recent. The essential new fact is that a developed society
and economy are less than fully effective if anyone is educated to less than the limit of his potential. The uneducated is
fast becoming an economic liability and unproductive. Society
must be an "educated society" today—to progress, to grow,
even to survive.

A sudden, sharp change has occurred in the meaning and
impact of knowledge for society. Because we now can organize
men of high skill and knowledge for joint work through the
exercise of responsible judgment, the highly educated man has
become the central resource of today's society, the supply of
such men the true measure of its economic, its military and
even its political potential.

This is a complete reversal of man's history within the last fifty years or so. Until the twentieth century no society could afford more than a handful of educated people; for throughout the ages to be educated meant to be unproductive.

A man who is now chief executive of one of America's largest businesses did not dare admit when applying for his first job, in 1916, that he had an advanced degree in economics. "I told the man who hired me that I had been a railroad clerk since I was 14," he says, "otherwise I would have been turned down as too educated for a job in business." Even in the late twenties, when I myself started, commercial firms in England or on the Continent still hesitated before hiring anyone as a junior clerk who had finished secondary school.

It has always been axiomatic that the man of even a little education would forsake the hoe and the potter's wheel and would stop working with his hands. After all our word "school"—and its equivalent in all European languages— derives from a Greek word meaning "leisure."

To support more educated people than the barest minimum required gross exploitation of the "producers," if not strict rules to keep them at work and away from education. The short burst of education in the Athens of Pericles rested on a great expansion of slavery, the intellectual and artistic splendor of the Italian Renaissance on a sharp debasement of the economic and social position of peasant and artisan.

Idealists tried to break this "iron law" by combining manual work and education—the tradition goes back to the Rule of St. Benedict with its mixture of farmwork and study. It found its best expression in the mid-nineteenth century, in Emerson's New England farmer who supposedly read Homer in the original Greek while guiding a plow. But this, of course, never worked. The Benedictines—imperiling their salvation to the lasting benefit of mankind—very soon left farming to

villeins and serfs and concentrated on study. Long before
Emerson's death those New England farmers who cared for
the plow had left both Homer and New England for the rich
soils of the Midwest, while those few who had cared for
Homer had left farming altogether to become lawyers,
preachers, teachers or politicians. The "iron law" was indeed
inescapable as long as manual labor was the really productive
labor.

Thomas Jefferson believed in higher education and in
equality as much as any American. He considered the found-
ing of the University of Virginia and the authorship of the
Declaration of Independence, rather than the Presidency, his
greatest achievements. Yet in his educational master plan he
proposed to limit access to higher education to a handful of
geniuses. It was obvious that only a few could be spared from
manual labor.

Today the dearth of educated people in the formerly colonial areas appears such a handicap as by itself to be adequate
condemnation of colonialism and proof of the "wickedness"
of the imperialists. But education did not come first in the
scale of social needs even fifty years ago; flood control and
land boundaries, equitable taxation and improved agriculture,
railroads and incorruptible magistrates, all ranked much
higher. If the colonial powers were then criticized on the
score of education, it was for forcing it on too many, for destroying thereby the native culture, and for creating an un-
employable, overeducated proletariat. The educated person
was then still a luxury rather than a necessity, and education
a preparation for dignified leisure rather than for productive
work.

In my own childhood forty years ago, schools still assumed
that education was for "nonwork." They preached that the

educated man should not despise the honest worker as schools
had preached since the days of Seneca in the first century.

## The Scale of the Explosion

Thirty years ago only one out of every eight Americans at
work had been to high school. Today four out of every five of
the young people of high school age in the United States at-
tend high school. Twenty years hence, when today's middle-
aged will have retired, practically every working American will
be a high school graduate. We have already passed the half-
way mark.

Even greater has been the jump in college and university
attendance. Thirty years ago it was still an almost negligible
4 per cent or less of the appropriate age group. Today the
figure is around 35 per cent for the nation; this takes in groups
such as the Southern Negro or the Southern "poor white," for
whom going to college is still all but unknown. In the metropolitan areas of the country—even in such predominantly
working-class cities as Detroit—the figure is nearly 50 per
cent. It will, barring catastrophe, be that high for the nation
as a whole in another fifteen years. By then two out of every
three young Americans in the metropolitan areas will, regardless almost of income, race or sex, be exposed to higher education.

In the American work force of thirty years ago there were
at most three college graduates for every hundred men and
women at work. There are eighteen today; the figure will be
thirty-five, twenty years hence—even if, contrary to all expectations, going to college becomes no more general than
it is already among the two thirds of our people who live in
metropolitan areas.

On top of all this, adult education is booming. Fifty years

ago only those adults went back to school who had been unable to get a formal education as children. Adult education was for the educationally underprivileged—the immigrant from Southern Europe who wanted to learn English or the man who had gone to work at age fourteen and wanted to improve himself. In England adult education was the "Workers Educational Alliance" or the "Home University Library," both offering standard school subjects to workers and clerks. The German *Volkshochschule* served the same purpose.

Adult education during the last fifteen years has been growing faster in this country than college enrollment. And now increasingly it means advanced education for the already highly educated. It is almost routine for the experienced and successful physician to go back to school for advanced training every two or three years. Refresher courses are increasingly demanded of our teachers. Some fifty universities—in addition to a dozen large companies and professional management associations—offer advanced management courses to successful men in the middle and upper ranks of business, who usually already have college if not advanced degrees. Yet before World War II, only two such programs existed, both new, and both struggling to get students.

The educational revolution has been even more explosive in Soviet Russia. Thirty years ago basic literacy was confined to a small minority—had probably fallen even below the low standards of czarist Russia. The educational push hardly began until the mid-thirties. Today, because of Russia's larger population, the proportion of young people in secondary or higher education is still quite a bit lower than in this country, but the absolute numbers are fast approaching ours.

In the total population of the Soviet Union educated people must still be a small group. Few if any of the top people in the

Soviet Union have had more than elementary formal schooling; certainly of those over forty in the Soviet Union, even high school graduates are still only a tiny fraction. But in Russia, too, it has become evident that education is the capital resource of a modern, industrial society. We know now that the Russian achievement does not rest on the Communist tenets of "socialist ownership of productive resources," the "dictatorship of the proletariat," "collectivization of agriculture" or "national planning." Every one of them has been as much an impediment as a help, a source of weakness fully as much as a source of strength. The achievement rests squarely upon the tremendous concentration of resources, time and effort on producing an educated society.

The two outstanding success stories among small nations, Switzerland and Mexico, have nothing in common save extraordinary educational development. Switzerland is the one European country where secondary education, in the last thirty years, has become almost universal. Mexico is the only country in the world that, since the mid-thirties, has spent no money on defense but has instead made education the first charge on its national income. And is it entirely coincidence that the major countries in the Free World that have found the going the roughest since World War II, Great Britain and France, are also the countries in which the educational revolution has advanced the least, in which the supply of educated people, though of high quality, is today still not much larger proportionately than it was in 1930 or even in 1913? In England the supply may well be smaller considering the steady emigration of so many of the highly educated young people.

We are undergoing the educational revolution because the work of knowledge is no longer unproductive in terms of goods and services. In the new organization it becomes the specifically productive work. The man who works exclusively or primarily with his hands is the one who is increasingly unproductive. Productive work in today's society and economy is work that applies vision, knowledge and concepts—work that is based on the mind rather than on the hand.

There will therefore be no permanent oversupply of educated people. On the contrary, the more there are, the greater should be the demand for them. Educated people are the "capital" of a developed society. The immediate impact of, say, using physicians instead of barbers is to uncover needs, opportunities and areas of ignorance, leading to the need both for more physicians and for more medical and biological research. The same process can be seen in every other field—and with particular force in the economic field of production and distribution. Every engineer, every chemist, every accountant, every market analyst immediately creates the opportunity and the need for more men who can apply knowledge and concepts, both in his own field and all around it.

This may sound obvious. But it is so new that it is not yet recognized. Our accountants, for instance, still base their terms and measurements on the eighteenth-century tenet that manual labor creates all value. They still call it "productive labor"; the work of men of knowledge is "nonproductive labor" or "overhead," a term reeking of moral disapproval. When economists talk of "capital" they rarely include "knowledge." Yet this is the only real capital today. The development of educated people is the most important capital formation, their number, quality and utilization the most meaningful index of the wealth-producing capacity of a country.

### The Impact on Society

What is today called "automation," that is the rapid substitution of work by knowledge and concept for work by human hands, is a first impact of the educated society. It is a moot question whether the essence of automation lies in specific machinery and technical ideas or whether it lies rather in basic concepts about the nature of work.

But there can be little doubt that the driving force in automation is the fact that people who have been exposed to formal schooling for twelve or sixteen years have expectations in respect to work and jobs which manual work, no matter how well paid, does not fulfill. They increasingly demand jobs in which they can apply knowledge, concepts and system. They increasingly refuse to accept jobs in which they cannot apply what they have learned, namely, to work with their minds. They may be satisfied with a job of little skill—and there are a good many semiskilled knowledge jobs—but they expect work that draws on mental rather than manual faculties.

In the United States, where most of the young people in the metropolitan areas go at least to high school, the assembly line is already obsolete. The labor necessary to run it is becoming scarce. Young people with a high school education do not want to work as human machine tools. Moreover, to use people with that degree of education for the semiskilled and unskilled manual jobs of the assembly line would be a gross waste of valuable, expensive and scarce resources.

Tomorrow everybody—or practically everybody—will have had the education of the upper class of yesterday, and will expect equivalent opportunities. Yet only a small minority can get ahead no matter what work they choose. This is why we face the problem of making every kind of job meaningful and capable of satisfying an educated man. This is why the new organization must create an effective relationship of function, rank, rewards and responsibility, not only for its professionals but for all those employed in knowledge jobs.

How new these expectations are is shown in the field of personnel management. Not yet fifty years old—it began in World War I—the discipline is already outdated in its concepts and its assumptions. Its principles, its rules, its practices and procedures all represent a distillation of experience with unskilled or semiskilled machine workers, largely from the metalworking industries. Today the majority of the personnel employed even in manufacturing industries are no longer of this kind, are rather people doing knowledge work, however unskilled. How far our personnel management theories really applied even to yesterday's machine workers is an open question. For managing tomorrow's employees, the products of the educated society, they are likely to be quite inadequate.

The educational revolution has had an equal impact on the world economy. Educational capacity, as much as natural resources or industrial plants, is becoming a crucial factor in international trade, economic development and economic competition. Educational development, above all, has become a central problem of the poor countries.

Many of these underdeveloped countries spend today a larger proportion of their national income on education than does the United States. Yet where we complain that one fifth of our young people still do not finish high school, many of these countries can barely keep one fifth of their young people in elementary school. They cannot finance the cost of a literate society, let alone that of an educated society.

This educational inequality is a serious international and interracial problem. Its inevitable result is to make inequality greater, to make the rich richer and the poor poorer. Even greater is the danger that it will push poor, underdeveloped countries into the totalitarian camp; for a totalitarian tyranny, so it appears to them, can raise enough money for the rapid development of education even in the poorest. (This is a delusion. Practically all the poor underdeveloped countries are much poorer than Russia was in 1917 and much further behind in education. They are unlikely therefore to repeat her performance in education even by faithfully copying every Russian tenet and action. But this may be found out only when it is too late.)

Here, it would seem, is a highly promising area for international aid and co-operation. There is need—and opportunity —for financial aid to help the underdeveloped countries pay for the rapid expansion of education. There is need for systematic co-operative effort in training and developing people, especially future teachers. There is need—and opportunity— to help think through the purposes, the structure and the methods of education needed in those countries. Above all there is need for the developed countries, and especially for the United States, to accept a national policy of assisting underdeveloped countries in building education.

## The Educational Competition

"The Battle of Waterloo," it is said, "was won on the playing fields of Eton." Perhaps; but no one asserts that it was won in Eton's classrooms. "The Prussian schoolmaster," another saying goes, "defeated France in the War of 1870 that created imperial Germany." But long ago this was exposed as empty boast; the credit belongs to the German railway and the German armaments designers.

With the launching of Russia's Sputnik, however, the old pleasantry became a grim fact. The higher education of a country controls its military, its technological and its economic potential. In an age of superpowers and absolute weapons, higher education may indeed be the only area in which a country can still be ahead, can still gain decisive advantage.

The greatest impact of the educational revolution is therefore on international power and politics. It has made the supply of highly educated people a decisive factor in the competition between powers—for leadership and perhaps even for survival.

*The conclusion from this is as simple as it is new: Educational development becomes a priority of national policy.*

International leadership is not a matter of power alone. It is as much a matter of policy. Power can never substitute for policy. But purposeful, principled, courageous policy is a potent substitute for power, has again and again given leadership to a weaker rather than to a stronger nation.

Concern for the quantity of educated people is therefore not enough for a national policy in this age of the educational revolution. Numbers of engineers and scientists, of language students and physicians, are not very meaningful in themselves. It is not even enough that national policy aim at the largest possible supply of highly schooled people. It is not enough, in other words, that the graduates know their engineering, their science, their law, languages or medicine. National policy is only possible if these are also highly *educated* people—that is, people who can formulate, understand and support purposeful, principled, courageous policies.

This leads us back to education. And indeed the greatest impact of the educational revolution is on education itself. It raises basic questions about the values, the purposes, the structure and the tools of education. On the one hand, education has become the central capital investment, the highly educated people the central productive resource in such society. On the other hand, education, while "higher" and perhaps "highest," can no longer be limited to an elite, but must be general education.

ꙅ   ꙅ   ꙅ

## 2 · SOCIETY'S CAPITAL INVESTMENT

To the Protestant Reformer ability to read the Bible was needful for salvation; elementary literacy of the masses was therefore to him a necessity. To the Humanist ability to read and write the languages of classical antiquity was the foundation of individual excellence and achievement; higher education of the upper classes was to him therefore a necessity. However watered down, these two approaches still dominate our educational thinking.

But in the educated society higher education for the general is a necessity. It is the foundation of the excellence and achievement, if not of the survival, of society itself.

To both the Protestant Reformer and the Humanist, the fruits of education were individual rather than social or economic. Education, while necessary, was a cultural overhead cost, a charge against society rather than a contribution to its productive capacity.

In the educated society, however, education is capital investment; on it rest the effectiveness and productivity of most other capital investments.

The educator usually distrusts economic discussion of education. He points out with reason that individual excellence, knowledge and responsibility, rather than goods and services, are the "products" of education, and human ideals and standards its true measure. And—again with reason—he suspects that anyone who tries to "put the dollar sign on education" really wants to cheapen it.

Individual excellence, knowledge and responsibility must remain the goals of education, and human ideals and standards its true measure. That education has become the controlling capital investment only reinforces these priorities and values. But the change from overhead cost to capital investment means that economic analysis of its function, needs and contribution has become appropriate. And whereas the economic approach to an overhead cost always implies the question: Isn't it too much?—the economic approach to a capital investment always asks: Is it enough?

## An Economic Analysis

The basic capital investment of a society must be given priority over all alternative uses of national income—excepting only national defense. On this all schools of economics agree. Such capital investment cannot be postponed; time lost by postponement is educated people and their contributions lost forever.

A capital investment if misrepresented as an operating expense always ends by being accounted an overhead expense or a fringe benefit of doubtful utility. It only "costs" and does not "return" anything. This is the way education is still organized today everywhere—even in Soviet Russia. Capital investments must be considered in contemplation of tomorrow's income that will not be produced without them. How much education is necessary now to produce results in fifteen or twenty years? Unless we approach education with this question, we will, by the rules governing capital investments, spend far too little and waste far too much, with little or no return on what we spend. We will at best get "training," that is competence in yesterday's minor skills.

Education has become the most advanced form of capital investment today. The more advanced a capital investment, the more productive it is, and the higher its rate of return. But also the more advanced, the longer the period between investment and full productivity. The more advanced, the higher also is the minimum initial investment needed to produce any results.

Educational investment per productive worker may already be a good deal higher than any other capital investment per worker. During the last thirty years the amount of money invested per worker in plant and machinery has gone up in American industry from well under $1,000 to well over $10,000. At the same time educational investment has gone up from the $1,000 or so which represented the educational cost of yesterday's worker with his five years of formal schooling, to the $25,000 investment in today's graduate of higher education with his sixteen years or so of formal schooling. Add to this as genuine cost to the economy what the man would have produced had be gone to work at fourteen instead of at twenty-one—another $15,000 or so. This amounts to a total educational investment of $40,000—or four times the average investment in plant and machinery per worker. (The physical support of the student would, of course, have to be added to arrive at the total cost of education. It is not, however, part of the capital investment in education—he would have to be fed and clothed anyhow, whether educated or illiterate.)

At the same time the productivity of this investment is also the highest, as befits an advanced investment. Half of the $40,000 or so is investment in higher education—about $20,000 including both the actual cost of education and the loss of production during these years. A college degree, however, adds on average some $200,000 to a man's earning power during the thirty years after graduation. There is no other investment that promises a tenfold return, an average yield of 30 per cent per year, and a thirty-year life.

This is of course a very poor way to measure the productivity of the capital investment in education—but only because it understates the actual economic return and the real "utility" of the investment. For the main beneficiary of the increased productivity of an educated society has not been the educated man who brought about the increase, but the rank-and-file worker, especially the semiskilled unionized industrial worker who, economically speaking, contributed little or nothing.

The exceedingly high return and long productive life of the investment can be obtained only if the wealth-producing capacity of the educated individual continues to grow for twenty years or so after graduation. If it stops growing sooner, the investment is likely to turn in a loss—individually as well as socially—rather than a profit. This does not mean that education has to be measured by the income it produces. Far from it. But we cannot afford education that does not make the individual a bigger, a better, a more dedicated, or a more excellent—that means, a more productive—person. We cannot afford any education that does not add to his ability to contribute.

Whatever does not add to the capacity for sustained growth of personality or contribution is impractical—and may indeed be deleterious. That this or that subject adds to a man's ability to get a job, or to do well on his first job, is not irrelevant. But as a measure of the effectiveness of a long-term advanced investment it may be the most impractical yardstick, may indeed cost heavily in terms of the really practical results. The practical test of education in educated society is whether it prepares for the demands of the work fifteen years after graduation. Since we live in an age of innovation, a practical education must prepare a man for work that does not yet exist and cannot yet be clearly defined. To be able to do this a man must have learned to learn. He must be conscious of how much there is still to learn. He must acquire basic tools of analysis, of expression, of understanding. Above all he must have the desire for self-development.

No educational system does a very distinguished or intelligent job by these yardsticks.

If the reports are to be trusted, the poorest job is that of the Russians. We are told that they do not train "engineers"; they do not even train "production engineers," nor even "steel-production engineers." They train "rolling-mill engineers" or "open-hearth engineers"—men who know everything about the narrowest possible specialty of immediate application but know little else.

It is not impossible that some of those Russian "open-hearth virtuosos" will remain capable of growth, and will give thirty years of increasing contribution. But the odds are against it; and many youngsters who would have been capable of making a full contribution, may be stunted and will forever be unable to do anything but immediate "open-hearth" production engineering; and, twenty years hence, the open hearth may well have become obsolete.

The Russians undoubtedly know what they are doing—their educational revolution has otherwise been purposeful and clear-headed. One explanation of their behavior may be that it is dictated by political reasons: the technician who has not learned to think critically is docile; the educated man may be a danger to a dictatorship. It is even more likely that the Russians' policy expresses their belief that they must, no matter what the future cost, overtake the technology of the Free World within a few short years. In such a situation, as in a

war, one subordinates everything, and especially the training
of men, to the immediate demands of combat and victory.
But if this is their policy, it is a desperate and risky gamble—
and one better not imitated by the Free World. Even in war,
an army takes great care not to sacrifice the long-range advanced education of tomorrow's leaders; it concedes defeat
when it throws into combat the men who should be in the
military academies or the command and general-staff schools.

But the Russians are only the most extreme, or at least the
most deliberate, example of the wrong kind of practicality in
education today. Every country faces the question what education is productive and therefore really practical.

### Teachers and Teaching

Education differs from most other investments in that all
its "critical factors" are human beings, their ability, their
competence, their dedication. Above all, it is the teacher who
makes education happen.

As long as education was a cultural overhead cost, teaching
was, economically speaking, a luxury trade. Luxury trades do
not employ many people. And though highly skilled, luxury
workers are badly paid; an economy pays for contribution
rather than for skill.

As far as numbers go, the situation has already changed. In
this country teaching is now the largest occupation; there are
more teachers—one and a half millions or so—than there are
steel, automobile or aircraft workers. Yet there are not nearly
enough teachers. Twenty years hence we may need twice as
many as we have now. Higher education—colleges and universities alone—will need at least 500,000 new teachers, which
is as many men and women as are now employed in the automobile industry. Even with these numbers, classrooms will

still be larger than they should be for effective teaching under today's best methods.

In respect to paying teachers, however, we have not yet changed. We still pay luxury-trade wages—as little as possible.

The only difference between Russia and America or the other free countries is that Russia pays its teachers the way an aristocratic society pays luxury trades, we the way a democratic society does. Both pay low wages. The Russian primary and secondary school teachers and even the younger men in the university faculties are, even measured by Russian standards, paid worse than they are in the West; their standard is just a little better than that of domestic servants in Victorian England. But an aristocratic society showers fabulous largesse on a few court favorites; hence the amazing incomes of a handful of academicians in the Soviet Union.

Clearly we shall have to raise teachers' compensation—probably double it—while we double the numbers. But this change though overdue will make sense only if, at the same time, we raise demands for performance.

Teachers have differed from all other traditional luxury trades in one essential respect: there have been no performance standards. The reason is simple enough. The performance of a goldsmith or of a fur worker can be easily measured. But how is a teacher's performance to be measured? When—now or twenty years later? By whom? And what constitutes good performance? Because we have never been able to answer these questions, there is no other field where mediocrity and incompetence are so patiently accepted, especially in secondary and higher education. The good teacher has always and everywhere been badly underpaid. But the poor teacher, especially in higher education, is probably not only overpaid; he may cause loss far beyond his "direct cost," i.e. his salary. But how to tell the two apart, except by purely arbitrary, personal judgment?

If education, and especially higher education, is the advanced capital investment of society, we need to know much more about the teaching process than we now know. We simply cannot depend for good teachers on natural talents—we need too many. We cannot depend on higher salaries alone to bring the most qualified people into teaching and keep them there. We need both a craft of teaching that people can learn, and ways to measure, however crudely, how they perform.

To develop a craft of teaching is a slow and difficult process; for teaching, as every good teacher knows, is as much a passion as it is a craft—and even Hollywood cannot teach passion. Therefore we also need better teaching tools to help bridge the gap. We need new and better tools as well because teachers are the critical factor in that expensive, long-term investment that is education. We must help them to concentrate on what only they, as human beings, can do, and to "automate" everything else.

The very people who will recoil in horror at this thought are the people who are proudest of the most complete automation in learning and teaching—the printed book. The printed book complements the human being in teaching by a mechanical tool. It makes possible the concentration of the productive efforts of teachers on those things only they, as human beings, can do. Printing is mass communication through automation. On this automation largely rested modern society and the modern world-view; on it rested the achievement of mass literacy.

We are not going to replace the book—any more than the book replaced the teacher. But mass education needs its own specific methods of awakening of desire, presentation of knowledge and thought, and multiplication of teaching excellence, as much as did mass literacy. The new tools of mass communication such as radio, movies, automatic data processing and television, which perceive and convey a whole configuration simultaneously, have great potential for mass teaching and mass learning. Here perhaps are the new tools that we need to raise standards and to convey to the student what is, in the last analysis, the true mark of great teaching: the intoxication of excellence.

### How to Pay

Because education has become the critical capital investment of society, its financial support is a major issue. The annual cost of education in the near future will not only exceed anything ever spent for education before, even in the richest country; it will exceed anything ever spent, except on defense, on any one item in the national budget. For a considerable time to come the charge will go up rapidly and steadily as, all at the same time, enrollment expands, teachers' salaries rise and physical facilities have to be added.

Two demands will have to be met:

The financial foundation of education, especially of higher education, must be on a mass, rather than a class, basis.

Education must not be entirely or even mainly financed by government—at least not in a free society.

Both demands follow from the character of education as advanced capital investment.

The sums needed are simply too great to be raised on a class basis.

Where the educational revolution is already occurring, as in the United States, this is obvious. The nongovernmental colleges and universities, whether private foundations or church-affiliated, receive today many times more money as gifts from business corporations than they ever received as donations from individual wealthy men. Yet this resource is patently inadequate even for their needs today. For the needs of tomorrow, with doubled enrollment and doubled faculty at doubled salaries, no private giving, no matter how lavish, can do the job.

In the countries of Western Europe where the educational revolution has barely begun, the costs of higher education are being born by the taxpayer. But the state contributes so little that higher education is stunted; and it is doubtful whether any European tax system could stand the necessary increase to expand higher education.

Only Soviet Russia has today a mass basis for general higher education. But would any free society want to have the government in control of its critical capital investment? Could it even tolerate this? Would even devout believers in government action, such as American New Dealers or European Socialists, want it? Or would it threaten both society and education?

There is a central political problem here. For elementary education the government is clearly the right agency—the only question is whether it ought to be the central government or, as in the English-speaking countries, the local governments. But how about higher education? Elementary education deals with skills, higher education deals with thought and knowledge. Can free society allow government the exclusive control of thought and knowledge? Political theory and practice have always answered "No."

But the crux of the problem may well lie in the economic field. Should any but a totalitarian society entrust its major capital investment to government? For all but the doctrinaire socialist the complete control of the central capital investment of society by government is unacceptable. It is incompatible with a free economy, and, as all experience indicates, also with a free society.

It is, moreover, incompatible with effective government. This is so big a job that it must be decentralized, or it may paralyze government itself by its bigness, its complexity, its issues of educational policy, values, directions—all of them the wrong issues for either political or bureaucratic disposition.

Finally government control of higher education, such as must follow from complete dependence on government for finances, would be very bad for education. We need new ideas, new educational policies, new currents, new methods. We need innovation; therefore we need experimentation. But can any government, no matter how intelligent, do anything but impose conformity?

What is desirable is easy to specify. The traditional pluralism of the United States and Great Britain, in which government bodies, religious denominations and purely private foundations compete with each other in higher education, is highly desirable and should be maintained. Of course higher education should never be organized on a private-profit basis—its profit is of necessity social profit, its utility public utility. But it should never be entirely controlled by government either; there should be a large and prosperous private sector continuously involved.

In other free countries, the creation of a similar pluralism would be desirable, which means self-governing non-governmental institutions in secondary and especially in higher education. Hand in hand with this reform should go encouragement of experimentation by the individual institution to replace the complete curriculum control by a Ministry of Education that now exists, for example, in France and Italy.

But how can this goal be reached? Even in Soviet Russia the state does not pay for education; it only prefinances it. The individual who receives the higher education pays for it through five years of compulsory service to the state after graduation—at very low pay, and in a job and place to which he is assigned. Essentially higher education is paid for in Russia in much the same way that prospective immigrants to this country in the seventeenth and eighteenth centuries paid their way across the Atlantic—by indenturing themselves after arrival as servants for five or ten years to a wealthy prospective employer who advanced the money.

A free society will not finance education by indentured labor. It will not control the individual's choice of career, except as the most short-run, wartime measure. But the Russian policy is relevant because it illustrates that one can usually finance a capital investment out of its future returns. Higher education has an exceptionally high and exceptionally certain return. In this country, where the supply of college-educated people is so large that they no longer have scarcity value, the college degree adds ten times its cost to the gradu-ate's average earning power. In other countries where going to college has not yet become as general, the incremental return is much higher. It should therefore be both possible and equitable to expect the graduate to repay, in dollars over the years, the cost of his education, that is the capital invest-ment that he represents. It would be a small burden—not much more than 2 or 3 per cent of his annual income in any one year. This measure would not eliminate the need for some government support—perhaps in the form of reinsurance for these obligations—though even this, in any reasonably well developed community, could easily be done through existing banking and insurance institutions.

Such a policy would be a radical innovation—and highly unpopular at first. But it would, in one stroke, solve the finan-cial problems of higher education and at the same time pre-vent government control of the central capital investment of the economy. It would express the fact that education, especially higher education, has become the central capital investment of an educated society, and can therefore no longer be regarded and financed as a luxury, as a social service or as a cultural ornament.

This is hardly more than a first try at a solution. It is presented here to show that the problem can be solved, not as the right or the only solution.

☙ ☙ ☙

### 3 · EDUCATION FOR WHAT?

"Education for what, is the wrong question," a teacher would—or should—say. Education is for some*body*, not for some*thing*. The product of education is not knowledge or learning; it is not skills, ability or virtue, jobs or success, dollars or goods. It is always a person, who acquires knowledge or skills or virtue, who gets a job and an income or who produces goods.

Only the individual can learn; and only the individual can be taught. Every teacher knows that his real reward over long years of teaching is the memory of those rare moments when "something suddenly clicks in a student." Every former student knows that education is what he himself put in rather than what the teacher gave out. Even an educational system that aims at the destruction of personality and at the creation of faceless robots, has to teach individuals.

The purpose of education in educated society therefore means first: What does an educated person have to be? What does he have to learn to achieve the most, make the greatest contribution, succeed the best and develop the furthest as a person?

*Society's Stake*

The moment there is a school, however, education is also social, is education for community and society. If there were no school, but only Socrates and a disciple sitting in the shadow of an oak, education might conceivably start with the individual, his talents and his needs. It might conceivably aim at the best development of the individual as a person. Rousseau's Émile dreamt of this as the ideal of education; but Émile, who was otherwise given the greatest freedom, was not allowed to go near a school.

Progressive education preached education according to individual ability and inclination. But even in its weirdest experiments it expected all children to acquire the same basic skills regardless of individual ability or inclination. It had to set limits to their free choice of subject matter, if only because of lack of teachers for everything. And its emphasis on the individual often concealed (as extreme individualism does) repression of the person and the collectivism of adjustment to the group.

A school must have a common ideal of the educated person. It must educate according to an ideal of society. Its educational policy, its curriculum, its structure, its methods, always represent what society is or what it wants to be. One may well doubt whether the schools really mean it when they repeat, *"Non scholae, sed vitae discimus"*—the old Latin tag that we learn for life rather than for school; it is rarely the spirit that governs a faculty meeting discussing, say, course requirements. But there is no doubt that the schools educate for society.

Education is not quite the matrix of society, as educators often have it. Education is not that effective; at best it is a hit-or-miss proposition. There are, moreover, in every society many other formative influences at work—the family and friends, the church and books, arts and nature. They can be limited, above all by taking the child over at an early age, especially from the family, as collectivist education from the Spartans down to the Russians has always tried to do. But these other influences can never be entirely eliminated. Indeed the very attempt to eliminate them may produce a hot-house faith that wilts at the first exposure to anything unexpected.

Finally education is not the absolute mold of society because the individual reacts individually to education; and that means he reacts differently from other individuals. "No one goes to school with the Jesuits and comes out indifferent to them," has often been said; "he either loves them forever or he hates them forever." If true, this would reflect a high educational impact, but one quite different from the intended one. The Jesuits would certainly not accept a society molded by anticlericalism as the society they want to bring about.

Still, education is a major social force. "Keep politics out of the schools" is an old demand. Insofar as politics means partisanship and patronage, it is a legitimate demand. But politics as belief in the structure of society, its values, its political process, cannot be kept out of the schools; for it is formed largely in and through the educational system.

The attempted re-education of Germany and Japan by American military government after World War II was bound to fail even if the re-educators had known what they were trying to do. A foreign army of occupation is hardly the proper instrument to teach peace and democracy; and the assumption of one's own superiority is hardly the proper foundation for teaching others not to be nationalist. But the re-educators were right in one premise: A society needs an educational system committed to its values.

Every educational system, no matter how much it stresses the educated person, therefore also expresses a social goal.

The three major educational systems of the Modern West are set apart largely by their social goals. Education for rulership, the social goal of the English public school and, until World War II, also of Oxford and Cambridge, underlay the individual goals of self-control, responsibility and character. Education for responsible, active and effective citizenship, the social goal of the American school since colonial days, underlies its emphasis on initiative, on respect for others and on working with others.

The school of continental Europe at first sight seems to have no social goal; its aims seem in part to be the educated person of the Humanists, in part (as in most of European university education) vocational preparation for earning one's living. But the Humanist had a social ideal—the "subject" who sticks to his work, or to his ideologies, and lets others do the dirty job of being responsible. Soviet Russia could therefore take over this educational concept almost without change; the Russian secondary school curriculum is the traditional curriculum of the German Real-Gymnasium or of the French Lycée as it was designed well over a century ago.

Therefore when the educated society asks what an educated person has to be, it is really asking: What must society demand of education? What is education for, as a force and power in such a society?

## The General versus the Special

Educational debates, here and abroad, have for years been arguing the same alternatives. Should education stress the generalist, or do we need advanced specialists? Should we stress the humanities or the sciences? Should we aim at knowledge or at ability to perform, at learning by learning or learning by doing? Should education be cultural in its values or practical and aimed at making a living?

These alternatives are no longer real and meaningful, even though they are still hotly debated. The educated person today

needs to be generally educated; he must also be a high-grade
specialist and he needs a general education the most in the
area of his specialty. He needs the humanities and the sciences
—but he needs a systematic discipline in the humanities and
a humanist approach to the sciences, an understanding of
their philosophical foundations, their logic, their values. He
needs systematic knowledge which only systematic learning
can give. But he also needs a very high ability to apply his
knowledge, which only performance—that is "doing"—can
give.

Certainly he needs both to be an educated man and to be
able to earn his living through a practical contribution in work
and job.

The debate over general education versus specialization is
usually carried out as a discussion of subject matters. Yet
subject matters are neither general nor special. There is
nothing more specialized for instance than Anglo-Saxon grammar; electronic circuitry, however, is a most general subject
integrating a good deal of physics, technology, mathematics,
logic, theory of perception and information theory. Yet the
first would usually be classified as general education, the
other as specialized or technical training. It is not a subject
that is general or specialized; it is how one teaches it.

I have heard Shakespeare taught as a specialized "nuts and
bolts" course—indeed his plays are taught this way more often
than as great dramatic literature. The most general education
I have ever had was in a course in a highly technical subject,
admiralty law, which a martinet of a teacher presented as a record
of Western society, Western technology, Western legal thought
and Western economy—yet never discussing anything but the
specific details of a case. And though I myself had previously
taught philosophy and history, my own venture in general education began fifteen years ago, when I took up the teaching of

management—usually considered a technical specialty, but actually one that can be taught as integrating discipline of human values and conduct, of social order and of intellectual inquiry.

To be an effective person in an educated society everyone, whatever his work, needs certain foundations. He needs a foundation in the knowledge of man, his greatness and his wretchedness, his personality, his history, his society. He needs a foundation in the knowledge of systematic inquiry that we call "science"— its methods, its history, its basic assumptions and its major theories. He needs a minimum of competence in using the skills of imagining, analyzing, formulating, interpreting and conveying *thought* which we call "language" —and which include, of course, mathematics. And he needs the skills of imagining, perceiving, formulating, interpreting and conveying *experience* which we call the arts. But he also needs to be able to strive for excellence in one particular area. This means specialization, since one cannot attain excellence in more than one small area. It means education for contribution in work, that is practical education.

The special skill, above all, becomes effective in and through a job as a professional in the new organization. Yet the professional is effective, that is practical, in organization only if he knows enough about the universe of knowledge to relate himself and his work to it. To be practical he must therefore have a foundation in general education and must be able to wield those tools of thought and experience that are universal rather than specialized.

Engineering and business schools do not include more and more of the humanities in their program just because these are "cultural." The least practical of men is the highly trained engineer who cannot convey his ideas because he can neither read nor write, or the highly trained accountant who cannot test the assumptions underlying his figures. Both are distressingly common today—in Europe as well as here.

Since fifteen years hence any of today's jobs is likely to be quite different from what it is now, to demand new knowledge and new abilities, to present new opportunities and new challenges, practical education is also education that fits a man to learn, to develop the new, to understand and to grow. It is the practical specialty in which a man intends to make his living that needs most to be taught in general, even in philosophical terms. The high probability that, within these fifteen years, the graduate will move out of the specialty for which he originally prepared himself makes this even more imperative.

To teach a student, say, "time and motion study" may give him a small but salable skill right away. But unless this skill has been embedded in an understanding of production as a basic discipline with its assumptions and principles, its limitations and unsolved problems, the student's training has been a waste of time, and impractical even in the meretricious sense. It may have unfitted him to learn what he needs to get promoted. It may even have unfitted him to learn what he needs to keep his job a few years hence.

We do not, so far, teach specialized subjects in contemplation of the general. We still teach them as skills rather than as knowledge, stress yesterday's solutions rather than tomorrow's problems, aim at the first job only rather than at the first *and* the last. But we increasingly understand that the specialty itself must have general meaning to enable a man to be effective as a specialist. We increasingly rediscover the wisdom that St. Bonaventura, the great medieval philosopher and teacher, expressed seven hundred years ago when he said that every knowledge and every discipline comes out of knowledge and love of the ultimate, and leads back to it.

Once this is seen, the old debate between general education and practical specialization ceases to have much point. We need a general education that is practical and makes a man effective, and a specialized education that is general and makes a man capable of growth, development and responsibility.

## Learning by Doing

Our colleges teach music history and art appreciation, but few teach playing the violin or painting a picture. Despite all the talk about learning by doing, the disciplines of performance are not considered legitimate or respectable by our academicians. Yet the educated person in today's educated society needs something only performance can give him: the challenge of workmanship.

The arts alone give direct access to experience. To eliminate them from education—or, worse, to tolerate them as cultural ornaments—is anti-educational obscurantism. It was foisted on us originally by the pedants and snobs of Hellenistic Greece who considered artistic performance fit only for slaves and women.

But this snobbery becomes a danger in an educated society in which people stay in school till they are adults. If they learn book subjects only they will not know standards of workmanship. In book subjects a student can only do student's work. All that can be measured is how well he learns, rather than how well he performs. All he can show is promise.

In the United States this danger is lessened by the tradition that young people, regardless of economic status, work in real jobs after school hours, during week-ends and vacations. It is further tempered by our respect for manual work and our emphasis on the shop in school or the basement workshop at home. But this is not demanding enough.

An old teacher of mine used to say: "When you sit down at the piano, there are no alibis—you either play well or you play badly. You do the same finger exercises as the greatest virtuoso and even though you will never play Mozart as well as he does, there is no reason why you can't do the exercises just as well as he does."

In the arts the lowliest beginner can measure himself against professional standards. The argument that few students will —or should—become artists is irrelevant. Few of the trigonometry or biology students in a high school will or should ever be mathematicians or biologists.

This plea for the arts as practical subjects takes a very narrow view. No artist would subscribe to it. Art should certainly be taught as "art," that is as man's direct expression of his experience, and as a creative act of order. But even the limited practical contribution of the arts as the student's only access to the demands and rewards of workmanship should give them a high place in the education of an educated person in educated society.

## The Educational Whole

*summary*

That education needs the humanities *and* the sciences *and* the arts; that it requires a general education aimed at effectiveness, and specialization aimed at an understanding of the whole as well as at skill; that there is no conflict between the practical ability to earn one's living and to excel in one's work and the philosophical capacity to know what one is doing— all these may already be commonplace.

Yet the old debates will continue until we can do the new job. In this we need unifying concepts and disciplines for our new post-Cartesian, post-modern world.

One of the pioneers of Operations Research, Dr. M. E. Salveson, listed, a few years ago, the skills which the Operations Research specialist needs to acquire, over and above the knowledge usually possessed by graduate engineers. The twenty-nine distinct major areas included advanced mathematics and formal logic, history and ethics, economic analysis and organization theory, creativity and program planning, physics and something called "individual and group motivation."

Dr. Salveson is a thoughtful and knowledgeable man. Yet his program is unteachable. There just would not be enough time to introduce a brilliant student to all these areas. Each one is relevant to the work to be done. But how does one organize these twenty-nine lifetime studies into one program? Four weeks of history, four weeks of ethics and four weeks of Boolian algebra, plus two lectures on creativity? To teach and to absorb anything like this program demands unifying concepts that pull together these bundles of knowledge into a few general systems, these skills into a few disciplines.

We also lack the necessary educational structure. By and large we still consider that education is something for the young. When one graduates one stops learning and begins working. At the same time the educational structure consists of three, perhaps four, school systems. Each originally was designed to be the end of formal schooling; each therefore crams into its curriculum a fair number of unrelated bits to introduce the student to important areas. As a result the formal schooling of the young, the preparation for working, takes longer and longer; when a physician finally starts practicing, he is young only compared to those about to retire. There is enormous duplication; and far too much study is done as a survey, once over lightly, instead of as serious discipline.

We need to accept two new rules. First, adult education is as normal in educated society as is the education of children in literate society. In educated society it becomes the mark of individual accomplishment and success for an adult to go back to school for advanced education. In educated society anything that is best learned by adults with some experience and maturity should therefore be taught only to them—just as in literate society we expect everyone to learn as a child what is properly learned by children.

In all professional disciplines there are such areas that are properly defined as advanced, adult education—in law and medicine, business and teaching, engineering, public administration and military service. Indeed some of them—business education or journalism are examples that come to mind—should perhaps be taught only to adults with an adequate background of experience. There are also many such areas in science and in the humanities. Today we try to cram them into the program of the young. The attempt lengthens unnecessarily the period of formal schooling, which becomes perforce a time of artificially prolonged adolescence and immaturity. It debases the subject matter, which has to adapt itself to the lack of experience in the student. It thus becomes not only expensive time but wasted time.

The second new rule is that higher education does not mean more years of education; it means a different aim. It assumes at the outset that the great majority of children who start in school at age 5 or 6 will stay in school for twelve and increasingly for fourteen or sixteen years—and come back as adults. This means that all subjects might be directed toward the goal of the educated person, and that all are seen in a sequence rather than as isolated, one-shot exposures.

Albert W. Tucker, the Princeton mathematician, suggests that basic concepts of modern higher mathematics, such as those of "number," "function" and "set," be introduced in primary school, together with the four elementary operations of arithmetic. This would be higher education. But it is not higher education when a girl spends four years in high school concentrating on "homemaking" and then four years in college on more "home economics"; it is only wasted years.

It was not higher education (or education of any kind) when I spent eight years of Austrian Gymnasium on Latin irregular verbs. There was no attempt made to relate this study to any language, living or dead, to literature, culture or history. There was hardly a hint from any of the teachers that Horace or Tacitus might be read except to find their grammatical mistakes. Such a study would have been excellent vocational preparation for a job as proofreader in a printing shop in the Rome of Augustus. Yet, partly because it had no usefulness, partly because it wasted so much time, it was—and still is—mistaken for higher education. Let me make myself clear: Latin may well belong in higher education; but it must be taught as something other than mechanical memory drill to be education at all.

We have to look at our educational structure not as a chronological sequence but as a configuration. Starting with the end point, the purpose, the educated person, we must ask what disciplines, what skills, what knowledge, what experiences, what perspectives should he have acquired by the time he passes out of adolescence? At what stage, from kindergarten to adult education, should each be introduced? What level should each attain? What is the best sequence? And what balance should we strive for at each stage between the three different definitions of education: the possession of knowledge and skill; the ability to learn and to use; the awe and wonder at the beauty, diversity, excitement of the world of work and knowledge, and the awareness how much more there is always to do and to learn?

Now that children in developed countries stay in school until they are sixteen at least, there is no point in adding on years; the job is to make each year fully effective.

The last two years of the American high school are clearly wasted even for those who do not go to college. Instead of building junior colleges to waste still two more years, we ought to use the last two years of high school for the work now done in the first two years of college. This in turn might make us reconsider the junior high school. How much point is there in what is known as "social studies" and "general science" in those years now that practically all the children go on to high school?

The same question applies to the European school. All the time spent, for instance, on mathematics in the stiff workout of the European secondary school in its upper grades goes into acquiring manipulative skills in old-fashioned, if not obsolescent areas, the mathematics of the seventeenth century. None is devoted to learning basic concepts. This seems a terrible waste of precious time; it is strictly vocational preparation—but for vocations that largely no longer exist.

I do not argue for "stiffer" work; I argue for better focused work. If children of ten are to learn basic mathematical thinking, as Professor Tucker suggests, it will have to be presented in a way suitable to normal children rather than to mathematical prodigies. I propose that we accept what every good teacher knows: Beginners' work must be slower, simpler, clearer—but it must be just as serious and just as workman-like. Above all I argue for a view of education as a continuing process determined by its goal and end purpose, and for its measurement in terms of what it aims at and contributes, rather than in terms of years spent. The struggle for more years available for schooling is won; how do we now use these years most effectively and most economically?

We will have to build the new structure of education on the foundations we have. We will, I hope, keep the best of our educational systems but avoid their worst features. Take from the English public school its stress on character and responsibility and avoid its tendency toward class-conscious superiority; take from the continental European school its emphasis on knowledge and work and avoid its tendency toward pettiness and intellectual arrogance; take from the American public school its stress on responsible citizenship, individual initiative and freely given co-operation and avoid its tendency toward "adjustment" and sentimentality.

We will have to experiment. We will have to try many

things that will not be completely successful. We will even have to try a good many highly uncertain approaches.

Visitors from Europe tend to criticize our advanced management education for its lack of uniformity. General Electric for instance, tries to teach a formal theory of the work of a professional manager. Other programs such as the management courses at Harvard focus on typical situations in daily business life. Some use mainly lectures, others only discussion of case examples, still others rely mainly on the student's own written work, and so on. But this competitive experimentation is strength rather than weakness. It makes it possible for prospective students to find the program that best fits their needs. It makes possible rapid exploration of a number of approaches to a new, big, difficult and still fuzzy task.

Finally, we will have to compromise. We can only use the schools and the teachers we have today. At best we face therefore a long period of transition; the educational system of the modern West after all still bears heavily the imprint of the schools of the medieval monk even though it started out by repudiating the monk's way of life, his religion and his educational aims and methods.

## The Social Responsibility of Education

Now perhaps we are ready to answer the question underlying all other educational issues: What are the social demands on education, the educated and the educators in educated society?

First, responsibility. Education cannot teach everything; to expect it to do so endangers it, as the recent history of the American high school shows. But in a free society it must teach responsible citizenship. It must fit a man to rule himself and to take responsible initiative for the actions of his society.

Society must also demand that education be considered by the educated as a responsibility rather than a right, and as a high responsibility by the highly educated. It must demand of them commitment and dedication, the attitude "What can I contribute?" rather than "What's in it for me?"

Society must, finally, demand responsibility of the educators. There will not only be so many of them; in an educated society they occupy a position of high visibility and symbolic impact. The academicians today worry a good deal about "mass culture." Perhaps they might better worry about the "academician's culture," if only because it may become the mass culture of tomorrow. I am not sure they would find it all it should be.

The oldest complaint in this country is that America is "anti-intellectual." Insofar as the complaint alleges a national failure to value knowledge and education, it is nonsense. There is a good deal wrong with our educational system; its greatest weakness is that it tries to do a little of everything rather than do superbly a few essential things. But if we were really hostile to, or contemptuous of, knowledge or education, why would everybody try to get as much as possible? Why would we have come so close to being an educated society, in numbers at least? Why would those practical people, the businessmen who run our large companies, so generously endow and support the colleges and universities? Why would they bring into their businesses highly schooled men from all branches of knowledge, or use, in unprecedented numbers, university professors as their consultants? Why would they, finally, in a profound though naïve act of faith in the educator, leave the decisions on their future managements so largely to him, his judgment and his grading? "We select our management trainees from the upper third of the graduating classes

of colleges of high intellectual standing" is fairly typical business policy today. It hardly reflects lack of appreciation of
knowledge or education.

But insofar as we, in this country, are reproached for failure
to appreciate the "intellectual," the charge is true. The intellectual has always been suspect in this country—not, however, because of his knowledge or his education but because
of his social irresponsibility and his claim to privileged status.
We have never accepted the Cartesian split between the
created universe and the world of the mind. We do not
accept a claim based on status rather than on contribution.
But the European intellectual—and his American imitator—
is a Cartesian and takes no responsibility for the crude, disorderly world of affairs in which people live and work. He also
claims special status, claims indeed a modern equivalent to
the medieval "benefit of clergy," because his concern is with
"things of the mind."

An Italian friend, every inch the "professor," recently told me
of a fashionable Roman hostess who introduced one guest as a
"distinguished poet"; he was a well-known lawyer who once in a
great while translates, for his own amusement, French symbolist
verse. She introduced another guest as a "well-known art critic";
now an official in the railway administration he had once, when
still a student, published two articles on modern architecture. My
friend went on to talk of the slight but distinct contempt of
the intellectual for the man who takes his work seriously. "Even
the lawyer, the doctor or the civil servant," he said, "though having a high status as a professional, is considered by us somewhat
uneducated or provincial if his work becomes more important to
him than being a dilettante of literature, of art or of other things
of the mind."

The American rejection of the intellectual has its dangers to
be sure. It may lead to an underrating of the power of ideas
and to a tendency to dismiss what one does not understand.

But it is not contempt for knowledge and education, or for those who possess either. It only holds that education does not confer privilege but creates responsibility, does not justify claim but owes contribution.

An educated society must demand that this be the conviction and commitment of its professional educators.

Education must take a high view of its function, must set high standards for its objectives, its own seriousness and its products, the educated. This is the second social demand on education.

It is charged today that the standards of the American schools have fallen these last thirty or fifty years, as higher education became mass education. The evidence for or against the charge is somewhat confused—if only because there is no agreement by what standards one measures. But two points are clear.

First: whatever lowering of the standards has occurred, it has not been the result of mass education. Standards have fallen where no increase in enrollment has taken place; they have remained unchanged in places with an almost explosive rise in enrollment. Whatever deterioration there has been has resulted from acts of the educator: the emphasis on "adjustment"; the attempt to do a little bit of everything; the refusal to take seriously the student and the community, and a resulting conscious downgrading of demands and expectations. It did not result from the press of numbers. And where, in recent years, attempts have been made to raise standards, for instance in the teaching of English, they have had the full support of parents and students, and have been successful regardless of numbers.

The second and more important point is that there has been no attempt to *raise* standards as education became general. As the educational level of the public keeps going up, its educational expectations for the next generation and its educational capacity should also have kept going up.

It will be argued that the great majority of people—those with an Intelligence Quotient of 100 or less—do not have the intellectual endowment to go to college; to make college education general education must therefore debase it. This sounds plausible. There is no denying that there are tremendous differences in individual ability. As in every effort and on every level, some will have to try harder; and some will not make it at all, no matter how hard they try. There is also no doubt that high competitive pressure is not educational. The annual suicide wave among French students before the final secondary school examination is not a sign of high educational standards; it is a sign of barbarism.

Still, the argument is a fallacy. Had we known of I.Q.'s a hundred and fifty years ago, we would have argued that the great majority clearly did not have the intellectual endowment to learn to read and write, and that general literacy must destroy the elementary school. (This was indeed a common argument then, even without modern testing techniques.) The I.Q. does not measure the potential of a certain intellectual endowment; it indicates only what a certain intellectual endowment has, traditionally, been expected to achieve.

It is a delusion that college education in the past was confined to the exceptionally brilliant. Selection was—and still largely is, even in Russia—by class rather than by intelligence. There is no evidence that having a wealthy or influential father results in higher intellectual aptitude for the son. What evidence there is indicates that one thing that does make a difference in the capacity to learn, regardless of I.Q., is the support of, and respect for, knowledge and education in the child's home—as witness for instance, the record of the New York, first-generation Jewish youngsters with their background of desperate slum poverty but traditional respect for education. In an educated society the student population should have the same capacity as the earlier class-based sample, and greater motivation as society itself comes to expect more from the school.

Natural inequality of endowment may require alternative but parallel paths in higher education—maybe even differential speeds of progress. But all paths should be higher education, and should demand high standards.

To raise standards of any large group one must simultaneously raise the performance of both the average and the outstanding. What the outstanding few alone can do today, the great many average performers will be able to do tomorrow. What is considered average performance today becomes the springboard from which the outstanding take off in their sprint for excellence. For the gap between the two tends to remain a constant, regardless of level. Both have therefore to rise, in a kind of ratchet action, for the level to go up.

Athletic records exemplify this principle as do medical education and performance. Today's great doctor is no more above the average than the great doctor of 150 years ago was above the average of his day, the village barber. The advance in medicine has been achieved by lifting both the competence of the outstanding medical leader and that of the average practitioner. Education also exemplifies the principle in its evolution from literacy for the outstanding to general education. The brightest student of today is certainly no brighter than Socrates' "golden boy," Phaedrus. But I am not sure that Phaedrus could write; and he certainly could not multiply.

The most important demand of society is, however, that education have an ideal of the good man, the good life and the good society. It must have a high and pure ideal of what constitutes success and failure, goal and achievement.

Thirty years ago Dr. William Dodd, a distinguished historian and Franklin D. Roosevelt's first ambassador to Hitler Germany, recorded with incredulous revulsion in his diary that Dr. Goebbels, the Nazi minister of propaganda, had a Ph.D. degree. What appalled Dodd was not the individual but the lack of values in the system that had produced him. He was frightened by the sudden realization that the German university to which he had looked up all his life had become vocational preparation for a job rather than embodiment of ideals and commitment to values. This is indeed the ultimate depravity; this is, as Julien Benda, a French contemporary of Dodd's, called it, the "high treason of the learned" (*La Trahison des Clercs*).

Education in educated society must be education for virtue, and must aim at creating the desire for it. Education that does not strive for the "good man" is ignoble and cynical. Anyone as highly equipped with knowledge, with ability to learn, and with ability to do—and with income—as is the educated man of educated society, is equipped with so much power as to be a menace, if not a monster, unless he have virtue. He must have high ethical values, strong moral responsibility and a commitment to serve no mean end. He needs spiritual values founded in the knowledge of man's fallibility and mortality, in man's imperfection and man's aloneness, and in the knowledge that freedom is but the responsibility to choose between service to a true and to a false master.

This discussion has not attempted so far to pass judgment on the development that is giving us the educated society. The educated society is by way of becoming accomplished fact. To become an educated society is a necessity for every country that wants to remain able to compete economically, militarily or for political leadership. It is a necessity to the advance of every underdeveloped country. To the development of the educated society, and of the education it requires, a high priority has to be given. There is not much point in arguing whether we want it, nor in bemoaning its problems; let us rather take care not to fall short of its demands.

But in conclusion one might well ask: Is an educated society good and desirable?

It is certainly full of difficulties, full of doubts, full even of great dangers. One does not have to be anti-intellectual to wonder whether human happiness lies in higher education, or human achievement in the ability to destroy humanity. This educational explosion occurs at the very time when knowledge itself is becoming a threat, its control a metaphysical and spiritual problem. The doubling or tripling of our college enrollment within the next twenty years will by itself pose staggering problems. Will we have the wisdom and courage to solve them? They certainly require hard work, demand the abandonment of old, cherished habits and traditions. Were I president of a university I would feel the way a Roman bishop must have felt during the invasions of the Barbarians: They were God's just and necessary punishment for the sins of the Empire; they were Christians or receptive to the true faith; still they were about to sack his familiar city. The bishop may have gone out and blessed the invading host; but I doubt that his heart was in it.

Still, the new intellectual frontier has opened up. There is deep faith here in education, its values and its value. There is great achievement in freeing man from the iron law that had to deny access to learning and knowledge to all but a few throughout the ages. There is great promise too, great boldness and great vision.

# CHAPTER SIX

# "Up to Poverty"

## 1 · THE FRONTIER OF DEVELOPMENT

"Nothing ever changes here," said the manager of the Bangkok branch of a large American manufacturing company to the young man who had just come out from the Chicago head office to make a study of the changes in Far Eastern markets. "And nothing ever will change here," he continued; "these people have no initiative, no ambition, no vision. All this pushing of new products, new methods and new ideas from Chicago is just plain foolishness."

The two were sitting in a restaurant in one of the city's main streets; and the young man was idly looking out at the noisy throng of cars, buses, trucks, motorcycles and bicycles—the traffic jam that characterizes all cities in the Free World today in sharp contrast to the regimented emptiness of city streets in Communist countries. The branch manager—an elderly man who had spent most of his adult life working for American companies in the Far East—went on with his theme of the changeless, shiftless East. But the young man hardly heard him; he watched the traffic. Suddenly he turned his head and asked: "And how are you getting your goods to the customer today?"

"About 90 per cent by truck, the rest by motor launch; we have the most up-to-date delivery system in the city," was the immediate answer.

"And how did you move them twenty years ago when you first came to Bangkok?" the young man continued.

"Oh, mostly on bamboo poles carried on coolies' backs," was the answer.

"Yet you then also had the most up-to-date delivery system in the city, I imagine," the young man murmured.

This story, with slight variations, fits every city in the so-called underdeveloped countries: Leopoldville in the Belgian Congo or Salisbury in Rhodesia; Belém at the mouth of the Amazon, La Paz high up on the Andean Plateau, or Fairbanks, Alaska, at the rim of the frozen Arctic; Konya in Central Anatolia; Beirut in Lebanon, Meshed in Persia, Baghdad, Bombay, Rangoon or Gauguin's Tahiti. It might have to be changed before it would fit in the Communist world. But there too the overnight leap has been made from Abraham's time into the machine age, from the storyteller under the banyan tree to the radio, from the wooden hoe to the fifty-ton drop forge in the steel mill.

And yet the real change is not physical; it is not trucks and radios and machine tools. It is not even in the way people's lives have been altered: the sudden transformation of the Peruvian Indian living in the pre-Inca Stone Age into a skilled machinist in an automated paper mill; or the sudden transformation of the Mongolian nomadic herdsman into a bookkeeper.

The real change is in vision, beliefs and expectations.

For the first time in man's history the whole world is united and unified. This may seem a strange statement in view of the conflicts and threats of suicidal war that scream at us from every headline. But despite the reality and danger of conflict, mankind today shares the same vision, the same goal and the same hope; it even believes in the same tools.

This vision might, in gross oversimplification, be called *economic development.* It is the belief that man can improve his economic lot through systematic, purposeful and directed effort—individually as well as for an entire society. It is the belief that we have at our disposal the technological, the conceptual and the social tools to enable man to raise himself, through his own efforts, at least to the level that we in the West would consider poverty, but which for most of our world would be almost unbelievable luxury.

This vision is the important, the central fact. It is a vision not of individual wealth, but of a productive society. It is a vision of freedom from the slavery to want and the bondage to material destitution in which the human race has always existed. The aim is not luxury. It is a level just above mere material subsistence, where man is no longer controlled by starvation and at the mercy of every cloudburst, hailstorm or drought. The promise is that one's children will not forever be forced to go to work as mere infants to contribute to the meager subsistence of the family, but that they will have a chance to learn and to develop. It is the hope that man will not forever be caught in the quest for the next meal, but will be able to put material things in their proper, subordinate place as means to higher human ends.

This to be sure is a material vision. But the ends are not material fulfillment for the individual but material independence for individual and society alike. What impresses the outside world about the United States today is not how our rich men live—the world has seen riches before, and on a larger and more ostentatious scale. What impresses the outside world is how the poor of this country live.

*"Up to Poverty"* is the proper slogan for the great world-wide vision and improvement.

## The Agents of Revolution

"I can always tell an Indian who has driven a truck or a tractor," the old, experienced manager of a big sugar estate in South America said to me once. "He stands straight and talks back at me." The manager was a Spaniard, proud of his Castilian speech and his pure lineage. He had always been kind to the Indian field hands. But he had always looked down on them as an inferior race, had treated them with the care and affection a good husbandman gives to his horses, had, at best, thought of them as irresponsible children. "But now," he said, "we must realize that, in another twenty years, one of them will have to be able to take my place and do my job. For the internal combustive engine is doing what neither Spanish Crown nor Catholic Church could do. It is making a man out of the Indian."

Similarly, in this country, it was the automobile that gave momentum to the Negro's drive toward racial equality. "We had no troubles until the depression years when the Negroes first started to have cars," said a Southern newspaper editor, himself of the old school and bitterly opposed to racial integration. "White folks around here blame the New Deal, the government in Washington, Northern agitators or education. They are all wrong. Segregation was dead when the first Negro found out that a white man better get out of the way of an old jalopy even though a colored man be at the wheel. Up till then he accepted inferiority no matter what his leaders told him. After he'd made the first white man wait for him before crossing the road, he knew he wasn't inferior."

And a petroleum geologist adds to this: "The jeep means the end of the Bedouin tribe. It can go where no camel can go. There is no longer any hiding out for the nomad subject to no law but his tribal code, obedient to no command but that of his tribal sheik. When I first came to Arabia, in the thirties, we cocked our rifles when we ran into Bedouin tribesmen. Now we drive over and ask them whether we can listen to the news on the battery radio that the lead camel carries."

The agents of the revolution that has created the vision of economic development are the new tools of communication, the new agents of physical and psychological mobility. There is the radio which brings the whole world with all its ideas, its excitement, its dreams, into the most remote hamlet. The battery radio on the Bedouin's lead camel may well be the best symbol of this revolution. There is the dirt road which for the first time in history makes it possible for goods and ideas to reach the isolated villages—and for people to leave life in isolation and to move to the city with its companionship, its lights, its jobs, its schools. And then there is the truck, the jeep, the old jalopy fitted out with a wooden body to serve as a bus, and increasingly the plane, destroying distance and fear of the unknown, creating mobility, knowledge and desire.

These new tools are changing the very meaning of "economic necessities." Economists maintain that economic development starts with subsistence needs: food, clothing and shelter. As people shift from the peasant's natural economy to the money economy of the city, they should thereby create a constantly growing demand for, say, cheap textiles. Luxuries supposedly come much later. This, at least, is what the Industrial Revolution did in Western countries; when it first began, the textile industry was *the* growth industry. To a large extent the Point Four program of the United States has been based on this axiom of the economists.

But it does not work out that way in the growth countries of today. It is indeed amazing how well dressed the urban masses are in the burgeoning cities of these countries. The shopgirls may live in miserable rat-infested shacks. But they wear the same patterns one sees in Milan or Milwaukee. The styles and patterns Lancashire (or its imitators in Japan and India) used to make for the Indian or the South African trade cannot be sold to those countries today, not even at bargain prices. Yet they do not buy more clothing. I know of half a dozen large cities in the growth countries where textile sales have actually fallen these last ten years, despite doubling of the population and boom-time prosperity. The same goes for other "essentials" of subsistence living such as food and even housing.

The goods and services for which the demand increases disproportionately fast are such things as radios and household appliances, gasoline and electric power. The greatest increase in demand is for schools for the children. And the dream of every peasant who moves into the city is to own a car, however ramshackle, or at least a motor scooter, or at the very least a bicycle.

These are, in truth, the real consumer necessities in today's economic development. They symbolize its vision: a break through the age-old walls of isolation, a new, wider horizon, power over physical forces instead of enslavement to them, and opportunities for the children.

Indeed these new necessities show that economics itself is assuming a new meaning. Economists have long emphasized that the true measure of economic advance is not material—that is, a higher standard of living—but human: increasing freedom to choose and to act. In the old developed countries of the West, economic development did not contribute such noneconomic, human values to large masses until fairly late in the process. At first it contributed the old necessities, subsistence goods which provided material satisfaction for material wants. In the development countries of today, however, the emphasis right from the start has been on creating alternatives of choice and freedom. The means, to be sure, are material. But the new economic necessities are the keys to doors that lead out of immemorial bondage in isolation, want and ignorance to freedom of movement, freedom of knowledge, freedom of choice and opportunity.

## The Promise and the Danger

The full measure of the power of industrial society is its ability to stir the imagination. Even in the remote mountain villages of Tibet or the Andes, the promise of economic development possesses man with the force almost of a Messianic vision. He may not be able to realize the vision; but that he can believe it attainable releases tremendous energies.

But this vision also creates a new problem: international economic inequality. It creates a new danger: international and interracial class war between the underdeveloped poor countries and the developed rich.

We, on the North American Continent, including our Canadian friends and neighbors, are a mere 10 per cent of the world's population. But we have about 75 per cent of the world's income. By contrast, the 75 per cent of the world population whose income is below $125 per person a year receives altogether perhaps no more than 10 per cent of the world's income.

The twenty largest underdeveloped countries produce well over half of the Free World's industrial raw materials. But they themselves consume less than 5 per cent of what they produce. All of them excepting Brazil are "colored."

The inequality is increasing. Income per person in the fifteen developed countries with the highest standard of living (all "white" except for Japan) was in 1938, on average, seven times the income per person in the twenty largest under-developed countries. By 1955 this disparity had widened to a ratio of eight to one. Yet, there had been large-scale war-time destruction in major developed countries and an unprecedented raw-materials boom in most of the underdeveloped ones. This international inequality of income contrasts sharply with internal high equality of income in the developed countries, especially in ours where we are in the process of proving that an industrial society does not have to live in extreme tension between the few very rich and the many very poor. What used to be national inequality and economic tension is now rapidly becoming international and unfortunately also inter-racial inequality and tension.

We are engaged today in a race between the promise of economic development and the threat of international world-wide class war. Economic development is the opportunity of this age. Class war is the danger. The two are the essential economic realities of this industrial age of ours. Whether we shall realize the opportunity or succumb to the danger will not only decide the economic future of the world—it may largely decide its spiritual, its intellectual, its political and its social future.

### Is Economic Development Possible?

This new situation poses the question: Is economic development possible? Or is it a mirage?

There are many reasons for wondering. Anyone looking for scientific proof of a trend toward economic development would search in vain. During the last fifty years the majority of mankind has hardly improved its lot; in many parts of the world, for instance in China or in India, there may actually have been deterioration. In the least developed rural areas, where most of the "colored" races live, population is growing so much faster than the economy that there is danger of economic collapse.

Economic development is seriously hampered by all kinds of economic superstitions and delusions that are taken for gospel truth in most of the world today (including our own country). Perhaps most dangerous is the confusion between equality of opportunity and equality of income and rewards. The first is a dynamo of economic development. The second is deadly poison in the early stages of development. Soviet Russia has shown this most convincingly; but few people understand the lesson.

Yet, though it is neither easy nor automatic, economic development is possible.

The most visible evidence that it is not an impractical dream is Soviet Russia. This is, however, a misleading example, since the Soviet Union started out at a much higher economic level than most of the underdeveloped countries of the world. The economic level of European Russia in 1913 was almost as high as that of northern Italy. Soviet Russia also started out with plenty of open, empty space. Indeed, up till World War II the Soviet Union was a good example of misdevelopment.

The economic development of Latin-American countries, especially of Mexico, Brazil and Colombia, in the last twenty-five years is more impressive evidence that economic development is feasible. Perhaps even more meaningful are Turkey and Puerto Rico—two areas with singularly unfavorable natural conditions for economic development, in which, nevertheless, real progress has been made.

But the best example is the oldest: Japan. A century ago Japan was a feudal anarchy; she was one of the poorest and most backward of all economies—and at the same time already densely populated. Within forty years she had transformed herself into a modern economy with tremendous growth potential. She did, apparently instinctively, all the things which we now know to be essential to rapid economic development. As a result the progress of Japan during the fifty years up to World War I was faster than anything the Soviet Union has ever been able to achieve. In many ways therefore it is Japan, the Japan of the Meji Revolution, that should serve as our model.

Today, for the first time, we have a tested theory to describe what went on in Japan a century ago. Since the end of World War II, economic development has not only become a major goal of national and international policy but its study has become central to economic theory.

The understanding of economic development, and the new ability it gives us, rest on the new world-view. We can understand economic development because we see it as a purposeful process, as a pattern rather than as a mechanism. We can organize economic development because of our concept of innovation. Economic development does not come about by evolutionary imitation of the experience of the developed countries. It does not go from mercantilism to "putting-out" system to steam-driven machinery and so on, or from making necessities by hand to making the same necessities by machine. It leap-frogs from primitive to developed economy. The new organization is the engine that powers this economic leap. The ability to organize men for skill and knowledge is the basic resource of economic development, and conversely the lack of men capable of doing this, both as professional specialists and as managers, is its greatest obstacle. It is not, however, the only obstacle. Thanks to our new logic of innovation, we can predict what various other difficulties will be.

*The "Take-off Crisis"*

The first predictable difficulty grows out of the process of economic development itself. This is the crisis that confronts any nation at the first stages of development.

Gradual improvements never bring about economic development. There must be a leap. Economists call this the "take-off crisis." They speak of the "self-sustaining chain reaction" that must be released if there is to be economic development. And they carry analogy with physics to the point where they speak of the "critical mass."

What they mean is that economic development is a "threshold phenomenon," a term of the scientist. Until development efforts reach a certain level they are wasted; there is no development. Once they pass this point they become effective. If they are maintained above this level for a number of years development begins to feed on itself, begins to be self-generating.

This threshold can be stated in fairly precise quantitative terms: By and large there will be no economic development until at least one tenth of national income is put into productive investments over and above the investment needed to maintain a growing population at the same standard of living. There is a wide choice of investment possibilities; and there is ample room for disagreement whether schools, roads, houses, candy factories or petroleum fields should come first, or what the balance should be between them. But the threshold below which there is no economic development remains more or less the same regardless of investment policy. And the problem is the same in all underdeveloped countries: how to obtain that much capital in a poor country.

The answer is that the take-off crisis cannot be overcome without some capital investment from the outside.

The economic development of the United States, despite all

our empty land and mineral resources, rested on the massive European investments during the nineteenth century, especially in the railroads. Even more important, though impossible of measurement: The immigrants who came here were predominantly grown men and women in whose wealth-producing capacity their native countries had invested a lot of capital for a long time. A sixteen-year-old boy must have cost $500 to raise, feed and clothe, even in poorest, nineteenth-century Sicily. With allowances for the old and the children, the lame and the halt, the annual immigration of a million people into this country during the forty years prior to World War I represented therefore a capital contribution to our economic development of at least a quarter billion dollars a year.

Japan too relied heavily on foreign capital for the take-off. But the country in which foreign capital played the greatest part was Russia. It is never stressed in Soviet literature that the Communists inherited one of the best railway systems in the world—a system so good that it lasted through World War II without much addition and with a minimum of maintenance. This system was almost entirely built by foreign capital. Altogether czarist Russia obtained in the twenty years before 1913 about as much capital from Western Europe as the United States through Marshall Plan loans and investments contributed to European recovery. Even after the Revolution Russia continued capital imports; the "foreign concession" during the twenties provided the capital foundation for the first Five-Year Plan.

The problem is therefore not whether a country needs foreign capital to develop. Economic development is not possible without some dependence on outside capital during the take-off time. The problem is how much it needs, for how long, where it will get the capital, and what use it will make of it.

The problems of economic development are not over once the take-off crisis has been passed. Nor are they confined to problems of industrialization. A few years ago most people believed that the two were synonymous, and today most people in the underdeveloped growth countries still believe that building plants and training workers to man them are their only concern. On the contrary, economic development requires balanced and simultaneous change in four sectors: agriculture; "social overhead"—that is, public and community services such as roads, transportation, communications, water and power, schools and hospitals; industrial development; and the development of effective systems of distribution and credit. So much has been written and said about industrialization that no discussion seems necessary here. The other three areas, however, still demand more attention than they have received.

### The Agriculture Problem

The most difficult challenge to development is actually in agriculture.

Agricultural technology has been advancing in the last thirty years at tremendous speed. It has given us new methods, improved seeds, new crops and new techniques which are infinitely more productive than anything scientific farmers knew only a generation ago. Moreover, agriculture is so backward in most parts of the world that tremendous improvements are possible fast and with modest investment of capital. More than half of the world's harvests do not even get to the consumer but are destroyed on the way, rotting in the rain, eaten by insects and rodents, spoiled or wasted in processing. In many parts of the world, approach roads to get the products to market and a simple marketing system can double actual agricultural yield.

But technical improvement may only aggravate the real

problem of agriculture, which is social. To improve agriculture means getting people off the land. Agricultural overpopulation is by itself a major cause of agricultural underproduction. It encourages, indeed demands, concentration on the less productive crop, which however usually provides the most jobs.

Rich soils in Bulgaria are planted to tobacco of such low quality as to be almost unsalable. They would be well suited for the production of badly needed vegetables or edible oils. But the need to find something to do for the surplus farm labor is simply too great to permit a switch from the highly labor-intensive but worthless tobacco crop to more valuable high-grade oil crops.

Overpopulation on the land also inhibits the use of modern tools. It creates uneconomically small plots and wide dispersion of individual holdings. Altogether it makes improved farming methods practically impossible. If the farm population in the underdeveloped countries could be halved overnight farm production might double within a year or two, without much additional incentive, change or capital investment.

Agricultural overpopulation thus prevents any increase in the production of food and raw materials. Such increase is, however, a necessity for industrial expansion. How else can the growing urban population be fed or the growing industries be supplied with new raw materials?

Agricultural overpopulation also prevents economic growth because it keeps the needed labor in unproductive though strenuous idleness. Altogether it can be said that the number of people needed on the land to feed one family in the city is an index both of the economic level of a country and of its ability to grow further.

That France still requires half of her population to work on the land is a major reason for France's economic difficulties, going far beyond political incompetence or international involvements; and at the same time it is a major brake on France's economic development. By contrast American economic development in the last generation would have been impossible without the halving of our farm population. This both released the workers for the growing industries and provided, by more than doubling total farm output, a steadily increasing per capita supply of food and industrial raw materials.

But how can the surplus population on the land be moved out without large-scale upheaval? It is not enough to move people off the land—not even if there are jobs for them. Those who remain must have an incentive to produce more. And the means used to bring about the shift must not themselves impose a new rigid and frozen pattern of agricultural organization which, in turn, becomes a brake on development.

Here the Soviet Union has failed so thoroughly that, all outward indications to the contrary, Russia's economic development is seriously stunted and permanently weakened. Collectivization was partly a political move—to obtain control of the recalcitrant farmers whose opposition made precarious the tenure of any Communist government. Collectivization was also a means to force people off the land and thus provide workers for the new Soviet industries. The brute force with which peasants were driven off the land, and their farms collectivized, destroyed the incentive of those who remained instead of stimulating them to greater production. It permanently lowered productivity. Even today, thirty years later, the loss has not been made good, despite heavy capital investment, despite police terror and threat, despite scientific agriculture.

At the same time—and in the long run the effect may be even more damaging—collectivization makes rural overpopulation permanent. It freezes at a high level the work force that has to stay on the land, with low income and low productivity. The Russians have, for twenty years, tried without success to reduce farm population to less than 50 per cent of the working population—which compares with 12 per cent in this country today. Instead they have had to force people in fairly large numbers out of the cities and back to the farm. Yet they have not been able to bring about any real increase in the supply of farm products; farm production has risen more slowly than population. This is a narrow and precarious foundation for a first-rate power—and in the long run a fatal weakness.

China today is making the same mistake. Forcing young Chinese from the city to "volunteer" for farmwork will not increase farm yields; it will only starve industry of needed workers. The story is the same in the European satellites.

There are at least two countries that have done better than the Communists, though by very different methods and in very different ways. One was Japan seventy years ago. The other is Mexico today, where the collective-farm system that was the sacred cow of the revolution in earlier years has been allowed to collapse quietly. As a result large numbers of surplus farm workers have left the land for the cities to supply the labor force for Mexico's growing industries. The remaining farmers have greatly improved their productivity and output and have responded to the incentives offered by the growing demand for their product.

But the task of reducing the surplus farm population without impairing the incentive for the remaining farmers—and without creating the social poison of an uprooted, unemployed, new proletariat—is a central problem of economic development.

### Distribution and Credit

Economic development demands the rapid growth of distribution and credit systems. In our preoccupation with industrialization, and influenced by the age-old feeling against the middleman, we tend to slight both.

A handful of Sears, Roebuck stores in Latin America—in Mexico, Cuba, Colombia, Venezuela, Brazil and Peru—has had as great an impact on the economies of these countries as all the very much larger investment in steel plants. The Sears stores have brought into being several hundred small, local manufacturers turning out all kinds of goods, and have set for them advanced standards of quality, cost control and production methods. They have created new consumer demands.

In Southeast Asia there is everywhere a striking correlation between economic growth and the extension of installment credit to consumers. And, contrary to all predictions, installment loans are being repaid as faithfully as in the United States, defaults are as uncommon as here.

In country after country, simple farm credit has had more impact on farm productivity than any improvement of methods—except better methods of marketing. I know at least half a dozen underdeveloped countries where industry could easily produce twice as much if only marketing were more effective.

An effective marketing system not only enables the producer to get his product to the consumer at least waste, loss or cost; it enables him to produce for the market by providing him with credit, standards, quality demands and product specifications. It makes the consumer capable of discernment, that is, of obtaining value for his limited purchasing power. Economic development in any growth country requires an intricate distribution system:

a system of physical distribution;
a financial system to make possible the distribution of goods;
actual marketing that integrates wants, needs and purchasing power of the consumer with capacity and resources of production.

An efficient marketing organization in small and poor markets is the only way to foster small industries. By itself the market for any one product is too small for efficient distribution—and without efficient distribution there cannot be efficient production. Without a distributive organization, many products for which there is a demand cannot be supplied. At the same time a distributive system is the quickest way to develop a middle class.

Unlike agricultural development, development of distribution and credit systems poses few social problems. It thus deserves very much more enthusiasm than it usually gets in the plans of underdeveloped countries.

## *"Social Overhead" Costs*

Rapid economic development is not possible without heavy investment in what the economists call the "social overhead" of an economy and less erudite people might call the basic foundation: roads, water supply, power supply, harbors, housing and, last but not least, schools. These are all long-term investments. Ten or fifteen years may elapse before they begin to produce economic returns in the form of goods and services for the consumer. At the same time building these basic foundations requires a large work force, consisting usually of people who, only yesterday, lived as subsistence-peasants and almost entirely outside of the money economy. This is one reason why every government in an underdeveloped growth country stresses the basic foundations—they supply jobs. But at the same time they put new money into the hands of exceedingly poor people, who immediately will want to turn this income into goods they never before could buy. These goods, however, are not yet being produced—and thus there is a permanent excess of purchasing power created by the very process of economic development. The obvious result is inflation.

This is not something that can be overcome by sound financial policies. Sound financial policy would argue that no such basic foundation investments be made at all, or at the very most that they be severely limited. But if they are slighted no economic development is possible. Nor can the problem be shrugged off with the old saying: "Why worry about inflation? The houses that inflation builds will still be there after the boom has burst." Inflation misdirects capital investments into unproductive channels. It destroys a country's ability to get foreign development capital; even the Russian loans to satellites are charged in dollars or gold rubles after all. It creates dangerous and lasting social bitterness. Economic development is impossible under rapid inflation. Every growth country is therefore caught for a long time in the dilemma between not spending enough on the foundation, and thus starving economic development, or spending too much and conjuring up inflation that will as effectively kill it off.

## The Problem of Attitudes

Economic development cannot exist without public support. On the one hand, economic development is a major effort, and therefore requires impatience, a desire to have things changed, a willingness to get big things done. On the other hand, the results will not appear overnight—in fact, the more important the investment, the longer the result may be in coming. There is therefore need for patience and public spirit.

To mobilize public support for economic development, a symbol is called for, a "spectacular" to catch the imagination of the people. A good example in the United States was the Tennessee Valley Authority (TVA). Ten years or more were required before this great effort had any real impact on the economic life of the mid-South. But from the beginning it symbolized the new day. It mobilized energies. It created hope and vision where there had been despair and shortsighted greed.

Yet the TVA also illustrates the problem of the spectacular. How much uneconomic effort is justified for the symbolic and emotional yield?

Could Egypt's Aswan Dam be justified as a spectacular? The future of its water supply depends on the underdevelopment of the countries in which the Nile starts; as soon as these countries themselves begin to develop, the water supply to Aswan might well fall off. On the other hand would not a spectacular have been justified in Iraq, where an intelligent and well-planned development effort—an effort which, if allowed to take its course, will have changed the miserable poverty of one third of the total population in another ten years—is in danger of being repudiated because of the absence of any such rousing symbol?

Attitude problems lie at the heart of economic development; for the attitudes needed tend to run counter to the superstitions and emotions of the great majority of people, especially in the growth countries.

There is need, for instance, for both public and private efforts, regardless of the nation's political commitment to private ownership or state control. Soviet industry was largely built by people who had come up in the private enterprise system before the Revolution. But unlike the Russia of 1917, most of the underdeveloped, growth countries of today still have to produce the private entrepreneurs, businessmen and managers whom the Communists inherited in sizable numbers and high quality. Government, regardless of who is in power, must therefore encourage a private sector in all these countries. It must provide the proper incentives in it; must, above all, provide the assurance of respect for contracts and for private property without which private business cannot produce at all.

It is not very relevant whether the government of the Indian Republic controls more or less of the economy than the U. S. government. What is relevant is that the Indian government, while fully aware of the need for the development of private business in a large sector of the economy, is not willing or able to accept this fact. It is not willing or able to look upon private business as desirable. At best it looks upon it as a necessary evil that will be suppressed as soon as it is no longer absolutely necessary. With such an attitude the necessary development of the private sector will not take place—and without it the entire economic development of the country is likely to fail.

But economic development also requires large-scale government action, especially in the years of the take-off crisis. No matter how deeply wedded one may be to the free enterprise system (and I for one am married to it for life), one has to accept the need for positive government; one has to consider government action on a sizable scale as desirable rather than a necessary evil.

Another attitude problem is the dangerous tendency in underdeveloped countries to confuse creation of jobs with economic growth. All these countries desperately need job opportunities. But uneconomic investments made to create jobs always deplete the resources of the country. India is a good example. Unemployment is a danger; but stagnation is more dangerous still, and will in turn produce even more unemployment.

Domestic industry must be protected if, in its early stages, it cannot compete with the industries of more highly developed countries. But an economic nationalism that encourages permanently uneconomic developments is a danger to economic development. Growth countries need to think clearly about which industries should be encouraged because they can be expected eventually to stand on their own, and which industries had better not be pushed in a small, poor economy.

Money spent on atomic energy in a small, underdeveloped country, for instance, might well be a total waste. Yet atomic energy promises to become a major development factor in many of these countries. Its exploitation might therefore be tackled through regional or international co-operation.

A steel mill in Chile deserves protection during its early years; it has excellent coal and iron-ore resources available and is close to cheap transportation. But the steel mill which Perón built in neighboring Argentina—without ore, without coal and without transportation to its remote markets—was sheer folly. A common steel market between these two countries would have given cheap steel to both from the Chilean mill, and would have in turn permitted bringing together the Argentinian surplus of foodstuffs and the chronic Chilean food deficit for mutual advantage.

Still another important problem is the attitude toward profit. In most parts of the world (including most of the United States), profit is a dirty word. It is commonly believed that there are ways of running an economy without profit. This is nonsense. Profit is an absolute requirement of economic activity and especially of advanced economic activity. For the essence of such an activity is to commit present scarce resources to future and therefore highly uncertain results, to create and to take high risks. Profit is necessary to cover these future risks, which would otherwise become loss, that is destruction of economic capital and of the wealth-producing capacity of the economy. Profit of course is also the source of the additional capital needed for future expansion, and as such another genuine cost of economic development. There is no way to eliminate this need for profit; it is greatest if the economic development is based on central planning. But there will have to be a real change in attitude before this is generally accepted; and in the meantime resistance to profit endangers economic development everywhere.

## The Ultimate Resource

The ultimate resource in economic development is people. It is people, not capital or raw materials, that develop an economy. The greatest need in the underdeveloped countries is people who can do the new organizing job, the job of building an effective organization of skilled and trained people exercising judgment and making responsible decisions.

The great conflict in the world will be decided in this area. It can be decided neither by military might—we should have known this all along—nor by economic power by itself, though the use of this power will have a real bearing. It will indeed not be decided by anything that happens in the developed countries, including Russia. It will be decided by the people who in the underdeveloped growth countries will take leadership, the very small numbers of able, educated, dedicated people on whom any such economy must depend. In the last analysis the great world conflict today is over the values, the beliefs, the competence and the vision of these people.

## 2 · BUILDING AN INDUSTRIAL SOCIETY

Twenty-five years ago the basic premise of the Marxist "theory of imperialism" was widely accepted even by non-Marxists. The premise was that the industrial economy of the developed countries had reached, or was at least inevitably approaching, the point where it could grow no further but must stagnate. Keynes—anything but a Marxist—accepted this. The slogan of the "mature economy" that was so popular in this country during those years rested on the same premise.

Today even the dedicated Marxist has his doubts.

The main reason for the change is not the shift from the Depression of the thirties to the prosperity of the fifties. The reason is the emergence of economic development. The theory of imperialism assumed subconsiously that economic development could take place only in the old industrial countries of the West; it expressed racial bigotry, much as it would pain the Marxists to admit it.

Today the central economic premise is not maturity but immaturity, the central economic problem is not stagnation but growth, and the stimulus to economic growth is not in the developed but in the developing economies.

In the fall of 1957 the Committee for Economic Development, a group of American business leaders founded to study economic problems and to formulate economic policy, asked fifty highly distinguished men—economists, philosophers, political leaders—all over the world to write an essay on the question: "What is the most important economic problem to be faced by the United States over the next twenty years?" A full third of the writers, despite the differences in their nationality, background and professional interests, agreed: the most important problem will be the economic development of the underdeveloped countries. More important: every one of the papers dealing with the subject stressed that the economic development of the underdeveloped countries was an opportunity rather than a problem.

"Up to Poverty" is as much the growth opportunity for the developed as for the underdeveloped countries. It means that there need be no danger of stagnation for those countries that have already, in the course of the last two centuries, overcome the take-off crisis and started the chain reaction of economic growth. The vision of economic development in the under-developed countries first and foremost creates a new frontier for the already developed economies. It is capable of banishing the specter of their own economic decay for at least another century of productive work and continuous growth.

Economic development of the underdeveloped countries is not only an opportunity for the developed countries but a necessity. While the former remain underdeveloped, the threat of stagnation for the latter is real. For only a developing or developed country offers major opportunities for both investment and trade.

The whole Indian subcontinent of 500 million people buys no more from the developed industries of the United States than does little but highly developed Switzerland with fewer than five million inhabitants—and yet we are India's biggest supplier. All American investments in Indian industry during the last ten years, despite strong U.S. government support, total only a third of the American investments in Swiss business and industry during the same time.

Economic development of the underdeveloped countries is also the only way to obtain the increasing supplies of raw materials on which the development of the industrial countries depends. In turn it is the only way to obtain larger markets for finished products and therewith the means to pay for larger raw-material supplies.

Rapid and sustained economic development of the under-developed areas is therefore as much a concern of the developed countries as it is of the underdeveloped. It deserves as much attention in American, British or German national policy as in that of India, Brazil or Rhodesia. To support it is not "aid" to the underdeveloped countries but "investment" in the future of the developed ones; it is not philanthropy but self-interest.

What then does it require from the developed, industrial countries of the West?

## The Role of Money

Economic development demands a supply of money—for the capital investment needed for the take-off; for expenditures on the "social overhead foundation" such as schools, roads and transportation; for the inevitable growing pains of an inflationary or balance-of-payments crisis; and above all for productive investments in agriculture, commerce and industry.

But leadership in economic development is not primarily a matter of the amount of money that is made available. Nor is raising the money the central problem.

In the first place the amount that can be usefully spent is very small. Ten per cent is a very large chunk of the national income to be invested in economic development; but the national income of the underdeveloped countries is so small as to make this a fairly minor sum for a developed country. The experts agree that no more than six to eight billion dollars of outside capital a year could be invested productively by all the underdeveloped countries in the non-Communist world. Taken together this is less than 2 per cent of the annual national income of the United States alone, and just about 1 per cent of that of the entire free West.

By contrast Great Britain invested overseas on an average 4.5 per cent of a much smaller national income in the years between 1880 and 1913. In the period between 1909 and 1913, British capital exports rose to 8.5 per cent of her annual income. Yet these were the years of greatest prosperity and most rapid growth of the British economy, and especially the years of most rapid advance for the British worker.

Moreover, we are already investing as much in the under-developed countries as they can put to productive use. The United States capital exports to these areas alone has been running at six billion dollars a year, two thirds of which represents private investment.

The great need is for right direction and productive use of the money already available.

This requires, first, a commitment on the part of the developed countries—a clear, unambiguous and consistent policy of support of, and leadership in, the development of the underdeveloped areas.

It requires, further, a clear priority on economic development in foreign aid. The criterion for making a loan, an investment or a grant must always be: Will this contribute to the ability of the country to develop itself?

American policy over the Aswan Dam project in Egypt will go down in history as a classic blunder. But the mistake was not the abrupt withdrawal of the loan offered. The mistake was to offer one as a bribe to Egypt not to do business with Russia or not to nationalize the Suez Canal. Even if the Aswan Dam could have been justified as productive investment, this would have been futile appeasement. And since, in the opinion of the experts, it could not be justified as a sensible contribution to Egypt's economic development, the offer was folly.

The productive use of development money is a problem above all in respect to government expenditure.

The worst waste of scarce capital resources has been to use them to build up armies of dubious military value. Perhaps this can be justified in countries that are directly in the path of the Russian juggernaut. But what can be said for Argentina's or Colombia's attempts to build up the largest second-class armies and air forces in the Western Hemisphere? Or for Chile's wasting money on light cruisers rather than on improving her desperately backward agriculture and food supply? India would still be in need of foreign loans if she had no army at all. But the crisis of India's Five-Year Plan is primarily the aggrandizement of the Indian Army. Equally wasteful and equally common is the division of economic growth capital into building up huge, totally unproductive bureaucracies of underpaid government clerks.

This immediately raises the ticklish issue of national sovereignty. It had better be faced squarely: Dependence on outside capital limits freedom of action. The businessman who borrows from the bank to finance seasonal inventory accepts limitations on his freedom; at the least he has to use the cash from the sale of inventory to repay the bank rather than to expand his plant. The management of a family-owned company that sells stock to the public accepts limitations; at the least it has to render a public accounting of its stewardship each year.

Similarly the country that accepts capital from abroad has to accept limitations of its freedom of action. It makes no difference whether the money is a gift, a loan or a direct investment; whether the donor or the recipient is a government or a private concern; whether the money comes from the United States or from the Soviet Union. There are, of necessity, strings attached. Gratitude is not a measure of the relationship; the American Congressman who expects to buy thanks with foreign aid is wasting the taxpayers' money. But obligation is of the essence of the relationship.

Yet we are dealing with independent countries; and the weaker partners are understandably jealous of their sovereignty and entitled to respect for it.

We need therefore informed international public opinion to express the necessary limitations and to define the necessary safeguards. Above all we need to establish that these limitations are dictated by disinterested, objective concern with the best self-development of the underdeveloped world.

The governments in those countries are often not the real problem. Everyone in public life in Chile, for instance, knows very well that the country's own best interests demand less navy and more farm roads, fewer government clerks and more work. But who dares say so publicly? Almost any government in an underdeveloped country needs someone with outside authority to speak the unpalatable truths. Even the truth is not acceptable, however, if it comes from the "rich uncle." For the United States to tell Chile to cut down the navy while herself engaged in building superaircraft carriers is far too much like Marie Antoinette's "Let them eat cake." Nor can the prospective foreign investor say these things and be heard; all he can do is decide not to invest. But there are plenty of examples to show that they can be said effectively by the outside expert with no ax to grind and no profit at stake.

This is what makes it so important that we today are developing a theory of economic development that is generally accepted. The American banker, the German industrialist, the Western government official, may be suspect as a "capitalist" or "imperialist." But would the same suspicion be aroused by a West Indian such as W. A. Lewis, the brilliant development economist who is now adviser to the government of Ghana? By an Indian Socialist such as Masani? An Argentinian like Prebisch? A Puerto Rican? A Turk? An Iraqi? Yet all of them agree on the essential points.

To mobilize this new knowledge, experience and agreement is an important requirement for effective Western leadership in economic development. Western governments too, of course, would be helped in their own domestic affairs, in their own relations with their legislatures and their voters, by effective and respected impartial advice. But above all, such advice (and it should be that rather than outside decision) might help create what is lacking today: the conviction that the developed and the underdeveloped countries are united by mutual self-interest, common vision and common goals.

## Leadership by Example

The oil-rich sheikdoms of Arabia or oil-rich Venezuela have all the money—much more than they could possibly use. But they show little economic development. Money by itself can buy Cadillacs and concubines; it cannot buy development. The motor of economic development and its driving power must be the power of people. And people must come from the inside, must develop in and from the countries themselves.

The greatest contribution which the developed countries of the West can and must make is therefore to give leadership through example. They must be able to show the growth countries the example of a functioning industrial society and of a worth-while industrial civilization.

Here the free West should enjoy a decided advantage over the Communist countries. Financial aid the Soviet Union can supply. She can also supply technicians. But she cannot supply an example of a free and functioning industrial society. Russian Communism denies that such a society is possible, that its problems exist and are real. It must deny this or else give up the belief in its own tenets, and especially in the dogma that all social and economic problems are automatically solved by the mere establishment of the dictatorship of the proletariat.

The Soviet Union has not even attempted to tackle the problem of the relationship between worker, work and enterprise, clinging instead, in the face of all evidence, to the dogma that the only problem is "exploitation" of the worker by the "capitalist." As a result the real problems of status and power, of satisfaction and responsibility, have simply been suppressed. But release the tension only the least bit, and, as in Soviet Germany, in Soviet Poland, in Soviet Hungary, in Soviet Yugo-

slavia, or in Red China in the spring of 1957, the ugly reality
of worker bitterness, suppression and class hatred for the
new, Communist "bosses" comes to the surface immediately.

Communism denies also that there is need for managers.
Officially it accepts only the need for technicians. This does not
get rid of the manager. It only stops any work and thought on
his role and his function. As a result the Soviet managers not
only have near-despotic powers; they do not learn how to
manage and are incompetent to do so.

One of the strangest phenomena was the collapse of the Polish
economy when the yoke of terror was lightened in 1957. That
collapse took place in Hungary as a result of the uprising in Oc-
tober, 1957, could perhaps be explained by the weeks of bitter
fighting, the occupation by a foreign, invading army, and the mass
exodus of trained people. But in Poland there was a great upsurge
of patriotic exultation. And yet the economy collapsed. The explanation is that there was no one, after ten years of Communism,
who knew how to do the simplest managerial tasks: to purchase
raw materials, to schedule work, to sell products, to route freight
deliveries, and so on. The moment people had to do any of these
things for themselves instead of having them done for them by
order from above, they collapsed into enthusiastic incompetence.
No greater indictment of the basic inability of Communism to
build a society could be imagined.

Finally, Communism can build only a war economy. It
cannot allow the fruits of economic development to accrue to
the citizen as a consumer. To do so would create a crisis of
inefficiency that would bring down whole industries in mass
unemployment and bankruptcy; for a Communist economy
can only work if costs of production are irrelevant, that is if
there is chronic shortage of goods and chronic unsatisfied
demand. Furthermore, any real improvement in the consumer's lot would destroy centralized planning which cannot
operate if the consumer has any choice—quite apart from the

fact that, as said before, centralized planning can only function if the goal is clearly defined, such as the eternal "more" of a war economy.

Of course, the very weakness of Communism as a social system, the fact that it denies the need for, and possibility of, an industrial society makes it also a danger. Underdeveloped countries will not go Communist if they believe that they can develop, believe that they are developing. But they will be profoundly attracted to Communism if they fail. For in the promises of Communism lies an alternative to failure of economic development. And people will try any alternative before abandoning so dazzling a vision as that of economic development.

In the long run Communism cannot solve the social question of the worker in society and economy. But in the short run it promises to suppress it. Communism does not, in the long run, produce the professional managers and entrepreneurs that are needed. But for the short run it promises to do without them; a completely controlled economy is, whatever the long-run cost, a manager-saving device. Communism has never built a self-generating economy that is capable of sustaining its own growth and innovation; but it promises to extort the necessary capital to build a war machine.

Even these promises may prove to be false in the really underdeveloped countries, whose economic and intellectual foundations are so much lower than those Soviet Russia inherited. Communism in such a country may only mean despotism; but by the time people find this out it may be too late.

On balance, however, the Free World clearly has the advantage. Unlike the Communists we have tackled the job of building an industrial society. Though we have by no means finished it, we have gone far enough to know that the job can be done, and to know what needs to be done to make our advantage fully effective. We know, in other words, what our major unsolved problems are.

## The Problems We Face

One problem we face is the political one of the power, role and function of the labor union. All developed countries accept the labor union today as necessary and legitimate to an industrial society. But what should its power and function be? No labor union in any developed country is still the persecuted underdog of its own rhetoric. But by law and custom it is granted privileges, powers and exemptions from the laws such as can be allowed only to a weak and powerless minority in need of special protection. It enjoys a right of coercion over the citizen—whether in the form of the closed shop, restrictions on apprenticeship, or even the right to discipline members for their private lives or political opinions. These, at the very least, demand regulation in the public interest and control by the guardians of individual liberties, the courts of law. And how far can any private association, however beneficial, be allowed the right to strike? Is there not need for a sharp line between strikes against an employer and those increasingly frequent strikes which coerce the public?

In all developed countries the labor union has obtained for its members the first call on the fruits of enterprise. If permissible at all, this calls for union responsibility for the economic performance of the union member and for the economic welfare of the community. The "underdog" who fights against exploitation can shrug off such a demand. The union leader who asserts right and power to determine economic policy cannot.

In every developed country the labor union has learned that the job and welfare of the union member depend on the welfare of the enterprise and the performance of management.

Twenty-five years ago American labor leaders were unique in understanding that the labor union needs free enterprise as a fish needs water. Today, as a result of experience both with Communism and with nationalized enterprises, all union leaders in industrially developed countries know that. But how many dare admit it? How many dare slough off the outworn rhetoric of class war, hatred and negation? How many, in other words, think of their responsibilities instead of their privileges, their contribution instead of their demands, their future impact instead of their past injuries?

This is a crucial problem for industrial society. All of the underdeveloped countries are evolving unions—and they should. But their unions demand in poor, underdeveloped countries what the union gets in rich, developed ones; when they are "against" rather than "for," obstacles to development rather than forces for it, they are only following the example of the labor union in the developed countries. They need a new example of effective, responsible, constructive unionism.

Union leadership in the developed countries can still take the initiative in thinking through the problems of unionism and the role of a powerful and accepted labor union in society and economy. The capacity exists, as was made manifest in the contribution of some American union leaders to the success of the Marshall Plan. But is there enough intelligence, enough imagination, enough courage? Or will the job have to be done by legislation restricting the labor unions, that is by social action such as every free society has always taken in the end against groups who subvert power into privilege rather than use it to serve?

Another problem of industrial society is that of productivity in administration, distribution and service industries.

Unlike the problem of unionism this is a new one.

We know how to increase the productivity of work in agriculture and in manufacturing. We know that it means not harder but more effective work, that the factors of increased productivity are better tools, especially machines, and better management. But we do not know how to increase or how to measure the productivity of other work, especially in distribution; we know more about office work but not nearly enough.

In the United States the productivity of work in manufacturing has risen at the rate of 3 per cent compounded each year since the end of World War II—for a total rise of 80 per cent in twenty years. The productivity of work in agriculture has risen at a perhaps even faster rate. Yet few people would assert that there has been much rise in the productivity of office work, selling, distribution or the service industries. If common experience of Christmas shopping is an indication, productivity in retail trade has certainly gone down.

At the same time, incomes of employees in these fields, as well as those of manufacturing employees, have risen with the rise in manufacturing ways and productivity. Fifty years ago this would have been a minor problem. At that time about three out of every four Americans at work were either in manufacturing or on the farm. Today, however, farm and factory labor together are less than half of the work force. More than half the total are in office work, in distribution or in service industries. Thus the rise in all incomes with the rise in manufacturing productivity creates a constant inflationary pressure, constant increase in costs and increasing economic distortion. The same development has occurred in all developed countries.

This new problem cannot be solved by the remedy of the classical economist: to pass on gains in productivity in the form of lower prices rather than higher wages. This would only shift the impact of dislocation without lessening it. What is needed is a rapid increase of productivity in the lagging areas. It is in these areas rather than in manufacturing that the greatest opportunities of such new concepts as automation and of such new tools as the computer lie.

For the underdeveloped countries this problem is even more crucial than for the developed ones. They need rapid growth of administrative, distributive and services work. But their economies do not have the reserve to stand much dislocation. Because we in the developed countries do not have any measurements the underdeveloped countries have no yardsticks at all; they tend therefore to build up huge forces of office and distribution employees who contribute little or nothing. But because they have no reserves, they have to pay these people starvation wages; the entire economy is depressed and, at the same time, put under inflationary pressures which it cannot withstand.

The common vision of economic development means that the whole world is dedicated to a business civilization. It makes little difference whether the legal or ideological forms are those of Socialism, Communism or free enterprise—however profound the moral and political cleavages. Regardless of the system, the business enterprise is the productive unit in a business civilization—in Soviet Russia as well as in the United States, in Great Britain or in the emergent economies of Latin America.

As a result the basic decision on the political and moral values of this world of ours may well be made in judging the business enterprise, its values and its performance. The crucial, world-wide political choice between freedom or tyranny, the central moral choice between truth or lie, could well depend on the values of our business civilization.

What then are the values that business enterprise has to stand for in this age of economic development? It has to demonstrate that while it is an economic instrument, designed to produce goods and services economically, it can serve the social end of a better and a juster society, of a fuller and more responsible individual with more and more equal opportunities. It must use the material as a means toward a society that is both more humane and more human.

This does not mean subordination of economic performance—the first job of a business, under free enterprise as well as under Communism, is to produce economic goods and services.

But it does mean that the ultimate test of a business enterprise and of a business civilization is not the goods and services they produce. The ultimate goal is not profit, which is rather a necessity and a condition of survival. The ultimate product of a business enterprise and of a business civilization must be people. The maxim by which it lives and operates must be the establishment of harmony between individual and social good and business interest. This is something that Communism cannot do at all. In this area we in the developed countries of the Free World should have the decisive advantage of leadership.

This is perhaps nothing very new. It is what people mean when they talk about the capitalist revolution that has taken place, especially in the United States, in these last twenty years. If the Free World can convince the growth countries that this is really what a business civilization stands for, it will have won, will have given the foundation for economic development in freedom.

But to convince others we have to be convinced ourselves and have to act true to our own best knowledge and conviction.

# CHAPTER SEVEN

# Modern Government in Extremis

## 1 · THE END OF THE LIBERAL STATE

Modern government, the nation-state, was born with the Cartesian world-view of modern man, just three hundred years ago. And it has died with it. But where we have, at least in its beginnings, a new world-view today, no successor to modern government has yet emerged. We are without an effective institution of political integration and order.

This, at first, may seem paradoxical. The new nations coming into being all over the globe are organizing themselves as nation-states, complete with all the trappings of sovereignty and constitution, supreme court, central bank and propaganda ministry. In the modern totalitarianism, the nation-state seems to have become all-powerful. And—perhaps the most striking fact—the countries of Western Europe all restored and rebuilt traditional nation-states after the cataclysm of the Second World War.

But this triumph of modern government is more apparent than real. At the very time at which its dominion is becoming universal, the concepts and assumptions on which the institution rests are collapsing, and with them the ability of modern government to govern.

195

*The Definition of Modern Government*

Fundamentally four major concepts characterized the insti-
tion of modern government. Together they defined it.

First is the tenet that *government has an exclusive monopoly
on organized power in society,* that it is the only power center
of modern society. This is the meaning of the term "sovereignty" which, around the sixteenth century, appeared as
the new key to the old problem of government. This is also
the meaning of the legal theory of "positive law" which re-
fuses to accept any social power or legal sanction unless it
derive by delegation (express or imputed) from the sovereign
government—a theory which still dominates the legal and
political thought of Europe.

Not since the days of the Greek polis had any government aimed at such monopolistic concentration of power as
did modern government right from its first appearance in
the France of Louis XIV and the parliamentary oligarchy
of Whig supremacy in England. Modern government swept
into its own hand exclusive control of all the levers of community organization and action: foreign affairs and armed
forces; coining money, levying taxes and duties; communications such as the postal system, the roads and later the railroads; legislative and judiciary power. Except in England,
it took full control of education. It even reached for—and
in large measure attained—control over religious life, over
the creed of the country and its inhabitants, and largely over
the personnel and organization of the official state religion
and of its rites of worship.

The second tenet of modern government held that it was *by
nature and definition self-limiting in its scope.*

The government of the nation-state was the central and supreme government. But everywhere it tried to limit its sphere of action to the "national" tasks. Everywhere it tried to set up dependent but functioning local governments for local tasks. These differed greatly in their composition and powers. Some, like those of nineteenth-century France, were mere agents of the national government; others, like those of England, were local self-governments supervised and limited, but not controlled by the national government. But every national government, while legally omnipotent, delegated local operating responsibilities to local governments. Even the Soviet Union today is, legally, a federation of autonomous republics; and within those republics districts and municipalities are supposed to be self-governing local governments.

*At the same time (the third basic concept) modern government was, by definition, limited in its power.* (3)

It was "government under the law"—and even the Soviet Union today holds officially that the law is supreme and that government is limited by it.

The sovereign government of the nation-state, being a power monopoly, represented a greater concentration of social power in a single institution than the West had seen in fifteen hundred years or more. Yet it also represented up to recent days a smaller aggregate of power than the system it replaced. It left a much larger sphere of the individual's existence in society outside and beyond organized and institutionalized power.

Modern government established itself by destroying, subordinating or neutralizing a host of local power centers: feudal manors and petty princes; bishops, abbots, cathedral chapters and religious orders; chartered "free cities," merchant and craft guilds; private armies, the independent universities, hereditary judiciaries responsible to no one, and a myriad others.

Individually, none of these institutions had much power; indeed, power was so fragmented that organized community action had become impossible, even in the face of so great and imminent a danger as the Turkish imperialist drive into the heart of Europe in the sixteenth century. But taken together these institutions presented an aggregate of power and domination that all but snuffed out the sphere of the individual. There was little or nothing he could do—whether in his political, in his social or in his economic life—that he did not have to do in or through one of these organized institutions, and subject to their control, supervision and veto. Yet none of these institutions was ever strong enough to see beyond its own shortsighted and parochial self-interest, let alone strong enough to allow the individual more than the most limited freedom of action. Even in the most ruthlessly totalitarian state today, the individual may not be as completely "socialized" or "institutionalized" as he was in the system of fragmented but ubiquitous power centers which modern government destroyed and to which it succeeded.

From the point of view of society as a whole, the government of the modern West represented a tremendous monopoly concentration of power. But from the point of view of the individual, it represented a tremendous decrease in domination by organized, institutional power. Precisely because it held a monopoly on power which it guarded jealously and vigilantly, modern government was able to limit its own power to the minimum needed for effective control. The very concentration it represented thus resulted in a sharp decrease of the total power charge of society. This explains why the new modern government, even at its

most capricious and despotic, was so enthusiastically sup-
ported everywhere by the rising middle classes, to whom it
was the Great Emancipator.

The greatest innovation of modern government was its
fourth tenet: *that the government of the nation-state was the
unit of an international community.* This made possible something new: a rational concept of international affairs.

Not one of the great political philosophers of earlier times
—from Plato to Dante—had included foreign policy and
international relations within the scope of his theories of
government and politics. Every one of these men was fully
aware that foreign politics are crucial; many of the great
political thinkers had been personally and deeply immersed
in foreign policy. But there was nothing one could say, there
were no concepts, no theories, no purposes, no sense—there
was no polity outside the scope of domestic government. One
simply had no choice but to ignore foreign affairs in discussing the purpose and function of government and the nature
of politics. Even Machiavelli (perhaps the most accomplished
professional diplomatist of Western history) concluded, after
devoting the best part of his great book on *The Prince* to
foreign affairs, that to make government possible, foreign
affairs would have to be eliminated by what we today would
call a "world government."

The theory and practice of modern government, however,
assumed an international community of sovereign and equal
nations. In that community only governments would be acting; but it also assumed—a very bold assumption—that only
governments would be acted upon. Nobody else—whether
individual or group—would have any standing in international
affairs. But nobody else—whether individual or group—would
be exposed to international affairs and be affected by them.

This idea—breathtaking when it appeared—made possible a theory and practice of foreign relations. It made possible international law and international order. It made it possible —for the first time in man's long history, and maybe for the last time also—to organize war as an instrument of government and policy, and to subordinaate organization for war to the ends and the organs of civilian peacetime government.

We are only too conscious today of the failures and shortcomings of this concept. Every student of international law knows that it abounds in contradictions and inconsistencies. The "international order" never worked. But this affects neither the novelty of the attempt nor the magnitude of the achievement. Even at its most successful the concept fell far short of realization. But it established a frame of general theory and habits of general practice that made it possible to organize international relations, to integrate warfare into government without subordinating government to incessant war, and to establish rules of law which set the norm of conduct even when being violated.

### The Rise of the Liberal State

For two hundred years—from the mid-seventeenth to the mid-nineteenth century—modern government developed steadily along its original lines, becoming both increasingly the exclusive power center of its society and increasingly self-limited.

The power monopoly of modern government rested on military technology and a money economy. Their juxtaposition, for two hundred years, made possible the self-limitation of modern government as well as the modern concept of international relations. But the very trends that permitted the emergence of the institution ultimately destroyed its foundations.

With the introduction of gunpowder into military technology around 1450, offense had gained decided advantage over defense. Until then a petty knight in his hilltop castle could sit out most attacks. As long as his supply of food and water held out, his position was impregnable. It is no accident that so many of the defeats of medieval and Renaissance warfare were inflicted by the traitor within the gates rather than by trial of arms. But against siege guns, even the fortified castle and city were virtually defenseless. At the same time the new military technology was much too expensive for anybody except a national government. It required arms that had to be paid for and cared for, and men trained for long years in their use. It required a standing army.

The monetization of the economy—brought about above all by the vast imports of silver from the new Spanish Empire in America—enabled government to levy taxes in money and thus to pay both its soldiers and the new professional administrators of modern government. Since Europe itself produces practically no gold and very little silver, the fall of the Roman Empire, which cut off the West from the Oriental supply of monetary metals, would by itself have forced Europe into the fragmentation of power institutions that characterized the twelve hundred years between Diocletian and Richelieu. If administrators can only be paid in kind, and if soldiers have to be armed locally and have to live off the land, power can only be petty and fragmented. In 1500, at least three quarters of Europe's population still lived essentially in a nonmoney economy. A century and a half later, all but the most isolated and backward of Europe's people —such as the Scottish Highlanders—lived in a society that was, to all intents and purposes, fully monetized. Without the money revolution, modern government would not have been possible.

These two together—military technology and the development of a modern economy—gave to the modern state the means to make good its claim to a monopoly on organized power.

For two hundred years the economy grew so much more rapidly than the demands of military technology that government, while growing absolutely in its needs and demands, appeared to shrink in relation to the total of economy and society. That meant also that the concept of foreign affairs as a sphere affecting only governments could be maintained for two hundred years.

Military technology did, of course, advance rapidly. Armies not only became much better equipped; they also became much larger. There is no comparison between the armies of the Thirty Years' War that ended in 1648 and the armies of Napoleon a century and a half later—whether in size, in fire power, in the length of their campaigns, or in the distances over which they could move and could be supplied. Navies— first organized by the Dutch around 1600 and becoming general by 1690—were an even greater burden: in the capital equipment they required; in the scarce materials they consumed both afloat and ashore; in the technological skills needed to build and to maintain them; and in the permanent trained establishment needed to man them.

But the economy, and with it the population of Europe, grew even faster—perhaps the single most important reason for the emergence of the liberal state of nineteenth-century theory and practice. Despite the rapid increase in its scale and complexity, warfare required a steadily decreasing proportion of a steadily increasing national income. We have no figures—national income statistics are an invention of the twentieth century. But Napoleon's monstrous armies, engaged in incessant warfare, ate up a very much smaller share of the income than those of the Thirty Years' War. Even of the national income of France—the country that bore the brunt—Napoleon's wars certainly took less than the armies of Louis XIV had consumed a century earlier. Yet Napoleon ranged from Egypt to Denmark and from Spain to Moscow, whereas Louis XIV's armies rarely ventured more than a hundred miles beyond the borders of France.

A more graphic way of saying the same thing might be that during the wars of the seventeenth century there were probably few skilled metalworkers in the entire European Continent who were not working full time on the production and repair of arms such as muskets, guns, body armor, lances or stirrups. During the Napoleonic wars we hear again and again of serious unemployment in the metalworking crafts and industries. While Great Britain was engaged, isolated and alone, in her desperate struggle against Napoleon, in the course of which she built and maintaned both the largest army and the largest navy she had ever mustered, none of Jane Austen's heroines was forced to go without any trinket she had the money for; none of her country gentlemen complained about the lack of able-bodied men for hire, or of coaches, horses or building materials.

Small wonder, then, that the same power monopoly of the modern state and its government that had appeared as the Leviathan to the men of 1660 could appear to the early nineteenth century as a domesticated pet. The only function which the government really discharged in the eyes of that generation was that of "traffic cop"* who makes sure that all cars stay on their side of the road, do not exceed the speed limit and stop at red lights, but who has no concern with where they go, why they are on the road, or what the passen-

---

* The famous "Nachtwaechter" (nightwatchman) state of German liberal theory.

gers will do when they get to their destination. Even this role seemed to be self-liquidating; at least the historical trend seemed to go toward making the power of government always smaller relative to the increasing sphere of individual action, which was not subject to any organized or institutional power.

The best illustration of this unique combination of exclusive power monopoly and relative insignificance of modern government in the nineteenth century world is the European government of a non-European country—British India. The British government in India was absolute; while it was carefully scrutinized by Parliament in London, there was no one in India to whom it was in any way accountable. It had a monopoly on power which went far beyond anything seen in the West itself; a word from the Viceroy and the most imposing native prince, supposedly the hereditary, absolute and sovereign ruler over twenty or thirty million people, was quietly deposed or exiled to a remote island.

It was also the most active government with the widest scope of control. It organized and operated, except for religious worship, whatever community activities there were throughout the entire subcontinent: police, justice and education; all means of transportation and communication; irrigation, flood control, forestry, agricultural improvements, surveying, disease control and hospitals. It dug wells, built cities, determined land boundaries and arbitrated between religious denominations. It collected and published the ancient literature of the country, both Hindu and Moslem; and it restored and protected her ancient monuments.

That the peasant addressed the District Officer—often a mere lad in his twenties—as "my Father and my Mother" was, of course, nothing but ancient and meaningless rhetoric. But there was substance to the joke of the juniors in the British service that they were expected by the government of India to be not only father and mother but also midwife and wet nurse to the Indian village. For British India was, a century before the term was coined, the first Welfare State.

The prevailing comment on the Indian government during the

nineteenth century, especially from the Liberals in England, was how monstrously swollen a bureaucracy the Indian Civil Service was. And yet this all-powerful, all-embracing, absolute government, administering an entire subcontinent, never employed more than a thousand Europeans for all its functions and in all the branches of the Indian Civil Service (even though, until fairly recently, Indians themselves were not admitted into the professional ranks of the Service).

It should not surprise us, therefore, that Karl Marx, writing in the 1860's, confidently predicted the "withering away of the state." Nor was there anything in this prediction to startle his generation; he only expressed in his own rhetoric what was already commonplace.

## The Decline of the Liberal State

Yet at the very moment at which Marx wrote, the tide was already running heavily in the other direction.

There was one more old-fashioned war: The Franco-Prussian War of 1870, like its predecessors for two hundred years, took a smaller share of the national income and drained off a smaller share of the national manpower than had the previous major war. Yet by then the first of the new total wars had already been fought, the first war that absorbed the entire economic capacity of a nation and forced it to mobilize its entire able-bodied population either for military service or for war production. The Confederacy fought the American Civil War as a total war. Our historians, dazzled either by the dominant figure of Lincoln or by the gallantry of Confederate generals, have done but scant justice to the psychological, economic and administrative efforts of the Confederacy which made possible five years of such unprecedented exertion. Nor have they always understood that it was this exertion—rather than the abolition of slavery or the (by present-day standards, almost negligible) physical destruction —which brought Southern society down in ruins, destroyed its political tradition and drained its vigor.

The decline of the foundations of modern government actually began with an even earlier American event: the American Revolution and its two political innovations, paper currency and the people's army.

There had been paper monies before—all the way back to the paper money of the Mongol Khans in the days of Marco Polo. All these had, however, been simply receipts for deposits of specie, that is not money issued against the credit of a government or of anybody else, but limited to the amount of specie actually on deposit. The Continental dollar did not even pretend to have any backing, but was simply paper issued against the credit of a nonexisting government.

Paper money enables government to expropriate the citizen legally by inflation or repudiation. It thereby gives to government the means for complete economic mobilization, that is for unlimited government control of the citizen in the economy. Paper money was one of the greatest of political inventions; it was also the fastest-spreading one, having been adopted within twenty years in France and within another twenty years by every other major European country. But it is doubtful that it was a constructive invention.* Its permanent effect was the abolition of the traditional obstacles to unlimited government control. Though paper money does not make unlimited government inevitable, it definitely makes it possible.

The second major innovation of the American Revolution

---

* The old Goethe, in the early years of the nineteenth century, had no doubts. In the second part of *Faust*, the work of his old age, he has the Devil invent paper money to destroy government, community and individual decency.

was the "people's army"—maybe the "people's war" might
be a better term.

Modern government, as it emerged in the mid-seventeenth
century, assumed a professional standing army as a matter of
course. But the American Revolution was fought—and won
—by amateurs, by the "embattled farmers" with their own
arms, their own tactics and their elected junior officers.
Though the idea of the "armed citizenry" was ancient, its
revival was revolutionary. It was the beginning of the end of
the concept of "war as an instrument of policy," and therefore controllable and capable of being subordinated to
civilian government. It meant the beginning of the end of the
concept of the international community as one of governments rather than of individuals, and of international events
as not affecting the individual citizen in his private capacity.
And since a people's war is possible only as a popular war, it
meant the end of wars of limited objective; henceforth wars
had to be fought for causes rather than for objectives—and
only a scoundrel compromises on a cause.

It is no longer original to observe that the United States
is simultaneously truly conservative and truly radical. But it is
rarely realized that this has been true from the beginning.
Politically the American Revolution was truly conservative—
in the best sense of the word. It was also the occasion at which
America gave birth to economic and social forces of revolutionary radicalism and of world-wide impact.

George Washington, most civilized of soldiers and most
moderate of rebels, would be horrified at our reality of total
war, totalitarian government and garrison state. Yet the innovations of 1776—paper money and armed citizenry—produced ninety years later, in the war fought for the preservation
of Washington's Union, the first total war, the first total
inflation, and the first total defeat and unconditional sur-

render. With Appomatox the crisis of modern government was on.

For two hundred years, from the mid-seventeenth to the mid-nineteenth century, the demands of warfare on the economic capacity of a Western country decreased steadily. Government could discharge its first obligation—the defense of the country—and yet steadily increase the sphere of non-government, the sphere of individual freedom and liberties. Modern government could also increasingly control the military, asserting the principle of its subordination to civilian authority. And war could increasingly be conceived as "the continuation of policy by other means"—Clausewitz' famous definition, written appropriately enough in the first decades of the nineteenth century with their tremendous economic expansion of Europe.

But for the last hundred years the tide has moved swiftly the other way—and the tidal wave is engulfing us now. The Korean War of 1950-51, which President Truman could call a "police action," imposed strains on the American economy almost as total as those of the all-out mobilization in World War I only a generation earlier.

The qualitative change in the demands of warfare on society has been even greater than the quantitative one. Particularly important has been the shift in the sinews of war from weapons requiring primarily ordinary peacetime products, made in ordinary peacetime facilities, to weapons requiring primarily special-purpose products that can be made only in special-purpose facilities which are of no use except for the production of military equipment and material.

The early nineteenth-century army was still literally able to "live off the land" for well over 90 per cent of its needs. Wellington's army fought in the Spanish Peninsula for five years, from 1808 to 1813. All the special-purpose equipment it required was guns and—the only big item—a siege train. The rest was procured locally even though Spain even then was an "underdeveloped" country.

The only "preparedness" necessary in the Napoleonic age was trained manpower. After the defeat of Jena in 1806 Prussia was disarmed and had all her armaments industry destroyed. The French Army in the country actually supervised the destruction. Yet seven years later, Prussia could put a large and effective fighting force in the field within three months, simply because, by a ruse, she had managed to keep up the training of reservists—and very skimpy training it was by our standards.

Whatever special wartime products were needed, were usually both easy to produce and durable. Right through the nineteenth century, cavalry was the most highly specialized and most highly trained branch of any land army. It was almost exclusively manned by long-serving regulars who were heavily armed compared to the infantry soldier. Yet the cavalry soldier of 1850 or so required only three pieces of special-purpose equipment: a horse, a saber and a pistol. It was standard practice to consider the working life of the horse to be about the same as the enlistment period of the individual regular—that is, ten to fifteen years—and to figure on both saber and pistol outliving the individual trooper, if indeed not three or four troopers.

In their early stages, the World War I armies were still largely of this kind, though by 1914 equipment suitable only for warfare constituted about one fifth of the total material equipment of what was then considered the modern army. By the end of World War I the situation had changed radically. As much as 40 per cent or so of the equipment needed to put an army in the field, and keep it there, was special-purpose; and to a large extent this equipment had to be produced in special facilities. But the bulk of it could still be produced in peacetime facilities after a brief period of conversion. Hence the problem of preparedness up till World War II was the problem of maintaining a small special-purpose stock, adequate to equip the army for a period of conversion, after which ordinary productive capacity would do the job.

Today, at least three quarters—in the Air Force considerably more—of the equipment needed for a fighting force is unusable for anything else. Most of it can only be produced in special facilities that are not capable of producing anything else. Conversion is no longer possible. To be capable of defense, a country has today to build a productive machinery which is exclusively, or at least heavily, designed for warmaking alone. Defense requires not only an increasingly larger share of the total national income; it also requires a permanent diversion of a larger and larger share of national productivity to strictly war purposes. And to survive in the event of a conflict requires that these special-purpose industries be built during peacetime rather than after the outbreak of hostilities.

Hence military technology has exploded the concept of war and society on which modern government based itself.

※ ※ ※

## 2 · The New Pluralism

The exclusive monoply of government on organized institutional power in society has been so seriously undermined as to be in a state of near-collapse. The agent of this collapse is our new power to organize. It is rapidly creating new autonomous power centers within the body politic.

In an industrial economy the individual is, by and large, productive only insofar as he has access to an organized institution of production and distribution, the enterprise. By himself, the individual in an industrial system can work, but he cannot produce. Only the institutional system organized for performance and survival beyond the lifetime, and independent of, any one individual is capable of production.

This is not the result of a sinister plot. Nor is there any alternative if we want industrial production and its fruits. What has caused this development is precisely the factor that is responsible for our industrial advance: the modern ability to organize men of high skill, knowledge and judgment for joint work and performance. This both makes possible and requires a scale of operation beyond the ability of any single man to direct, let alone to do. It requires such a variety of skills, knowledges and temperaments as can be supplied only by a large group of different people in organized, permanent effort. It requires the commitment of present resources to a futurity of such length as to be beyond the working life of any individual. It requires capital far beyond the means of any man, were he even a modern Croesus. Above all, it requires managing, that is systematic planning, organizing, integrating and measuring of the efforts and work of highly skilled and highly educated people which can be done only by an organized and disciplined body of men.

It requires a power center, partial in its purposes, to be sure, but largely autonomous.

As a result, new institutional power centers have shot up like Topsy. To take our own country as an example: Fifty years ago the federal government was a shadow of its present self. It spent less in a year than it now spends in a day. All its civilian employees could have been housed comfortably in one of the Washington buildings now occupied—and overcrowded—by one of the smaller agencies. The state governments were, as a rule, one-man shows. And the job of being state governor, while honorific, was so little burdensome that in some of the sparsely settled states the incumbent could still keep in touch with his private law practice.

But—and it is a big "but"—there was no other institutional organization of social or economic power. There were a few very rich men, a Morgan or a Rockefeller, who had great personal power and influence. There were a few "trusts"; but even though they so badly frightened our grandfathers, the largest of them were so small, whether in assets, in sales or in number of employees, that they would go unmentioned in any list of "five hundred largest corporations" today. Only a few railroads and telegraph companies were then so large that we would today consider them "big business"; and they were already being brought under effective governmental regulation. Otherwise, there was nothing. Big business, the labor unions, national farmers' organizations, the National Association of Manufacturers, the American Medical Association, the National Education Association, all these were still to come.

The world of the American citizen in those days looked very much like the Kansas prairie. Except for one hill, the individual citizen was the tallest thing as far as the eye could see. And even this hill, the federal government, while it looked imposing, was only a few hundred feet high.

Today the power charge of our society has been built up as it has never been before. Instead of the Kansas prairie, the citizen has the Himalayas around him. Here are the towering institutional peaks of big business, there the rugged and almost sheer cliffs of organized labor closing off access to trades, crafts and jobs to all but the dues-paying members. The farmers are dominated by national farm organizations, medicine by the American Medical Association, and so on. Even religious life, almost without power charge in the America of fifty years ago, is today increasingly organized in strong national institutions which speak for the individual denominations, lobby before Congress and conduct their own campaigns.

Within the government itself the administrative bureaucracy and the armed forces have largely become organized—though not yet autonomous—institutional power centers.

Of course, the federal government too has grown and expanded in size as well as power. It is clearly the Everest amongst the Himalayan peaks. But in relation to the total power charge of society as expressed by the other new institutions, the federal government may well have become less, rather than more, powerful. Certainly its power monopoly has been broken.

The development of the new power centers within society may have gone furthest and fastest in this country. But the growth itself is not specifically American; it is the result of the emergence of modern industry. Even in Soviet Russia, Stalin, while absolute despot, could only maintain his personal power by playing against each other the major power centers of Communist party bureaucracy, Army, Secret Police and industrial management. Since his death there has been an increasing power play between them, making and breaking governments. Even behind the façade of "monolithic" Communism, the new institutional powers have therefore become the actual political reality. Even there, the exclusive monopoly of organized institutional power, which had been one of the foundations of modern government, has been undermined.

### The New Metropolis

The emergent industrial society has had another major impact on the foundations of government: It erodes local government. It creates a new social community: the metropolis. And we do not know how to govern it.

Local affairs must be handled locally. Otherwise, they will not get done. If they do not get done locally they drift "upstairs" to central government. This may be called the "law of political gravity"—and it is as inevitable as the physical law of gravity. But local matters cannot be disposed of centrally, or they clog the wheels of central government to the point where they cannot turn at all, and where the major tasks of government—the formulation of national policy, national welfare, justice, defense or international policy—go by the board. Centralized planning, as we have seen, soon degenerates into no plan at all.

One reason why local affairs must be done locally is their mass of detail, of paper work, of regulations, of bureaucracy—especially as the burden of these things seems to increase with the square of the distance from the local scene where the need exists and where the action eventually has to be taken. Another, more insidious reason is that any issue, if removed "upstairs," acquires political connotations which might be quite lacking at the local scene. The simplest technical matter, if referred to the top level, turns into a major philosophical issue and threatens thereby to become insoluble.

We have known all this since the earliest days of organized government. During the last twenty-five years, we have learned the lesson all over again, in the organization of the big business enterprise. What we today call "decentralization" in business is nothing but the creation of local government within the business enterprise, so as to have the proper organ to handle and to decide operational problems at the scene of action. The major purpose of decentralization is not to make local, operating management stronger—though that too is necessary. It is to make possible effective top management. Without decentralization top management simply cannot do its own job, but gets mired in a mass of details and torn to pieces in a welter of emotional and personal squabbles.

In preindustrial society, local government tasks are few and simple, and their performance tends to be governed by well-established custom. In an industrial society, however, local government tasks rapidly multiply. They become highly complex, requiring technical knowledge and professional competence in their planning and execution. They also have greater impact; industrial society falls to pieces without a transportation system, without adequate sewage or power, let alone without a functioning school system.

Industrial society, therefore, more than any other society, needs strong and functioning institutions of local government. Yet in every society that has undergone the process of industrialization, local government has fallen to pieces; and inevitably the tasks that local government defaulted on fell into the lap of central government.

This often looked as if it were a deliberate reach for new powers on the part of central government. This illusion has been strengthened by the traditional Leftist (or rather, French Revolution) distrust of local government and preference for central government, as the more uniform, more elegant and more "rational." Of all the many follies of the Leftist tradition, none is greater than this preference for centralization. Of all its many illusions, none has been blinder than the belief that the extension of central control over local affairs represents the success of a deliberate policy, rather than unintended failure, if not bankruptcy, of government altogether.

To be sure, the central government in an industrial society has to be strong. It has to do a great many things which earlier governments never dreamed of, or perhaps never heard of. But precisely because it has to be strong, central government in an industrial society has to free itself from the jobs that require local knowledge, local decisions and local action—for the same reason that the top management of a big business, in order to be strong, frees itself from operating decisions through decentralization to local managers in charge of operating units. No central government today has assumed more of the local government functions than that of France; indeed, local government in France hardly exists any more. Yet no central government has been more obviously paralyzed, more impotent, than that of France. To a large extent this results from the domination which local concerns, issues and prejudices exercise on all levels of the national government, and from the political and emotional heat which they generate.

One major reason for the crisis of local government in an industrial society is that the unit of settlement in an industrial society is not the village or even the city, but the metropolis. The metropolis is not just a very large city. It is quite different from the city.

The metropolis cannot be confined within pre-established political or administrative boundaries. It rapidly cuts across all such lines, whether those of city, county, province, state or even nation. Its boundaries are not fixed but changing; above all they are different for different tasks—for schools or for water supply, for transportation, for sewage disposal or for power supply.

Every industrial city has become such a metropolis, ever since the mushroom growth of the industrial cities in the English Midlands produced the first crisis of local government a century or more ago. Whether it is metropolitan New York, San Francisco, London, Moscow, Tokyo or Johannesburg, it outgrows whatever boundaries exist; and so do all the smaller metropolitan cities in any industrial society.

Economic and social life in the industrial metropolis also has a degree of interdependence unknown in earlier, preindustrial times. Of course, to provide common services—common defense, common law and justice, a common market, common coinage, common weights and measures, common churches or even a common god—has always been the rationale of the city. But in his basic economic activities the stone mason of ancient Athens or eighteenth-century London was quite independent of the tanner or the weaver. Today, however, all are dependent to an unheard-of degree both upon common services and facilities and upon each other.

The metropolis must, therefore, organize activities and services across and beyond any traditional boundary line. Even a "sovereign" state of the American Union may have ceased to be an effective unit for something so essentially local as highways.

That the State of New Jersey is building an efficient system of superhighways only means that the traffic problems of the neighboring states, New York, Pennsylvania, Maryland and Delaware, are becoming that much worse; New Jersey's new roads, with their superior traffic capacity, disgorge motorists and trucks into the already overloaded and inadequate road facilities of these states. Engineers today talk of the "Eastern Sea Board Megapolis" stretching from Portland, Maine, to Norfolk, Virginia, and embracing fifty million people, as the "minimum" unit for highway and power supply planning. But power supply must also take into account such strictly local matters as the effect of smoke from the powerhouses on public health, air traffic, or even on the market gardens which feed the inhabitants of the metropolitan area.

There is today increasing concern with the social and cultural problems of metropolitan living. We are conscious of the destruction of the countryside wrought by metropolitan expansion, and of the decay of the center of the old city as the metropolis pushes out its suburbs. We are concerned with the sterility of life in the dead uniformity of ranch-style houses within easy commuting distance. We wonder whether the increases in cancer, heart disease and mental illness reflect the tensions of metropolitan living. We complain about the traffic problem, about inadequate community services, about high local taxes.

The metropolis does indeed present basic problems of civilization. It may well have all the traditional problems of the city and none of its advantages. But the central problem is its government. It can solve none of its problems, cannot even tackle them, unless it has effective political organs for community decision and action. It is fashionable among social scientists today to play down the importance of government and to stress rather the role of society, habits, culture. But all these are inert, chaotic and impotent without the formal and organized structure of government.

The metropolis today has no government. The traditional organs of local government are not adequate to the new tasks. This is at the bottom of the problem of metropolitan civilization and culture. But it is also a major factor in the crisis of national government. Because there is no effective local government in the metropolis, local problems inevitably become central government concerns, which paralyze central government.

## The Crisis of Government

The modern government of the nation-state finds itself increasingly unable to function as a result of the explosion in military technology, abetted by the complete monetization of the economy and by the "people's war"; the rise of new autonomous power centers within national society; and the collapse of local government.

Government everywhere has become a swollen monstrosity —yet increasingly incapable of making or executing policy. There are probably few cases of such extreme malfunction as that of the Social Security system of Chile where administrative costs eat up fifty cents of every dollar paid in—with the rest destroyed almost immediately by inflation. But the disease is universal. At best the central government can mediate between power groups; at best it can be honestly bureaucratic and administratively efficient. Policy and its execution become increasingly difficult.

Everywhere we see power move into the hands of administrative agencies—regulating and controlling transportation, power, housing and so on—all essentially local matters. But administrative agencies are by nature uncontrollable. They must decide individual cases rather than dispense general, impersonal law. They can neither confine themselves to general policy nor adjudicate disputes; they create or destroy individual property, privileges and profits. At their most scrupulous they are agencies of endless delay and red tape. At their most efficient they go by individual "pull" or influence, or become corrupt. They are a necessity in industrial society with its organized power centers and pressure groups and its metropolitan communities. But they are a cancer in the political system, and a denial of the basic concepts of government by laws and of government in the interest of the whole.

Everywhere the individual is becoming the captive, if not the slave, of the garrison state. To be prepared for defense, government today claims the right to embrace and to control all efforts of the citizens, and to commandeer their resources, skills, property and persons—practically without limitation. To be prepared for defense, government today irrevocably controls a very large part of the total national income—taxing away for armaments in peacetime many times more than any government has ever taxed away for all purposes, warlike or peaceful. It takes an increasing share of the citizen's productive adult life for military training. It demands that scientific inquiry and progress largely be subordinated to the needs of bigger and

better warfare. Above all, it claims—perhaps it must claim—
the power of veto on all activities, pursuits and discussions of
the citizen that, in the government's opinion, "endanger the
national security."

An attempt in the United States to forbid publication of a
government document in peacetime on grounds of national
security would have been laughed out of court less than twenty
years ago. Today we only question how to prevent abuse of
this power. Education has in most Western countries been
state-controlled for centuries. But it would have been inconceivable a generation ago for government to tell a university
that this or that man could not be hired for any kind of research work on grounds of national security. Today all we are
concerned with in a free society is to make sure that this veto
power only be applied to research that is really of military
significance, and that any man so attacked obtain a fair, impartial and judicial hearing. All we seem to be concerned with,
in other words, are the proper procedures for the exercise of
the new veto. The principle itself, despite its momentous
implications, we have conceded.

By so doing we have abandoned one of the foundations of
modern government: that it be strictly limited even though
the only institution of organized power; that indeed it encompass in its scope of organized institutional power only the
smaller part of the individual's life and sphere of action. The
less government can actually accomplish, the more it claims
today.

The worst breakdown has occurred in the international
sphere—the very sphere where modern government made its
greatest and most original contribution.

As a result of the explosion of military technology war has
gone completely out of political control. It is no longer possible to subordinate war to the demands of policy. On the

contrary policy has everywhere to be subordinated to the demands of modern warfare, has to be focused increasingly upon the military needs of survival.

At the same time war has ceased to have any rational meaning for society and individual alike. It no longer can make its one and only contribution: to bring about a decision in international affairs. No country can risk total war; no country can hope to survive such war even if it wins it. Hence no country can use total war as an instrument of policy—perhaps no longer even as an instrument of international blackmail. International affairs have again become irrational, beyond and outside any theory or practice of government. They have become an unpredictable gamble, a series of improvisations. At the same time they have become total in their impact upon nation and individual. In the name of foreign affairs, government today must demand a control over the citizen which denies the self-limitation of power on which modern government in its theory and practice was founded. Yet government today cannot give the citizen the protection in international affairs which has always been among its first duties, and which is a major justification and purpose of organized government.

A subtler, but perhaps more insidious, poison is the militarization of thinking, of public opinion and of policy. John Foster Dulles, President Eisenhower's Secretary of State, hated war as deeply as any man in the world today. But he was not able to develop a foreign policy other than military alliances. During the same period Senator McCarthy rode high until he attacked the Army. In the American tradition the military has always been the safest target of political attack; but even though the Army cringed before McCarthy he was finished three months after he first tackled it. That American education is in serious trouble had been known for a decade. But general concern with it only began when Sputnik showed our educational weaknesses to be a danger to military security. President Eisenhower, though himself a military man, was so impressed by these trends that he solemnly warned against them in his Farewell Address. But there has been little change since.

Unlike similar militarization in the past, this is not the result of military arrogance. On the contrary our military men, at least in this country, are appalled by it, and are indeed more "civilian-minded" than the civilian public. It is not the result of undue admiration of the military man; while not as bitter as after World War I, the reaction against the "brass" is as pronounced today as it was in the twenties. Yet we are all forced to become militarists; military technology threatens to swallow up civil society.

The crisis of modern government is not a matter of republic versus monarchy, of separation of powers versus paramount power, of written versus unwritten constitution, or of this or that system of elections. It is even less a matter of socialism versus capitalism, nor of democracy versus despotism. No matter how organized, no government functions adequately today.

This is clearly true of totalitarian dictatorships—the one major response to the collapse of modern government. Indeed totalitarian dictatorship, of all forms of government we know, is the least capable of satisfying society's need for effective government.

It cannot overcome the internal disintegration. We have learned by now enough of what went on behind Nazism's façade of emotional uniformity to know how thinly it covered a reality of extreme incompetence, deadly power struggle between autonomous power centers, and permanent crisis. The same is true of the Communist variety as events in Russia and in the Soviet satellites since Stalin's death have made abundantly clear.

At the same time totalitarianism cannot restore rationality and control to international life. All it can do is to make a virtue of chaos, make delusion a habit, crisis a necessity, lying the principle of right conduct, and paranoia a synonym for achievement.

Above all totalitarianism cannot solve the first problem of functioning government: It cannot provide for an orderly succession.

This has been, through the ages, the basic problem of all forms of government. From the succession by combat among the tribal braves to constitutional government, orderly succession has been the dominant concern. And rightly so. Before a government can be "good government," it must be able to function. This it can do only if succession is orderly, to the point of being automatic, and if it immediately establishes a government capable of governing.

So far, the American Constitution has provided one of the few effective solutions of the succession problem. Yet it is far from perfect. It establishes automatic succession of a legitimate head of the government with full control and in full possession of his faculties. But it does this only by building in the expedient of the Vice President: a "stand-by" and a mere cipher as long as the President lives, occupying the most frustrating political position human ingenuity could devise, condemned to burying his ambitions if an honest man, and condemned to praying for a dead man's shoes if an ambitious one. And, as we were sharply reminded during the Eisenhower years, we have not solved the problem of partial disability and diminished vigor in a President.

But few attempts to solve the succession problem have been quite so inadequate and futile as the trial by conspiracy to which any totalitarian society entrusts itself. This is not just the experience of our times; the totalitarian method of selecting successive heads of government has been attempted so often and has failed so regularly in history as to leave little room for doubt about the inevitable outcome.

Much more promising than totalitarianism is the other alternative to modern government which we can dimly see: political pluralism, which is government by countervailing powers under the rule of law. This is of course the original concept of the United States which never fully accepted the concepts of modern government and nation-state, just as it never accepted the Cartesian world-view of the modern west. Though greatly weakened by constant drift to a national concept, pluralism is still the governing theory of American political life; it is the governing reality of American social, economic, cultural and religious life.

## Pluralism and the Common Interest

The most successful creation of American pluralism is the American political party. It may also be of major importance for the future.

Only a few years ago it was fashionable to decry the American political party as an unprincipled anachronism. When Harold Laski, the late ideologist of the British Left, attacked it violently in the postwar years, he was only repeating what had been said for at least a hundred years by foreign observers as well as by American political scientists. Being nonideological, so the argument ran, the American political party stood for nothing. It had no ideals, no program, no convictions, no principles. All it did was organize "interest"—sectional or social—for the conquest of power.

Today we realize that it is its nonideological character that makes the American party an agent of national unity. Whenever one of our parties forgets this, as the Republicans did when they nominated Barry Goldwater in 1964, it invites—and deserves—disaster. The national convention every four years, we now understand, does an essential job behind its façade of pageantry and bombastic nonsense: It establishes a national coalition bridging across the cleavages. More important, perhaps, we are beginning to realize that the ideological party is the unprincipled anachronism. Willing to subordinate national welfare to doctrinaire righteousness, it increasingly becomes incapable of providing a government. In the free countries the major parties are either changing into nonideological coalitions like the Christian Democrats in continental Europe or the Conservatives in Great Britain; or, like the parties in France or the Socialist parties everywhere, they are becoming prisoners of the past and effective only in opposition. A free society requires parties. And effective government requires that there be an organized alternative government. With ideological parties moribund, only the nonideological party of pluralism can still discharge the job.

Altogether it is becoming clear that pluralism is the starting point for the new political theory and institutions we need. It still permits a sphere of individual freedom and choice—if only in the gaps between the giants of organized power. It, at least, accepts reality—political life today is pluralist everywhere. It has also given us so far the only effective—even though limited —and only new institution for the tasks of today's political life: the public corporation for specific metropolitan tasks. The London Passenger Transport Board, the Port of New York Authority, the Moscow Electric Power Board, the Ontario Hydro-Electric Commission, the Rheinisch-Westfaelische Electricity Works, the TVA, all are designed to serve the needs of the new metropolis. A little over a hundred years ago the Metropolitan Police of London (better known as Scotland

Yard) was founded as the first such body. Since then the public corporation has become everywhere the institution for technical tasks of the local but metropolitan community. The metropolitan public corporation is by no means perfect. It is local government without being local self-government; indeed it is all but beyond local control. But it is the best we have so far.

Major areas in international life, such as the rapid development of education in the poor countries and their rapid economic development, require autonomous and pluralist agencies of international policy and co-operation. The most effective international organ of recent years, the Marshall Plan, was such a pluralist institution.

Pluralism should again become a serious and important concept of political order—as, outside of this country, it has not been for three hundred years. But pluralism is not yet capable of supplying us with the new principles and institutions of political integration we so badly need. Whether it is at all applicable to the central issue—the collapse of international rationality—is highly dubious. American policy during the last decade has based itself on such pluralism—especially in the various regional alliances for collective security or economic development. No one will claim, I think, that its success has yet been so great as to prove the principle—nor, however, has it failed so completely as to disprove it.

More serious, there is still no cure for the old flaw of pluralism: the danger that the commonwealth will disappear under the conflict, selfishness, shortsightedness and sheer technical efficiency of pluralist institutions and partial power centers. No pluralist system has ever escaped this disease. In most pluralist systems it has been fatal.

That a policy in the general interest is bound—or at least is likely—to emerge from the attempt to balance and to compromise sectional and partial interests is old pluralist doctrine; highly developed in this country by Calhoun, it became all but the official philosophy of the bright young men of the New Deal. But can enough trust be put into this blithe promise that right vision will result from the canceling out of assorted short-sightedness, and that selfless action will emerge from the conflicts of selfishness?

Clearly this is a crucial question. Under today's conditions of industrial and international life, government's first job is to make the common interest prevail over partial interest and sectional power centers. Yet today's pluralist political reality, except in time of war, recognizes no overriding common interest.

The crisis of modern government is not the result of the incompetence of political leaders, or of their wickedness. It is not capable of resolution by better men, not even by great men; it is the essence of the crisis that it takes "supermen" in government to do even a poor job. Neither the American President nor the British Prime Minister can any longer do, even physically, all the jobs he is supposed to do. Yet he cannot delegate any of them; all are essential to the survival of the nation and the functioning of government. This is a crisis of basic concept; the very terms "sovereignty," "national state," "balance of power," "defense," "government by law," "parliamentary control," are rapidly losing meaning.

As such the crisis can be resolved only by new institutions embodying new political theory. But political theory today is sterile. The last great age of European political philosophy—the age of Hobbes, Locke and Harrington, of Bodin, Grotius and Montesquieu—is three hundred years in the past. Burke has now been dead over a century and a half. Even the brilliant but short outburst of creative political thinking in the United States—the *Federalist Papers*, John Adams, Jefferson, Marshall

—came to an end just over a century ago with Calhoun's theory of sectional pluralism.

Until recently there seemed to be no need for basic political thinking; the ascendancy of the modern government of the nation-state seemed to be so complete and so secure as to make redundant any concern with "the foundations of the common-wealth." Social theory, yes; economic theory, yes. But political theory could be taken for granted. In many universities polit-ical science is not even taught any more; instead we have com-parative government—which concentrates on the individual variations with which different countries play the same tune of modern government.

Now the time has come for another major Age of Political Philosophy, for creative, independent, fundamental thought, for new basic concepts and new institutions. It is a challenge first of all, perhaps, to the United States; for one major starting point must be pluralism which is a living tradition only in the United States. It is a task for statesmen; political thought has come from the men of large affairs rather than from the acad-emician. But it is also a task of the philosopher. And above all it is a task of the citizen.

We need a political theory that will give us effective, strong government, and substantial liberties and freedom of the citi-zen against government. We need new institutions of local government; and in a free society these have to be institutions of self-government. We need new institutions for the inter-national community. We have to accept the reality of the new power centers; but we have to make them subservient to the common good and to the freedom of the individual. We need pluralism; but it must be embedded in, and transcended by, objective, general law.

We have the beginnings in new political experiences. Most important of these, but also least understood, may well be the concepts of social order in the new organization. But the job itself still remains to be done. The crisis of modern government is not confined to this or that country—though it is the more acute the stronger the national tradition of centralized government and purely ideological parties (e.g., in France). The new job of political theory needs therefore to be tackled seriously in every country. On its solution will largely depend the life and freedom—perhaps the survival—of man. The decline of modern government affects all of us—and so will the principles, structure and institutions that will succeed. Here is a challenge to the conservative innovator. Here is a real "frontier" of the post-modern world—a common frontier.

# CHAPTER EIGHT

# The Vanishing East

East is East and West is West,
And never the twain shall meet.

So sang Kipling, laureate of empire at its high noon. Millions of people who never have heard his name know these lines. Many still accept them as folk wisdom.

It is always rash to say "never" to the future. Kipling has been dead only thirty years. But today "the twain have met"—in one chaotic, anarchic, explosive but common world disorder and world civilization. "East" and "West" have almost become mere geographic directions again rather than meaningful terms of politics, civilization and culture, "Commonwealth" has succeeded "Empire"; and the dominant figure at the Commonwealth meetings was, until his death in 1964, Nehru, the complete East-Westerner: fiery Indian nationalist and master of English prose, high-caste, proud Brahman and agnostic Fabian Socialist, idol of the Indian villagers and fervent apostle of heavy industry.

Yet Kipling was right—though not in the way he intended to be. *His* West and *his* East have indeed not met: the nineteenth-century West of the European power system, and the mysterious East of tribal village and Peacock Throne, of peasant following the bullock behind the wooden plow, and of

Confucian mandarin learning ancient texts by rote, have not met.

Both have disappeared.

Only fifty years ago the European power system was still substantially what it had been ever since the end of Europe's Religious Wars. The non-European great powers—Japan and the United States—were not accepted into full membership until World War I. For 250 years all great powers had been European; and all but Russia had already been members when the Westphalian Peace Treaties of 1648 first established the European power system.

It was the stablest power system the world had seen since the days of Caesar Augustus; and it became the most powerful. From 1700 on, it had been taken for granted that political sovereignty or economic control over entire countries with millions of inhabitants anywhere in the world could be bestowed or transferred by treaty between European great powers. In fact, the only successful challenges came from the United States, itself European by race and culture (in the Monroe Doctrine of 1823, and in John Hay's Open-Door Policy of 1902 which prevented the partitioning of China among the great European powers).

Just a little over seventy years ago nobody thought it extraordinary that a minor European potentate, the King of the Belgians, was given, largely in recognition of his family connections, personal ownership of one fourth of the whole Continent of Africa. Twenty years later he was allowed as a matter of course to dispose of this entire Congo territory with all its inhabitants by personal last will and testament. Even the First World War hardly seemed to dent the European power system. The victors divided among themselves the non-European possessions of the defeated in Asia, Africa and Oceania, without even a show of concern for the wishes of the inhabitants.

As late as the mid-twenties there was only one territory on the whole inhabitable globe that was not controlled by Europeans or their descendants: Japan. To be sure, there were seven other non-European countries that were considered sovereign and independent: China, Siam, Afghanistan, Persia, Ethiopia, Liberia and Haiti. But of these, Liberia and Haiti were wards of the United States. Siam, Afghanistan and Ethiopia were "buffer states" between territories of great powers and maintained by them deliberately for that purpose. Persia, while officially sovereign, had actually been divided into spheres of influence by Great Britain and Russia. China, the largest, was saved from a similar fate only by United States intervention; even so China's economic life and political institutions were run by Europeans who controlled courts and universities, ports, transportation, taxes and customs service, communications and industries.

Sometimes the buffoons of history tell us more than the tragic actors. Such a buffoon was the retired British Army colonel who around 1920 claimed to have discovered the "Secret of the Great Pyramid": The British were really the Lost Tribe of Israel, and therefore the rightful heirs forever to world domination. As proof he offered—quite seriously— that the Lord had promised Israel the land of milk and honey; and did not the British control the world's petroleum and the world's rubber? Of course he was a madman; but thousands of people in Great Britain, the Dominions and the United States took his ravings seriously—the movement was still going strong in rural Canada around 1940.

Even World War II, only two decades ago, was fought under the spell of the European power system. The pivotal decision in World War II was to throw the major energies of the United States into the European theater of war rather than into the Pacific. That this was both difficult and risky was well understood. The people who made the decision in the United

States knew that it might well mean the loss of China. The people who urged it in Great Britain saw that it might well mean the end of British rule in India. Yet it was inescapable at the time.

It was no longer correct, as President Roosevelt believed—in what was surely a major blunder—that world peace could be established by restoring the pre-1914 Concert of Europe, that is by ridding Europe of the danger of German aggression. But as late as 1943 or 1944, a world war could still only be won—or lost—as a European war.

One might even say that the first few years after World War II remained under the constellation of the European power system. For the traditional European countries it was a decade of weakness and power shrinkage. But the United States's military and economic hegemony during that decade filled the resulting vacuum. The situation could not last—hegemony never does. It was a delusion of Western, and especially of American, policy that it could endure or even that it should endure. But certainly in these first postwar years, during which the United States had a monopoly on atomic weapons combined with international economic predominance, the lineaments of the old Western-controlled world were still discernible.

By now they have all but disappeared. Japan's occupation of the European colonies in the Far East, Indian independence, the victory of Communism in China, the Korean War, the Suez debacle—each of these was another landslide burying the ruins of the European power system and creating a new world landscape. The final step would be European unification—both an acknowledgment of the end of the old system of European power balance and perhaps the first major step toward a new stability and order.

The Cold War could still be lost in Europe by either side. The Berlin Wall is a constant reminder—both of the threat to the West and of the fragility of the Communist empire in

Europe. The loss to Communism of Germany, France or Italy would be a severe blow to the Free World, and one from which it might not be able to recover. Similarly, the loss of the European satellites would be a heavy blow to Communism.

But the Cold War can no longer be won in Europe. It can only be won in the non-European world, the countries of Asia and Africa, which only yesterday were mere pawns in the European power game. Our side can win only if non-European peoples exercising their own independent decisions, and acting through their own governments, choose for themselves the values and ways of the Free World.

The European power system is gone so completely that the currently accepted view of the world conflict as one between two Western and white superpowers, the United States and Russia, may soon be obsolete. The ability of the Free World to prevail—perhaps to survive—may well hinge on the ability of the new and emphatically non-European Republic of India to maintain a free government and to develop an expanding economy and a stable society. It is even imaginable that, a few years hence, the threat of a new, and even less European, superpower, China—with a population of a billion people and growing industrial production—might force into close alliance the United States, Western Europe and Russia, despite their fundamental differences in principles, values and beliefs. Mr. Khrushchev, before his fall, was clearly moving towards such a re-alignment.

### Success or Failure of the West?

The European power system died of its own success. Every one of the forces that destroyed it was of Western origin, generated by the West and propagated by it. Nationalism is the West's very own *enfant terrible*. The campaign against colonialism only repeats the arguments and slogans of generations of European and American liberals. Everywhere it is being led by men trained and educated in the West, and Western in their thinking, their arguments, their principles. In the thirties it was said that only an honors degree from Oxford or Cambridge qualified an Indian to be jailed for resistance to British rule. Today this applies, with variations, to all the remaining colonial areas of the Western powers. Moscow-trained Communists are similarly the most likely leaders of resistance to the new Russian colonialism in the satellite countries. And, of course, Communism is entirely Western—a heresy, to be sure, but one that could only have grown on Western soil and out of Western heritage.

The world order that will succeed the European power system might well be anti-Western; but it will quite definitely not be un-Western. Every single one of the new countries in the world today—including those that have not yet shaken off colonial status—sees its goal in its transformation into a Western state, economy and society, and sees the means to achieve this goal in the theories, institutions, sciences, technologies and tools the West has developed.

Kipling and his generation could hardly have foreseen this development.

To them it appeared obvious that the non-Western peoples would reject the institutions, ideas and principles of the West. At the time this was a reasonable assumption.

Take for example the American Negro. Of all non-European peoples anywhere, he has been most completely divorced from any native culture of his own. He has had the longest and most complete exposure to a purely Western culture and tradition. Yet when the original promise of Booker T. Washington's "separate but equal" proved an illusion around World War I, the first reaction of the American Negro was to turn anti-Western—to change the slogan, so to speak, to "separate but really separate." Thirty years ago the movements with the greatest mass appeal among this largest non-European group in the United States were those that, like Marcus Garvey's, repudiated the values, institutions and customs of the white world. They proposed instead to develop a strictly separate American Negro culture on its own African foundation, and a community strictly apart from, and outside that of, the white man.

Today nothing is left of these movements. When the South African Boer talks about the same idea under the name of "apartheid," he is denounced as a disgrace and a danger by people of good will everywhere. Only a generation ago, however, this seemed the forward-looking, progressive position. As late as 1935 international Communism, after long and careful deliberation, adopted it in a calculated bid to capture the allegiance of the American Negro. Organizations that then stood for Negro emancipation and equality within white society, such as the National Association for the Advancement of the Colored People (NAACP), were denounced as "timid," "conservative" and "appeasers."

Western ideals and institutions proved too powerful not only for Marcus Garvey's dream but for any attempt to develop new, independent, non-European communities on their own non-European foundations. Regardless of the age and refinement of their own tradition, all the non-European peoples today have, like the American Negro, accepted that neither "separate but equal" nor "separate but separate" are the answer. Instead they acknowledge that to be equal with the West and with one another they must themselves be Western.

The second assumption of Kipling's generation has also been disproven: that non-European peoples are incapable of acquiring the ways of the West, and especially of acquiring proficiency in Western industrial and military technology.

At the beginning of World War II, people thought the Japanese constitutionally incapable of flying modern aircraft—"something to do with their eyes," they said. We soon found out that Japanese fighter pilots were second to none. Later, during the early stages of the Korean War, a good many high-ranking, professional soldiers believed equally seriously that the Chinese soldier could not stand up under fire or would not fight in the dark. The hoary superstition that the Hindu or the Chinese will not make an efficient industrial worker—the one because of caste, the other because he is "too individualistic"—is still around, though it was completely disproven by actual experience in both countries a century ago.

Fifty years ago the borderlands of the North Atlantic had a virtual monopoly on industrial and military technology, knowledge and skills. To assume a continuation of this monopoly was perhaps not unreasonable at the time. Technology is, after all, not something by itself, but the child of values, cultural traditions and historical development, all of which were distinctly Western. Yet—beginning with Japan —industrial and military technology has proven to be far easier of acquisition by non-Western people than Western political or social beliefs and institutions. All over the world, non-Western peoples are rapidly industrializing and rapidly building Western-style armed forces. The technological monopoly of the North Atlantic countries has been broken for good.

### The Failure of the East

The European power system has collapsed; but at the same time, the East has vanished.

This may seem paradoxical in view of the strong influence of, and high interest in, Eastern (or rather non-Western) ideas in the West today. It began with Gauguin and, a little later, with the impact of primitive Negro sculpture on modern art. It led to the emergence of jazz as a major musical influence. At the same time Gandhi became a powerful influence on Western liberalism and pacifism. Today there is the great interest in the cultures of that non-Western Westerner, the American Indian, and in his ancient civilizations in Central America and in the Andes.

And there is the influence of Japan on American art, architecture and design, and the interest in that most Eastern of metaphysics, Zen-Buddhism, with its strong affinities to our own new view of the universe.

More and more historians stress that "world history" is not simply "European history" writ larger. Thus we now increasingly see ancient Greece as one of the great archaic civilizations of the Orient rather than as a Western civilization all by itself.

It is true that the West has lost its old certainty of superiority and with it its old provincialism. But it is also true—and much more important—that no viable society today can be built on non-Western foundations.

This is not speculation. It is experience. In the three oldest, most advanced and richest non-Western cultures—Japan, China and India—the attempt has been made to base a viable society on inherited, non-Western foundations—and in all three it has failed.

Modern Japan grew out of an extraordinary effort to create on the spiritual and social foundations of Japan's own heritage a society capable of survival in the modern world. The aim was to preserve the substance of Japan through adoption of the forms and tools of the West.

There has rarely been an abler, more dedicated or more clear-headed generation than the men who transformed, in thirty or forty years, the stagnant, frozen and demoralized Japan of the last Shoguns, the Japan of 1857, into the dynamic, organized and proud Japanese Empire of 1900. Insofar as they Westernized the country they were a complete success. The Japan of 1857 could not protect its inland ports against a single foreign gunboat. Fifty years later Japan could decisively defeat both the army and the navy of imperial Russia. In 1857 Japan was almost totally illiterate. Fifty years later its literacy rate compared favorably with many European countries; and she had as large a proportion of her young people in secondary schools and universities as had Germany. The Japan of 1857 was one of the most backward and poverty-stricken economies in the world. Fifty years later she had the highest per capita income among all non-Western countries, was virtually self-sufficient in heavy industry and could compete on the world markets.

Indeed to this day, late nineteenth-century Japan is the outstanding example of the rapid economic development of an underdeveloped country. Her achievement was greater, her growth faster, than that of Soviet Russia since 1917. She had to overcome the obstacles of limited raw materials and of heavy overpopulation without empty virgin lands. Yet she developed without tyranny and terror, without concentration camps and purges.

But the attempt to build modern Japan on Japanese cultural, social and political foundations was a failure. It created strains and tensions that brought about the suicidal flight from self-control and sanity of the next generation, that of the twenties and thirties. When the collapse into defeat and humiliation came, it was not the Western forms and tools that disappeared, but any attempt to preserve a non-Western substance. Today's Japan stands or falls with the success of root-and-branch Westernization.

In Japan the attempt to build a viable society on non-Western foundations was essentially mechanistic—to join together elements of East and West. In China—the oldest, the proudest and the most adaptable civilization—Dr. Sun Yat-sen tried instead to distill out of China's own tradition guiding principles for her self-renewal as a modern society. The revolutionary impact of his teaching, its ability to loosen the bonds of the old regime and to inspire young people with a passionate desire for something new, can hardly be overestimated. Nor should the achievements of "Young China" between 1912 and 1930 be underestimated.

Still the attempt failed. What would have happened to Dr. Sun Yat-sen's China had there been no Japanese invasion can never be proven. But by 1930 basic weaknesses had already appeared, and it was by then clear that Sun Yat-sen's attempt could not revive the old, rural China, around which his whole doctrine had been built. The Chinese Communists repudiated this old China with its traditional values and beliefs. They demanded instead that peasant China be made over in a new, Western, though Communist image. And with this they denounced also any attempt to preserve China's own traditions or to build on them. Mao Tse-tung may himself write Chinese poetry in classic ideograms; but his regime has begun to introduce a Latin alphabet which is to be taught exclusively in the future, and which aims at making the classic writings a dead language accessible only to scholars.

The most significant failure is probably Gandhi's in India. Unlike the Japanese and unlike Sun Yat-sen, Gandhi was not content with merging East and West. He aimed at building on the foundations of the spirit a better, purer, stronger society that could be model and inspiration to East and West alike.

Here clearly was the greatest vision, the deepest understanding. Here also was a very great man, a saint and a shrewd political leader. His impact on the people of India was probably greater than that of any other man since the Prince Buddha 2,500 years ago. Not only the educated but the masses, in the hopeless isolation of their sun-baked mud hovels, caught the vision and were moved by it. Even untouchability and landlordism, which neither force nor reason had ever been able to weaken, showed signs of melting under his moral fervor.

British rule crumpled before Gandhi. Independent India is above all his achievement. Every Indian leader today claims to be his disciple—and most actually are. Even the Indian Communists pay lip service to his greatness. Yet only ten years after his death, there is little left of his social, political or economic gospel. India today sees her salvation in rapid industrialization, in steel mills, fertilizer plants, power dams and truck transportation—rather than in the self-denying, austere anti-industrialism of Gandhi's spinning wheel. A completely Western army, rather than nonviolent resistance, is her mainstay in international affairs.

The present Indian government, though composed of Gandhi's closest associates, seems singularly unimpressed by the power of nonviolent resistance such as threw the British into complete confusion. There have been many more "incidents," in which police and army were ordered to fire on demonstrators in the first ten years of Indian independence than in the last ten years of British rule. The present Indian government has given in only to violent rioting, not once— as the British so often did—to moral force. And instead of Gandhi's spiritual foundation, the present rulers base their ideas of society, economy and government on purely Western and purely secular ideas, such as, in Nehru's case, English Fabian Socialism of 1919 vintage. The only exceptions are the orthodox Hindu sectarians—but their ideal is to purge India of all innovations whether Gandhian or Western.

I am convinced of Gandhi's lasting impact—unless, indeed, independent India collapses into anarchy, civil war, totalitarianism, or before a new conquest by a foreign invader. But it is unlikely that there will ever be an attempt to realize Gandhi's society, that post-modern dream that was to be more truly a fulfillment of the basic values of the West than any Western country has ever been, and which yet was to rest on the non-Western foundations of India's own spiritual heritage. That attempt—despite its nobility and popular appeal—has failed.

Where Kipling's generation erred was in their belief that the East had such power, such deep, rock-bottom strength, that it would resist the corroding acid of Western ideas, Western institutions, Western technology and Western goods.

To the best of the West's representatives in the non-Western world this resistance was precisely its attraction. The great colonials—Gordon in China, Curzon in India, Lyautey in Morocco, Lugard in Nigeria, Lawrence in Arabia, Kipling himself—were all at odds with their own West, were strangers, rebels or misfits at home. They romanticized the East, they saw it as their mission to build it up and protect it against the West—Curzon's fantastic attempt to recreate the India of the Mogul Empire in the "Great Durbar" of 1906 was perhaps the most spectacular example, but by no means an isolated one. This explains their incredible inability to see, let alone to understand, the impact and importance of the Western-trained, Westernized lawyer, teacher, journalist or politician. To the very end the Western colonial administrators persisted in the delusion that these people were "scum," that they had no influence at all on the "masses," were indeed actually repudiated by them.

In a most perceptive book written by a former colonial about European rule in the East—Philip Woodruff's *The Men Who Ruled India*—this is still a recurrent theme. Yet the book was written in 1953, six years after the "Westernized troublemakers" had forced the last Union Jack in India to be struck. A similar delusion underlies French policy in North Africa. It determines much of American policy in the Arab world and explains our worst mistakes there.

The heritage and values of non-Western society will not be lost forever. Such deep traditions of old and advanced cultures cannot remain forever powerless, inert and ineffectual. But they will again become a living force only if the non-Western countries succeed in building viable societies on Western foundations: Western values and institutions; Western education, economics and technology; Western means of mass communication and mass organization. This is the lesson the non-Western countries themselves have learned—from Nehru in India and Mao in China to Nasser and Bourguiba in the Arab countries and Dr. Nkrumah in Ghana.

These men do not agree among themselves on values and institutions. They mean quite different things when they say "free government." But their differences are those of Westerners, the differences between the free West and the totalitarians; they all believe in the strong, central, professional government of the modern West. They do not agree on the principles of economic organization; but they all accept industrialization and organized large-scale enterprise, economic welfare and advancement as major goals of human society. They may not believe in "freedom of speech" or "freedom of thought"; but they all accept and exploit the printing press and the mass media of communication and propaganda. And they all accept—indeed they all worship—education in the Western sense and its product, the professional lawyer, doctor, scientist, bureaucrat or technologist.

### Can the West and the New East Meet?

This is a highly unfashionable question to ask today. Anyone who raises it is certain to be called a "reactionary," at Oxford or Harvard, in New Delhi or Tunis—let alone in Moscow where it is considered unthinkable to ask.

But, unfashionable as it may be, it is a very real question.

The Western institutions are not mechanical formulae. They are the fruit of long, painful development. They are not interchangeable machine parts that will fit any standard model, but living tissue in an organic body of values and experience, emotions and history, martyrs and precepts.

The Speaker of Parliament, in some newly organized government of a newly independent country on the West Coast of Africa, sports the wig and the mace of the Speaker at Westminster. He follows the procedures of the "Mother of Parliaments" with pomp, punctilio and relish. The spiritual ancestry of the Right Honorable Gentleman who sits in the Speaker's chair in Nigeria or at the Gold Coast includes all the political thinkers, statesmen and parliamentarians of the English tradition, back to the Barons at Runnymede. It extends beyond them into the dim antiquity of Greece and Rome.

Yet his father after the flesh was a tribal chieftain or a witch doctor, and his own roots are in a tribal society living in the Bronze Age. He may repudiate his physical father. But he cannot repudiate the society whence he came. This tribal Bronze Age society is his constituency. He can only be effective if he can convey to it what he stands for, if he can move it to follow where he leads.

In the entire country, with all the elaborate system of parliament, responsible ministers, law courts, civil servants and so forth, there may be only three hundred people with enough education and enough knowledge of the traditions of the West to understand what all these institutions are about, let alone how to run them. What will happen when these men are gone? Will they be able to bring up successors fast enough? Will there be enough time for these transplanted institutions to take root, and enough loving care and understanding to make them grow and prosper? How will they be integrated with a tribal community—can they be integrated at all? Will these Western institutions become means to unify the new nation? Or will they aggravate traditional hostilities and cleavages? Will they, in other words, become mere slogans to justify tyranny and terror, bloodshed and civil war, exploitation and paralysis, cruelty and lawlessness?

These questions must be asked not only of Tunisia or Ghana but also of India—and even more of China. The number of people in India with knowledge and understanding of Western values and institutions, and with real personal commitment to them, may not be so much larger proportionately than it is in West Africa. There is the same doubt that Communism can remain viable in a non-Western country like China, after the passing of the first Western-trained generation; but for us, in the Free World, this is cold comfort.

The speed and ease with which Western technology—industrial and military—is spreading throughout the non-Western world only adds to the seriousness of the situation. Technology is not a disembodied abstraction or a mere tool; it grows out of cultural and historical traditions and demands cultural and social foundations. Because of this, it cannot simply be imposed on an existing culture. Any culture that does not conform to the exacting demands of technology—whether African tribe, Indian caste or Chinese family—will be ruthlessly destroyed. But can technology, however productive of a higher standard of living or of a higher standard of warfare and dying, produce a culture and a community?

Technology in the West grew out of our own cultural foundations. The roots of the great technological changes of the last two hundred years go back all the way to the surge of the Middle Ages (the great cathedrals too were an "industrial revolution") and even further back to the Rule of St. Benedict. We have had a long time to get used to this "new growth," so that we could develop "antibodies." In the non-Western world, however, modern technology is a "foreign body." Its growth is explosive and much too fast to make possible the development of really effective antibodies.

This may make easier the adaptation of the non-Western world to Western political and social institutions by destroying those political and social traditions that stand in their way. It may force more thorough commitment to the basic values that underlie these institutions. But it may also uproot and weaken these non-Western countries before they can grow into cohesive societies.

In the disappearance of the East and in its Westernization the great themes of the post-modern world all come together. Education is the cause of Westernization; but the educated society is also the great need of the new world, the shortage of educated people is its great lack, and the development of an effective model of general education its great hope.

The vision of economic development is the driving force behind Westernization. The force that, in twenty years, made trucks rather than the backs of coolies up-to-date transportation in Bangkok also changes expectations, beliefs and ways of life unchanged since time immemorial. At the same time the new danger of interracial and international class war resulting from the failure of economic development is the great threat both to the old West and the new Westernizing countries.

These countries have no choice but to imitate the political institutions of modern government; they have to become nation-states. They can only survive if their political institutions become effective. Yet these institutions are just as inadequate there for the tasks of international affairs as they are in the West, and just as endangered there by the cancerous growth of military technology and the resulting militarization of society.

Above all these countries need the new, post-modern, post-Cartesian world-view. This alone can enable them to integrate the best of their own non-Western tradition with the beliefs, the institutions, the knowledge, the tools of the West. And no living civilization can clothe itself entirely in somebody else's cast-off garments.

The emergence of a common, basically Western world civilization is the greatest of our new frontiers—the greatest change and the greatest opportunity. But in whose image will it be cast?

# CHAPTER NINE

# The Work to Be Done

Policies and actions in today's world are already measured against the demands of the new frontiers; they are effective only as they answer to the new reality.

Yet our policies and actions are still largely molded by the reality of yesteryear, still aim at solving yesterday's problems, still assume yesterday's world. If we tackle the new at all, we tend to treat it as a "temporary emergency" that will go away again, or as a deviation from a norm that ought to be restored. We tackle the new tasks as disturbances and problems rather than as opportunities.

This, at bottom, is the crisis of the Free World—a crisis of vision and understanding, of leadership and realism. We are in mortal danger not because we are weak but because we misdirect our strength to fight over yesterday's battles and to repeat yesterday's slogans.

## Our Self-Delusion

A symptom of our delusion is the belief that there would be no problems if only there were no Communism, and that there are no tasks other than its defeat.

Communism is a formidable enemy bent on world conquest. It is an absolute necessity for the Free World to maintain its unity and military strength against the ever-present

248

threat of Communist attack. Kind words and good intentions can never substitute for power and preparedness in dealing with an avowed world conqueror.

Communism is evil. Its driving forces are the deadly sins of envy and hatred. Its aim is the subjection of all goals and all values to power; its essence is bestiality: the denial that man is anything but animal, the denial of all ethics, of human worth, of human responsibility.

But the great problems that face the world today are aggravated rather than caused by Soviet Russia or by international Communism. If both were to disappear overnight, the tasks would remain the same. The race for weapons of total annihilation, for instance, is not just the result of the conflict and tension between Russia and the West. On the contrary, the conflict is to a large extent the result of the unmanageable explosion of military technology and of the resultant collapse of the international system based on nation-state and obsolescent modern government. If military technology had not gotten out of hand, Russia, especially a Communist Russia, would still present a danger, and would still pose problems of defense in Europe and Asia alike. But the problems could be managed by conventional means of diplomacy and strategy.

To underrate the strength and achievements of an enemy is always folly. Yet everything is true that has been said and written about the internal stresses and weaknesses of Communism. Every glimpse we get into the Communist world, behind its façade of propaganda, shows sickness of the soul and torture of the body. Every opportunity given to the subjects of a Communist regime to register their real feelings has revealed hatred and despair. History knows no parallel to Hungary where an entire nation attempted to flee its homeland rather than stay under its own Communist government. Poland and East Germany show the same profound repudiation as do the thousands of refugees—most of them pro-Communist only a few short years ago—who manage to escape into Hong Kong.

We know that Communism's greatest achievement tends to undermine the regime rather than strengthen it. It is to her educational revolution that Russia owes her strength today. Yet whenever the iron hand of police terror relaxes for a moment in any Communist country, the educated rebel. The students, the writers, the scientists—the very group whom Communism cossets and on whom it showers privileges—led the Hungarian, the Polish, the East German risings. The students, the writers, the scientists rose up in criticism when Communist China, in 1956, relaxed for a few weeks the iron controls on thought and speech. The Communist rulers were right when they charged the educated with the high treason of repudiating Communism altogether. But this only means that Communism cannot allow the educated to use their education, it can only tolerate technicians. It finds itself, to use Marxist jargon, in a "basic contradiction": It needs the educated man yet cannot tolerate him. It needs the new organization of men of skill and knowledge yet cannot permit responsible judgment, let alone use the organization to promote human freedom.

It suffers from a similar contradiction in respect to economic development. A Communist government can survive only if it oppresses the farmer and supresses rural society. Yet it thereby undermines the agricultural foundation for economic development—and also freezes rural population at so high and yet unproductive a level as to endanger ultimate industrial growth.

The great opportunity of Communism is, of course, the emergent nationalism of the formerly colonial people. Yet

Communism cannot allow independence. It can tolerate only vassals and satellites.

Above all, it is the prisoner of its own rigidly mechanistic orthodoxy which must be proclaimed infallible. In the physical and natural sciences sheer necessity has forced the Communists to tolerate such heresies as quantum theory, nuclear physics and antibiotics—though even they were accepted only after considerable struggle. But can even necessity make the Communists accept similar heresies in social and political affairs—the new organization, for instance? Innovation with its risks and uncertainties and its need for decentralized, local, competitive planning? Or political and social pluralism?

The weakness of Communism, its internal contradictions incapable of resolution, its failure to build a society, are all shown up by one single fact: There has been no flight to the "Communist paradise." The Free World has no "people's police" to prevent its citizens from crossing the border into the Communist world. At every border point the flow of human misery runs in one direction only.

And yet not only does disenchantment with Communism come perilously late, but the very failure of Communism constitutes its present danger. For Communism is the exploitation of failure at the new tasks. It is the opiate of the defeated and the drug of the irresponsible.

Communism cannot accomplish the new tasks. But it can, for a time at least, suppress the problems, deny their existence, forbid their discussion. It cannot tolerate educated men, but it can breed technicians. It cannot create a society, but it can organize power. It cannot build an international order, but it can exploit disorder and make "crisis" permanent. It cannot furnish the resources needed for economic development. But it can channel despair and frustration into international and interracial class war.

For the short run we do not have to fear the strength of Communism but its weakness. In the long run, we do not have to fear the success of Communism but our own default. It cannot triumph; but we may fail.

## The New Frontiers

The Free World must remain strong enough and united enough to resist threat of Communist military aggression. But to contain Russia and to fight Communism, though necessary, cannot be our only policy. It cannot even be our principal policy. The policy of the Free World must center in the challenges of the new frontiers. It must aim at the demands of the new reality. It must be a constructive policy, out to build, to do and to lead. If we succeed in building the new:

> the educated society;
> the world economy of dynamic development;
> the new political concepts and institutions needed in this pluralist age, internationally, nationally and locally; and civilizations that can take the place of the East that has vanished;

we will have won. Otherwise, no matter how strong we are militarily, and how united in detesting the Communist evil, we may lose.

There is no doubt that we have the resources, human and material. We have the capacity to face reality and not to be blinded by dogma of our own making; the capacity to accept experimentation, diversity, dissent; the capacity to admit that we do not know all the answers and that we make mistakes; above all the power to encourage independence of thought and action in individuals as well as in government and societies.

Nor have we been wholly unsuccessful. It is no mean feat

that there is a Free World today. Few people would have
thought it possible, twenty years ago, when World War II
started. Our policies have not been wrong. On the whole
the Free World has been courageous, responsible and united.
But our efforts have been incomplete. We have been too
concerned with defense to give leadership, too busy with
propping up what we have to start building the future.

There is a striking parallel in the history of the American Civil
War. The war was decided in and by the West. The emergence
of the new West gave decisive strength to the antislavery forces.
It was the new Western railroads that gave the Union overwhelming strategic and economic superiority. It was the victories in the
West and Southwest that split and paralyzed the Confederacy and
deprived it of its economic basis.

Lincoln, himself a Westerner, knew all this—and so did some of
his generals. But the Union never acted on its knowledge, never
exploited its Western strength, never followed up its Western
victories. Prisoners of the memory of the Revolution and completely defensive in their thinking, the Union generals threw all
their forces into the Virginian Peninsula. The Peninsula is actually
so narrow that the Union's superiority in manpower became a
handicap rather than an asset; no decisive victory could be won
there. It was Sherman's march through Georgia, from the West
to the Atlantic, that decisively destroyed the Confederacy's ability
to fight; and, given adequate manpower, that might have been
done two years earlier.

The Union paid a terrible price for not using its strength and
knowledge, and for not exploiting its Western victories. The war
was prolonged for years and it ended in the unconscionable
blood baths through which Grant finally gained the Peninsula.

Military defense against Communist aggression is the peninsula of the great world conflict of today. We have to be
strong enough to hold the defense; but victory cannot be won
on this front—not even, any longer, by massacre and blood
bath. And it is much too narrow a front for us to deploy and

use our resources and our strength. Today's "West," where alone the decisive victory can be won, is the new frontiers with their new tasks.

The new tasks require much more than political decisions and government actions, though the leadership must, of necessity, be political. Governments throughout the Free World can—and should—make the development of the educated society a priority of national and international policy. But governments cannot create the new educational policies and methods needed. These must come from philosophers and teachers. And they require active concern with education on the part of citizens.

Governments similarly can only do a part of the economic development job (though an important part). Private business and private investment have a major role to play. The building of an industrial society in freedom that can serve as a model and inspiration is a task for every responsible manager and for every responsible trade union leader. And the development of a discipline and ethics of managing that can be learned, can be taught and can inspire is a responsibility only individuals can discharge.

Above all, governments cannot give us the necessary new thinking on the concepts and institutions of political integration. And it is people who, as politicians, teachers, artists, writers, judges or priests, will create, or fail to create, the civilization of the Westernizing East.

We must accept the tasks of the new frontiers. We must be committed to them—in our words and in our actions. We must give priority to them—subject only to the maintenance of free institutions and civil liberties and to the need for adequate defense.

This means overcoming the issues of the dead past, forgetting the slogans of yesterday, and sacrificing nineteenth-century promises which though empty today are still the cherished heirlooms of politics everywhere. Such abrogation will be most difficult perhaps for the Left in the Free World. Though nothing could be deader than the illusions of the European Social Democrat or the American Progressive, nothing engenders more comforting self-righteousness or a warmer glow of woolly-headed good feeling. But the traditional Right needs equally to grow up to reality; it too is enmeshed in emotional immaturity.

Educators everywhere will have to give up cherished notions; that higher education must be confined to a small elite is still, for instance, an article of faith for many. Businessmen and economists still tend to cling to preindustrial economics, still believe that encouragement of economic development in the underdeveloped countries is (or should be) charitable give-away or political bribe rather than hard-headed investment in our own economic growth and future. Labor leaders still believe that to produce less is the quickest way to get more, and so on. The problem is not selfishness but failure to realize where self-interest has come to lie. It is not evil designs but well-meaning mediocrity. It is not ignorance but failure to act on our knowledge.

Here leadership is needed the most, and here it is likely to be most effective. It can appeal to the desire to build. It can give renewed vision and focus. It can crystallize knowledge into action, and good intentions into dedication.

Finally we have to look upon the new tasks as opportunities rather than as problems, have to see them as chances of success rather than as threatening risks. Frontiers always are full of danger, unknown lurking terror and menace. The new frontiers of today's world are no exception. Their risks are largely the result of the success of the West—perhaps of too much success too fast. But while failure to resolve the difficulties that confront the post-modern world will endanger all the values of the West, if not its survival, the frontiers themselves offer the opportunity to build something new, durable and productive on the foundations of our beliefs, our values, our knowledge and our strength. There is hard work to be done; but it is work not of wrecking nor even of defending but of affirming, making, building and leading.

# CHAPTER TEN

# The Human Situation Today

So far we have talked of the universes around man: the universe of perception and ideas, and the universe of political order and social institutions. But man himself is a universe. Where does man fit into this post-modern world?

The universe of man has changed too—perhaps even more than the world around him. Two essential and unique attributes of man—knowledge and power—have changed their very meaning. As a result the meaning of man is changing. And yet—as in our philosophical systems and our social and political institutions—our ideas, our methods, our preoccupations, our rhetoric, are still those of an earlier age which is fast becoming obsolete. In respect to the human situation we are also on a voyage of transition. We are still trying to steer by the old landmarks, even though we already sail new, uncharted seas.

Twentieth-century man has achieved the knowledge to destroy himself both physically and morally. This new absolute has added a new dimension to human existence.

There is no danger that man will ever run out of ignorance; on the contrary, the more we know, the more we realize how little we know—in all areas of knowledge, in all sciences and all arts. Yet the knowledge we have acquired is absolute knowledge giving absolute power. There may well be even more "absolute" weapons of destruction than those we already

257

possess. But there is no going beyond total, final extinction; and that we can already inflict on ourselves.

Man has always been expert at mass slaughter. But even at their worst, his orgies of destruction were never "total," there were survivors who could start afresh. Even the worst slaughter was always quite localized. Now we can, in a few seconds of mania, make the whole earth unlivable for all of us.

By giving us this knowledge science has broken through to the core of human existence. If we are to survive, we must learn to live with a new demon in ourselves, must master a new, absolute power in our hands, must face up to the constant threat of self-annihilation through knowledge.

At the same time we are acquiring what is perhaps even more potent—and certainly even less controlled—knowledge: the knowledge to destroy man psychologically and morally by destroying his personality.

It is common belief today that the sciences that deal with man's behavior, such as psychology, have lamentably failed to keep pace with the advancement of the physical sciences. This, alas, is delusion. We have not, it is true, acquired the knowledge to make man better. We have not learned very much, if anything, to enable man to control himself. But we have learned how to make man worse. We have acquired knowledge how to control others—how to enslave them, destroy them, dehumanize them. And we are fast approaching the point where this too will become absolute knowledge capable of the total destruction of man as a moral being, as a responsible will, as a person. We all but know enough today to turn man into a biological machine run by the manipulation of fears and emotions, a being without beliefs, without values, without principles, without compassion, without pride, without humanity altogether. Through systematic terror, through indoctrination, lies and thought control, through systematic manipulation of stimulus, reward and punishment, we can today break man and convert him into brute animal.

A behavioral science that does not aim at making man capable of self-control betrays man. A behavioral science that does not affirm man as a rational and spiritual being betrays science. Such a science produces destructive results that can only be abused and have no legitimate use. But that does not affect the potency of the results.

Totalitarianism is the final result of science without morality. It is the systematic dehumanization of man, and the scientific exploitation of his animal nature. It is no less "scientific" for being wicked and for being a travesty on all the hopes and beliefs of the scientists. It systematizes old experience, as does any science; draws therefrom general theories of human nature; and then tests these theories in the large-scale experiments of concentration camps and terror, "brain-washing" indoctrination and thought control. Nor does the inherent instability of all tyranny invalidate the power of the pernicious knowledge on which totalitarianism bases itself. The knowledge is the danger;* and the knowledge remains available. Here too is a new absolute. Here too science has broken through to the core of human existence. Here too we possess, however limited our knowledge, enough power for total self-destruction.

The knowledge to destroy man's personality may have even greater impact on the human situation than the knowledge to destroy the physical life of the species. That he must die, man has always known; every one of his major religions predicts the eventual extinction of the species. But man, wherever and

* On this see the discussion between two eminent American psychologists, C. R. Rodgers and B. F. Skinner in *Science* (Vol. 124, page 1057, December 1, 1956) which should cure any reader of the comfortable delusion that this is not "science" and that only evil but not "decent people like ourselves" will ever use it to enslave, manipulate and dehumanize. Skinner, undoubtedly well-meaning, proposes to manipulate people to be "adjusted" and "happy"; but this is just as much destruction of man for being well meant.

whenever he started to reflect, has always asserted that to be a man is something different from being mere animal, that to live like a man is more than to survive physically. On this assertion he has built his religions, his cultures, his civilizations, his arts, his sciences and his governments—everything of this world that is not buried with the individual animal remains. It is this assertion that the totalitarian denies. He maintains instead that man is a domestic animal—remarkably clever, to be sure, but also remarkably docile. And he possesses enough knowledge of human nature to degrade man in the image of a domestic animal.

For two thousand years the Christian has taken on faith and revelation the end of the world and the Anti-Christ. Now the apocalyptic visions have become experience. We can see the Anti-Christ who turns all man's fairest promises onto his perdition and all his hopes onto his enslavement. And who among us today has not had the shock of *knowing*, if only in a nightmare, the moment of fiery cloud and deadly rain, the irreversible moment when a power-drunk dictator, a trigger-happy colonel, or a simple misreading of a "blip" on a radar screen will make us destroy ourselves?

## The Control of Power

We will not survive unless we learn to control these two new powers that knowledge has unleashed. Obviously we cannot survive our own physical destruction. It should be as obvious that we will not survive if we cravenly surrender our manhood and accept moral destruction to escape physical destruction; we will at best prolong physical survival by a very short time.

We cannot suppress the new knowledge. We possess it. Indeed every country today must try to advance it further, however much it fears or detests it.

Suppression of knowledge and of the search for it has always been the first reaction to "dangerous" discovery. It has never worked. But this time it cannot even be tried. The Russians had to give up the ban on the "heresies" of modern physics the day they heard that the atom had been split. McCarthyism in this country represented largely the traditional reaction against the threat of new, dangerous knowledge. But though the guilt feelings and self-doubts of the scientists greatly added to the effectiveness of McCarthy's campaign of blackmail, it was stopped, almost at the outset, by those unlikely champions of intellectual and scientific freedom, the professional soldiers. Knowledge has become power essential to military survival, and freedom of scientific search the foundation of national defense.

We cannot even, as has so often been attempted in the past, try to restrict the knowledge to a small group of the initiate, a priestly caste of the "twice-born," purified in the magic rites of Marxist dialectics, psychoanalysis or security clearance. On the contrary, we need more and more people in possession of this knowledge, more and more people of the highest education, more and more people capable of designing and building the means both of total physical and of total moral destruction. We have to accept the fact of the new knowledge; and we have to master it.

The starting point must be political. The new knowledge endows government with power that surely goes far beyond anything for which, in the words of the Declaration of Independence, "Governments are instituted among Men." By no stretch of the imagination can it be considered a legitimate power of government to be able to destroy the human race. By no stretch of the imagination can it be accepted as a legitimate purpose of government to dehumanize man. Yet today all governments have acquired these powers.

The first step toward survival is therefore to make government legitimate again by attempting to deprive it of these powers, that is by international conviction that either of the two powers is an intolerable abuse of power itself, and by international action to ban such powers.

This obviously will be easier in respect to the power of physical destruction than in respect to the power of moral degradation and destruction of personality. The first is directed clearly at the alien—though its exercise today is likely to destroy alike foreign enemy, neutral and one's own citizens. The second one, however, aims at a government's own citizens; to ban it is therefore clearly "interference with a sovereign state." Moreover, however difficult it may be to supervise atomic armaments at a distance, it is virtually impossible to supervise from afar the destructive forces that play on men's minds. Yet one is as antihuman as the other, one is as much a threat to the survival of man as the other. The attempt must therefore be made to forbid both to government. If this is incompatible with "sovereignty"—and it is—then "sovereignty" has become incompatible with human survival and must be limited.

This control and limitation of power cannot be achieved by unilateral disarmament. It cannot be achieved by the hegemony of this or that superpower; the last fifteen years should have taught all of us, including the Russians, that to aim at hegemony or even at preponderance of terror is a delusion.

But a world government cannot do the job either; it would only give us King Stork instead of King Log. It is impermissible and illegitimate for any government to possess these powers of destruction; they would be just as illegitimate if the government were global rather than national.

We need law to deny all government the use of the new powers. Such law must be based on the commitment of large and strong political bodies which, in turn, requires a multiplicity of large nations, each strong enough to have a policy, each united enough to be free at home, each big enough to count. But the task also requires true international institutions embodying the common belief that no government can be allowed to exercise the powers of physical and moral destruction of man. These bodies must be able to inspect and to seek out the facts. But they must also have the truly supernational power to hear appeals from the citizen against his government, or from government against government, and to give effective legal relief against governments transgressing the new limitations on their power.

I have no illusion that this will be easy. At the earliest it will become remotely possible only if and when the Free World has tackled the tasks of the "new frontiers." But it should even now be a goal and a commitment of the peoples and the governments of the Free World. We may survive, like the heroine of a radio serial, hopping from crisis to crisis. But each crisis will be worse than the last unless we have a goal. And the goal today can only be to deny to government effectively and without exception the powers of physical and moral destruction which are incompatible with any legitimate purpose.

Political action, however, is only delaying action. Where moral values and mental integrity are involved it may not even succeed in holding the tide, although the attempt must still be made. The problem created by the breakthrough of scientific knowledge to the core of human existence is not political. It is spiritual and metaphysical. It poses the question: What is the meaning of knowledge and power? Knowledge and power being specifically human among the attributes of the creature, the question really is: What is the meaning of human existence and of human spirit? These questions are as old as man. But absolute knowledge adds to them new urgency and new depth. They are metaphysical questions. "What we need," the answer will therefore come back, "is a return to spiritual values, a return to religion."

There is a revival of religion in the Western world today. It did not wait for totalitarian tyranny and the atom bomb but began at least a generation earlier—perhaps even with Charles Péguy at the turn of the century in France. I suspect that counting the number of churchgoers to measure the seriousness and intensity of the religious revival bears little relationship to the bookkeeping of the Recording Angel. But the trend away from, and against, religion that so deeply characterized the three hundred years of the modern age has certainly been reversed, at least for the time being. The historian a century hence—should there be one to record our survival—may well judge the return to religion to have been the most significant event of our century and the turning point in the crisis of the transition from the modern age.

Society needs a return to spiritual values—not to offset the material but to make it fully productive. However remote its realization for the great mass of mankind, there is today the promise of material abundance or at least of material sufficiency. There is the vision of economic development by means of which man can break the fetters of want that have always made Mammon the master rather than the servant of man. To what ends then should we use the material? In view of the grinding poverty in which the mass of mankind still lives, it is premature to talk, as some economists do, *of the economics of abundance.* The economist is concerned with reality; and abundance is still far from being reality. But it is not premature to think seriously about the philosophy and metaphysics of abundance; for philosophy and metaphysics deal with the vision of what can and should be.

Mankind needs the return to spiritual values, for it needs compassion. It needs the deep experience that the Thou and the I are one, which all higher religions share. In an age of terror, of persecution, of mass murder, such as ours, the hard shell of moral callousness may be necessary to survival. Without it we might yield to paralyzing despair. But moral numbness is also a terrible disease of mind and soul, and a terrible danger. It abets, even if it does not condone, cruelty and persecution. We have learned that the ethical humanitarianism of the nineteenth century cannot prevent man from becoming beast. Only compassion can save—the wordless knowledge of my own responsibility for whatever is being done to the least of God's children. This is knowledge of the spirit.

The individual needs the return to spiritual values, for he can survive in the present human situation only by reaffirming that man is not just biological and psychological being but also spiritual being, that is creature, and existing for the purposes of his Creator and subject to Him. Only thus can the individual know that the threat of instant physical annihilation of the species does not invalidate his own existence, its meaning and its responsibility. Only thus, above all, can he survive as a person under totalitarianism. Man, if he owns a spiritual nature in addition to his physical, psychological and social being, can never be entirely controlled by the "knowledge" of totalitarianism. The mere existence of spiritual man proves the knowledge of the totalitarians to be false and vain.

## Knowledge and Human Existence

Yet things are not so simple as the battle cry "Return to religion" might seem to imply. The crisis in which we live is not just one of the individual conscience. It is also one of metaphysical convictions. To be able to die as a man today it is still enough, as it has been before, to know and to believe that "Blessed are those which die in the Lord henceforth." But spiritual experience, however profound, does not by itself give the answer to the new questions of absolute knowledge and absolute power.

The Western world owes its emergence to the acceptance of knowledge. Right knowledge, the Greeks taught, will lead to right action. The two implications in this assertion—that man is capable of knowing and that knowledge is not vain but effective—are the specific Western metaphysics. A millennium and a half later, one of the greatest men of the Western tradition, St. Bonaventura, reaffirmed this position. His assertion that all knowledge comes from the Creator and speaks His truth and reality, became the charter of modern science. The modern scientist would say that knowledge is a value in itself and therefore "neutral" in respect to other values. But this is only a different terminology; he is still saying what St. Bonaventura said some seven hundred years ago.

This however is inadequate today. St. Bonaventura—and all philosophers of knowledge and science since—was concerned with the threat to knowledge. This is not our problem today; we know we cannot solve the problem of knowledge by suppressing it. We are concerned with the threat of knowledge. Only two or three generations ago knowledge was essentially a private affair. Science was the pursuit of knowledge for the sake of knowledge. Today science, whether we like it or not, is increasingly the pursuit of knowledge for the sake of power. No concept of knowledge we possess faces up to this new reality of human existence.

There is even less in our tradition to cope with the new reality of power made absolute through absolute knowledge. Altogether power, of all basic human realities, has been the least studied and is the least known. The student of politics has always taken it for granted. The philosopher and the artist, by and large, have dismissed it. The theologian and the moralist have suspected it. The politician has been concerned with organization of power rather than with its essence. Others have been concerned only with keeping it out where it does not belong. But what is it? And where does it belong? Power is a part of human life and a necessity of human existence. The traditional approach, purely negatively, attempted to keep power out of the really important concerns of man. But even if power were no more than brute force, a purely negative approach barely suffices. And power has always been much more than force alone.

Today the foundation of power is knowledge, and the essence of power is its potential of being absolute and total. Today we clearly need a metaphysics of power that is positive in its approach, that accepts power as a fact and a necessity, and thinks through its proper function and right purpose. If we do not know what power is for, we cannot say what its limits are. If we do not specify its proper use we will not be able to stop its abuse. Precisely because absolute power is so clearly beyond the limits, is so clearly intolerable abuse, we need to know the rightful sphere and proper use of power.

Power is no longer exterior to human existence and social purpose; it has become central to both. If we do not succeed in making it serve the ends of man and society it will destroy both.

Both knowledge and power, traditionally ends in themselves, must now become means to a higher end of man. Both knowledge and power must be grounded in purpose—a purpose beyond the truth of knowledge and the glory of power. We must demand that both control themselves, direct themselves, limit themselves in and through the purpose for which they accept responsibility. Nowhere will the break be greater between the new world and yesterday's modern age. It is here that we are likely to shift the most toward purpose as the ground of actions and events. It is in respect to knowledge and power that we will move the furthest from modern man's assertion of rights to a new acceptance of responsibility as the principle of freedom.

We cannot say any longer: "Knowledge is truth" or "All power corrupts." We must accept new propositions: Knowledge is power, and power is responsibility.

Knowledge and power have been problems of man since the Garden of Eden. Now they are in the center of his existence. The solution to them which the new age finds will, in the last analysis, determine its character and its meaning. If it fails to solve them, it will not only be a dark age without stars even to light up the night; it may well be the last age of man— and conquest of space will not alter this. If however the new age succeeds in solving these problems, it could become one of the greatest eras of man.

## Living in an Age of Overlap

The report on the post-modern world is now concluded. It has alternated between moods of optimism, if not enthusiasm, and moods of gloom, if not of despondency. For the post-modern world is an age of transition, an age of overlap, full of exciting challenges and opportunities, full also of terrible and terrifying dangers, an age which inseparably joins together the enchantment and the terror of the unknown, the challenge of new deeds to be accomplished and the penalties for old misdeeds come to judgment.

If I have stressed problems, questions, tasks, rather than solutions, answers and achievements, that too reflects accurately, I believe, a period of transition and overlap. What unifies an age, what gives it character, courage and confidence, are rarely answers but a common view of problems and tasks,

and the consent that these are indeed relevant to the generation. Achievements are for old men to remember by their
fireside. The work to be done, the hurdles to be taken, are the
important challenges for a young age as they are for a young
man.

We are in midstream today. Most of us still take the old
world for granted. But one thing is certain: The past is going
fast. If there is one thing we can predict, it is change. The
coming years will be years of rapid change in our vision, the
direction of our efforts, the tasks we tackle and their priorities,
and the yardsticks by which we measure success or failure. It
has been the thesis of this book that the new can already
be discerned, the purpose of this book to draw its lineaments.

A time like this is not comfortable, secure, lazy. It is a
time when tides of history over which he has no control sweep
over the individual. It is a time of agony, of peril, of suffering
—an ugly, hateful, cruel, brutish time at best. It is a time of
war, of mass slaughter, of depravity, of mockery of all laws of
God or man. It is a time in which no one can take for granted
the world he lives in, the things he treasures, or the values and
principles that seem to him so obvious. Those of us who have
been spared the horrors in which our age specializes, who have
never suffered total war, slave-labor camp or police terror, not
only owe thanks; we owe charity and compassion.

But ours is also a time of new vision and greatness, of
opportunity and challenge, to everyone in his daily life, as a
person and as a citizen. It is a time in which everyone is an
understudy to the leading role in the drama of human
destiny. Everyone must be ready to take over alone and without notice, and show himself saint or hero, villain or coward.
On this stage the great roles are not written in the iambic
pentameter or the Alexandrine of the heroic theater. They

are prosaic—played out in one's daily life, in one's work, in one's citizenship, in one's compassion or lack of it, in one's courage to stick to an unpopular principle, and in one's refusal to sanction man's inhumanity to man in an age of cruelty and moral numbness.

In a time of change and challenge, new vision and new danger, new frontiers and permanent crisis, suffering and achievement, in a time of overlap such as ours, the individual is both all-powerless and all-powerful. He is powerless, however exalted his station, if he believes that he can impose his will, that he can command the tides of history. He is all-powerful, no matter how lowly, if he knows himself to be responsible.